Donna + Mat

GW00838693

Elusive Growth

Eventually !

Jack.

First published by
Old Broad Street Press in 2011

ISBN: 978-0-9568881-0-5

British Library Cataloguing in Publication Data
A catalogue record for this book is available from the
British Library.

Text design and typesetting by Sally Osborn, editexpert.350.com

Printed in the UK by Good News Digital Books

Elusive Growth

Why prevailing practices in
strategy, marketing and
management education
are the problem, not the solution

Jack Springman

OLD BROAD STREET
PRESS

Dedication

This book is dedicated to my wife, Philippa, and children, Oliver and Clara, with my thanks for their patience over the weekends and holidays that have been consumed with writing it.

CLARA, PHILIPPA AND OLIVER SKIMMING STONES IN BEMBRIDGE HARBOUR, ISLE OF WIGHT

Acknowledgements

I would like to thank the members of my family and all the colleagues, ex-colleagues and friends who have helped (sometimes unwittingly) in developing or challenging ideas and supporting the publishing process, in particular: Adrian Ball, Martin Bean, Matt Boyd, Miranda Bromage-Henry, Vernon Bubb, Warren Chester, Graham Clapp, David Coleman, Peter Colman, Rich Coltart, Ian Copeland, Cathal Corocran, Paul Crick, Chris de Bruyn, Pamela Dickson, Paul Duffy, Mark Dunfoy, Maryam Ebadi, Nigel Eccles, Sarah Elton, Chris Freeland, Katie Freeland, Allan Gasson, Michael Gell, David Gilmour, Jo Golesworthy, Kevin Gothelf, Lucy Gottelier, Verena Gruenberg-Hoeltl, Marcus Hawkins, David Henderson, Vicki Herbertson, Meryl Hicks, Graham Hinde, Jacqueline Hoey, Ian Huckle, Rodrigo Hutt, Richard Ingleton, Kevin James, Stephen Jordan, Simon Keefe, Tobias Keller, Louise Knowles, Richard Koch, Robert Kynoch, Patrick Lee, Andrew Lindsay, Katy Lindsay, Joe Little, Ann Macdonald, Stewart Manning, Rosey Marsh, Ian Marshall, Chris Mathias, Rowena Maxwell, Kym McConnell, Lyn McKee, Kenneth McKelvey, Matthew McKennirey, Roy Mitropoulos, Fraser Munro, Nicky Oates, Sally Osborn, Alex Page, Mike Parker, Michael Pearson, Tony Peck, Barry Posner, Frank Proud, David Rankin, Philippa Reader, Mark Sacco, Tony Sadler, Paul Sanders, Richard Sanders, Deborah Saunders, Rick Seabrook, Tina Sell, Liz Shaw, Julian Sherratt, Tim Shorrocks, Derek Spence, Anne Springman, Michael Springman, Nicholas Springman, Sarah Springman, Des Sullivan, Linda Taylor, Tim Thorne, Niels van den Brink, Soizic Vangrevelynghe, Mark Waddington, Laura Watt, Graham Wederell, Jason Whitehead, Ken Whitton, Kim Wigglesworth, Nigel Williams, Graham Wilson, Philip Wilson, Patrick Woodrow, Paul Zaloumis and Wentao Zhang.

Contents

Introduction

The aim of this book is to start a debate about some of the basic, unquestioned assumptions that underpin modern management thinking. The seeds of this heretical objective were planted back in 2000, albeit on ground well prepared to receive it. The e-revolution of the late 1990s was metamorphosing into the i-revolution – e-business reclassified as one, dramatic example of innovation that was going to be the new engine of corporate profit growth. Probably the most famous book of this particular era was Gary Hamel's *Leading the Revolution*. One chapter contained a number of directives, the most striking being Surface the Dogmas, under which lay the questions 'What are the ten things that the top ten players in your industry would believe in common?' and 'What would happen if you inverted these beliefs?'

Asking these questions of the consultancy sector provoked a number of others about the process of strategy development that spilled over into the adjacent processes of management research, management education and marketing. One consequence of this was that I started to collect, summarize and classify marketing and strategy frameworks published in business journals or management books. This database has grown to several hundred entries and has provided useful context for this book.

During the intervening period I also changed career track, moving from strategy consulting and evaluating potential acquisitions to operational consulting, joining a customer management specialist called Inforte, which in its seven years as a NASDAQ-quoted company boasted Michael Porter, Philip Kotler, Al Ries and Al Kurtzweiler among its thought-leading board members. This shift from the world of strategic analysis and acquisition evaluation to the more operational world of developing and implementing customer-facing strategies both answered some questions and raised even more, most notably regarding the need for more design thinking in strategy development, to create value and to enable effective operationalization; and how far marketing had strayed from its supposed roots.

Not surprisingly, over this extended period the focus has changed a little more. In particular, the challenge of behavioural research to the neoclassical assumption of rational decision making that pervades both economics and its doctrinal offspring has moved from bit-part player to starring role. It has become the central pillar in the argument that serious scrutiny is required of the presuppositions underpinning management research, strategy and marketing.

The popularity of *Nudge* by Richard Thaler and Cass Sunstein, *Predictably Irrational* by Dan Ariely and *The Black Swan* by Nassim Nicholas Taleb has moved understanding of behavioural economics into the mainstream. Appreciation of the latter's relevance has also been furthered by the multiple dissections of the credit boom and bust, which highlighted how irrationality frequently prevailed. Finally, some of the themes of behavioural economics have started to penetrate management thinking, with a number of articles published in business journals in recent years.

Yet for all that, behavioural science remains an adornment, a means for adjusting decisions made using traditional approaches derived from assumptions of economic rationality. That the insights from behavioural economics fundamentally challenge the validity of those approaches has yet to be discussed (thankfully, for otherwise I would not have had the opportunity to write this book).

On the other hand, it is impossible to write about bias and distortion without recognizing one's own susceptibility, particularly when abstracting evidence that challenges or supports one's arguments. We are all prone to register only the evidence that supports our views. And while awareness promotes mitigation, it will never be complete. In an attempt to provide balance, I have tried to challenge my ideas via the experiences and perspectives of others. Consequently, during the writing of this book a few of my original hypotheses have been refuted, others reconstituted, a couple of new ones added.

What has stayed constant over this period is the belief that the biggest challenge facing large corporations is sustaining profitable organic growth. That may seem trite given the deep recession suffered by most economies from late 2007 to late 2009. Nevertheless, this challenge was also apparent during the boom period preceding the credit crunch, when traditional strategy and marketing approaches still failed to deliver.

However, my beliefs about the best way to resolve this challenge have changed markedly. Back in 2000 I believed that there were panaceas for the problem, initially in the shape of the internet and e-business, subsequently in innovation and corporate venturing. Experience has eroded such optimism, almost inverted it in fact.

The extent to which my views have changed became clear when someone volunteered: 'Growth is easy; all you need to do is stop doing stupid things.' This neatly articulated what I had come to believe. Much management time has been spent in searching for silver bullets: pre-packaged solutions, typically the secrets of successful companies as distilled by consultancies or business school professors that would magically solve the growth challenge. I fear such attempts to deconstruct success into approaches that others can apply are akin to alchemy – in all senses. Cutting out decisions that waste time, money and attention provides a huge impetus to growth, yet management science remains obsessed with codifying success more than eradicating failure.

That, of course, is easier said than done. But acknowledging the susceptibility to bias inherent in strategy and marketing frameworks, methods, models, toolkits and approaches is a starting point. Seeking out those that moderate rather than accentuate our innate biases by forcing us to play devil's advocate with our natural inclinations is a step further. That is what this book attempts to do

– it doesn't pretend that the approaches suggested are magical solutions, just that they are equally valid as alternatives and are less likely to result in expensive failure.

I will end this introduction by highlighting a couple of differences that you will find between this book and most others on the subject of strategy or marketing or management in general. A couple of years ago I read the advice that you should 'write the book that only you can write'. Given the research centricity of much business writing, the opposite could almost hold true. As will become apparent in Chapter 5, I do not hold in the highest regard the insights yielded by the research carried out in the name of management science. So the first difference is that you will find no case studies selectively constructed to support my views.

Equally, it is the aspiration of most business authors to write a book that is the final word on a subject – rendering it pointless for anyone else to do so, as there is nothing left to say (at least until evolution or revolution renders an updated edition necessary). Such books are popular because they purport to provide answers and, as Dan Ariely has pointed out, we prefer answers over questions: answers mean we can take action whereas questions mean we need to keep thinking. In business, however – and many other areas, for that matter – the more time spent in the thinking stage, the more questions we ask, the better overall answer we are likely to find.

My aim is for this book to raise questions – not to be the last word on its subject by seeking to prove its theories outright, but to be the first to make the case that some prevailing thought processes may have contributed to what in the pre-credit crunch era was hyperbolically termed the 'growth crisis'. Its ambition is to engage, challenge and open up debate. That objective is the real mitigation to my own biases, as acknowledged above.

As a result, I have tried to make this business book one that only I could write. That is not a mark of merit in itself, but it may go some way to explaining its quirks. Hopefully you will enjoy the difference.

One
Skimming Stones

It's an early evening in late summer and you are walking along the shore. The breeze scampers across your arms, playing hide-and-seek in the gaps between cloth and skin. The declining sun coaxes you across the stony beach, each step indenting the pebbles beneath your feet, reshaping the ephemeral terrain.

With gulls and children having departed for their evening feeding grounds, only the shingle stirs the stillness, each stride grinding pebble against pebble, triggering miniature landslides; and each ebbing swell provoking low screeches of complaint from the stones dragged to and fro.

The waves – if you can call them that – rise just a few feet from the shore before breaking like a gambolling puppy that scurries away. Further out, the water is so still that it scarcely dapples the reflections of the escaping sun, which conceals the far shore, as if slinking below the horizon to cower from the dusk.

Tired of squinting, you look down and your eyes are drawn by the gleam of a white, round pebble. You bend down, pick it up and start turning it over in your hand, savouring its smoothness. Then with an instinctive flick of the wrist, you send it spinning across the shimmering water – skip, skip, skip. You pick up another, five skips this time. Next time it is six; then just four. After that you lose track of the results as you settle into a rhythm of stoop, flick, skip, skip, skip.

Despite all efforts, regaining the remembered prowess of your childhood self proves elusive. Without you realizing it, ten minutes have passed, then another fifteen. By the time you look up, the sun has turned from yellow brilliance to orange glow. With a sigh, you pick up one final stone and almost casually send it skimming across the gold-flecked water – one hop, two, three, four, five, six, seven, eight – before you lose sight of it, unsure where it finally sank and whether you matched or beat the record you set when you were 10.

Turning for home, you imagine the stone still skipping its way towards the sunset, each hop generating ripples that spread and strengthen until they break as waves, once more rearranging the ever-shifting shingle.

Physicists would argue that skimming stones is science rather than art, citing the example of 'Upkeep', the bouncing bomb developed by Barnes Wallis in the Second World War to breach the dams feeding hydroelectric power to the German armament industry in the Ruhr valley. After many experiments – starting with a catapult, marbles and a tub of water on his patio, graduating to further trials at Nant-y-Gro dam in Wales and the National Physics Laboratory in Teddington, then full-scale tests at Chesil Beach and Reculver – Wallis came up with a precise equation: the cylindrical bombs weighing 9,250 lb each needed to be spun backwards at 500 rpm (to increase hop length and ensure they slid down the dam's retaining wall) and launched from an airplane flying at 240–250 mph just 60 feet above the water, 400–500 yards from their target.

For the non-physicists, however, skimming stones is more of an art than a science. So it is with the bag of pebbles that this book represents. It isn't a bouncing bomb; only others can add the weight of reputation or numbers to breach the dams that have been created by precedent and economic interest. And as with art, the intent of this book is to challenge and engage. Its ultimate aim is to change the way we think and talk about strategy, marketing and management research. But the first step in reshaping the shore is to create a few ripples.

Readers who enjoy the standard fare of pre-packaged solutions should be advised that this is not that type of book, for reasons that will become clear very soon. What it does seek to do is to illuminate the following paradox.

On one side, over the past 25 years the numbers of business schools and business consultancies have rocketed; and alumni numbers from these organizations have increased cumulatively too. On the other side, from the turn of the millennium to the inception of the credit crunch – which, due to a combination of the internet, globalization and easy credit, was a period of exceptional economic buoyancy – large companies still struggled to generate profitable organic growth. In short, never before had there been such a well-educated management workforce, yet never before had there been such pessimism about growing the revenue line in a profitable way, even before near financial collapse sank the developed world's economies into a long and deep recession.

There are two possible resolutions to this paradox. First, that the pessimism is misplaced: the 'growth gap' or 'growth crisis' was a belief forged by consultants and business school professors, creating a need for their elegant solutions. However, as Chapter 3 will show in more detail, stock market returns would appear to show this not to be the case. Secondly, that business schools and consultancies are part of the problem rather than the solution. Or, as Albert Einstein put it, 'Problems cannot be solved by thinking within the framework in which they were created.' In the same way that generals are always destined to fight the last war, the charge facing these organizations is that they are training people to conquer the battlegrounds of the 1980s and 1990s rather than to meet the challenges of the twenty-first century. (How the economic, technological and social trends of the last 25 years have influenced the way we think about strategy and marketing is examined in the next chapter.)

This book looks at some of the presuppositions that underpin management science, strategy and marketing. The intent is to expose these convenient assumptions to the light of contemporary challenge, and highlight the fact that much of our current thinking could well be built on cracked foundations, the result of which are a few contentions: pebbles skimmed across calm waters with the intention of creating a few ripples.

The behaviour of behavioural economics

The last few years have seen increased interest in the impacts that behavioural factors have on economic choices, best demonstrated in the way that books on the subject have become bestsellers. These insights from behavioural economics are gradually infiltrating management science. As far back as 2003, the *Harvard Business Review* published an article co-authored by Daniel Kahneman, a Nobel prize winner for his work in behavioural economics.

Nevertheless, for the moment this remains an adornment, seen as relevant to some elements of tactical marketing or as a means for reviewing and adjusting decisions generated using traditional approaches founded on the convenient assumption, borrowed from neoclassical economics, of rationality. The irony of seeing behavioural science as an adjustment mechanism is that one of its findings is that such adjustments are usually insufficient due to the process of anchoring. The original answer provides the starting point from which any change is made. And if the original conclusions are flawed due to bias in their construction, any such tweaking will be inadequate.

However, accepting that our rationality is limited should cause a more fundamental reappraisal. In particular, does the popularity of commonly used frameworks stem as much from their psychological appeal (fertile ground for bias to flourish) as from the economic value delivered, to the detriment of the latter? Two examples would be competitive strategy and brand-based marketing.

The idea that the purpose of strategy is to beat competitors appeals to the relativism that typifies testosterone-fuelled business leaders. As a result, in the strategy world military and sporting analogies are rife: business is a battleground and the purpose of strategy is to defeat your opponents. Despite lip-service to win–win thinking, the prevailing attitude to competition – which in Michael Porter's five forces model includes both suppliers and customers – is win–lose. The size of the pie is fixed and you need to take share from the competition. Success is defined in relative terms.

If beating competitors is treated as a direct objective, the potential for irrational decision making – concerning price wars and out-bidding on acquisition targets, for instance – is far greater than if it is regarded as an outcome of achieving other objectives (something that the economist John Kay calls obliquity). Profitable growth requires obsessing about customers rather than competitors, creating value for customers to create value for the business. If that is treated as the objective, relative success will follow.

Psychological appeal is also present in marketing's love affair with branding, specifically in how brands pander to our innate ego-centricity. Branding originated in the fast-moving consumer goods sector but spread to the rest of the economy over the course of the 1990s. Having seen the staggering sums attributed to 'brand value' in takeovers, such as that of Kraft by Philip Morris in 1988, the creation of brand equity became marketing's number one goal. But whereas within FMCG companies marketers control the necessary tools and organizational clout, in other sectors this is rarely the case. Worse, it has returned marketing to a pre-Copernican era, viewing everything as revolving around the corporate self.

Marketing's transition from Dark Ages to Enlightenment began over 50 years ago, the most famous milestone being the publication of Theodore Levitt's article 'Marketing myopia' in the *Harvard Business Review*. This introduced what has been described as the most influential marketing idea of the last 50 years, that businesses would do better if they concentrated on satisfying customers' needs rather than pushing products. (It also makes no mention of the word brand.) However, anyone reading it now could merely replace the word 'product' with 'brand' and see parallels with the state of marketing today. The focus on brands rather than customers marks a return to inside-out thinking, a preoccupation with an internal construct rather than an external constituency. And in the process it encourages marketers – their function charged with being externally oriented, a voice for customers at the management table – to look in the mirror rather than out of the window.

Marketing's ownership of all things brand related has other consequences, notably in the execution of brand strategy by what marketing controls. In multibrand FMCG companies, the brand managers are effectively general managers, so they can control or influence everything they need to. But in most other areas that is not the case. Marketing's sway over even the other customer-facing areas – sales and service – is often pretty limited, let alone over other parts of the organization. As a result, branding becomes about what marketing in these companies do have direct control over: communications, look and feel (or 'font fascism'), logos and tag lines. As a result, branding has tended to be more about image than reputation.

Reputation is a function of the experience that customers receive, while image is a function of the intangible benefits associated with the brand. The latter is a subset of the former, but outside certain sectors (such as consumer packaged goods or luxury items) it is rarely the defining factor. If brand, customer experience and reputation are to be one and the same – or at least inextricably interlinked – then ownership of 'brand strategy' should be vested with the CEO; or, if not, with the department that contributes most to a differentiated experience. That will rarely be the marketing function. Although marketers set expectations (or mis-set them), it is the rest of the company that is responsible for delivering to them.

Egocentricity is also unintentionally exhibited in two other favoured marketing terms: channel and route to market. Both very much display a corporate-centric view of the world, particularly the roles occupied by different players and their place in the pecking order. The businesses that make up the channel would naturally consider themselves to be customers and important elements of the industry value chain, not just a pipe through which their suppliers pump their products. Nevertheless, that is clearly what marketers intend when they use the term 'channel' – especially as demarcation of responsibilities means that channel relationships are usually managed by the sales team, leaving marketers free to concentrate on the far more exciting work of generating brand awareness with end users.

The problem is that, despite the internet's promise of disinter-mediation, the opposite has occurred. The mantra of simplicity has led businesses to reduce the numbers of customers they deal with and attempts to boost returns on capital have resulted in their exit-ing asset-intensive or low-margin components of the value chain. As a result, the reliance on distributors has increased. In addition, while the scale economies of distribution are less compelling than those of manufacturing, they still exist and consolidation is rapidly occurring, led by the large supermarket groups: Wal-Mart, Carrefour, Tesco and the like (and no one is so foolish as to call Wal-Mart a route to market). This process is being replicated in all the sectors of the economy that these businesses don't touch, resulting in the need for marketing to start thinking in terms of their businesses having layers of customers and creating value propositions for each different layer.

The logical conclusion of acknowledging innate bias – such as relativism and egocentricity – is that we should seek frameworks that counteract rather than compound that bias. Selection based on intuitive appeal is likely to accentuate the inherent distortions of such frameworks. Instead, we should seek approaches that take us out of our comfort zones, force us to take a less natural perspective and challenge us to be our own devil's advocates.

Best practice isn't necessarily best

Protesters will of course highlight case studies of top-performing com-panies that have used competitive strategy or branding to profitable effect. With any approach there will be some good practitioners, some less good and some poor. But management science's preoccupation with 'best practice' – codifying the experience of successful companies into lessons that others can learn – means that only the first of those three groups are focused on. As a result, they cannot be used to validate the approach in and of themselves. This selection bias is frequently compounded by false attribution of causality, by which an excessive amount of the company's success is attributed to whatever is being studied, while the role of other factors (such as luck) or other seemingly unrelated initiatives is underestimated.

In the process, what is missed is the damage suffered by average or poor practitioners of the same approach. A clear implication of acknowledging irrationality is that when selecting frameworks, particularly those used to allocate scarce corporate resources, susceptibility to behavioural bias should be a critical consideration. Purists (including Panglossians and the arrogant) would argue that such an analysis should not be necessary. However, risk assessment of a strategic *approach* is just as important as risk assessment of any strategic *decision*. How badly an approach can be implemented – and the associated damage – should be of equal if not greater consideration to how well it can be.

At the core of this is the issue of uncertainty. Wherever uncertainty prevails, so does the potential for bias and distortion. But while we acknowledge that the future is uncertain, we are less prone to seeing the past in the same way. Obviously the outcomes of history are clear, but the process that created them rarely is. In attempting to explain what happened and why, historians have fallen victim to a number of fallacies, first identified by David Hackett Fischer in the early 1970s. He identified over 100, classified into a number of groups, including the fallacies of selection and causation that were touched on above, but also fallacies of question framing, factual verification and significance, generalization and composition.

Nevertheless, appreciation of this range of pitfalls – and the humility that such knowledge typically brings – has yet to transfer from the faculty of history to the faculty of business. Management research is backward facing, typically seeking to codify the success of superior-performing companies into lessons that others can learn. Like historians, researchers seek to reverse engineer the reasons for success after the fact, not to observe them at the time. Such research is particularly prey to Fischer's fallacies of framing, causality and selection. And failure to recognize how these fallacies can distort conclusions results in another trait about which behavioural economics warns: overconfidence, most notably in how readily the universal form 'best' is appended to a favoured practice.

Any supposed best practice should be subjected to the following three tests. First, who has defined it as best and what qualifications do they have to pass such a judgement? (Subsidiary questions to this would include what practice set it has been compared against, which organizations make up the comparators and so on.) Secondly, in what context has it been deemed best: for what type and size of organization, business gross margin model, size of investment, volume of activity? Thirdly, what purpose (e.g. reducing costs, improving the customer experience) does the practice achieve best? Most so-called best practices have far narrower application than their proponents might assume. The adjudicators may also lack the experience or expertise to make such judgements; and rarely will they have all the data required to use a term such as best or worst in any case.

More fundamentally, any activity or practice can be performed at a number of levels – basic, standard, good or great – each of which is a perfectly valid choice, depending on the business context. Compounding the flaws in defining best practice is the implicit assumption that businesses should automatically aspire to it regardless. Businesses should love basic or threshold practice, selectively aspire to good, even great practice, but be intelligently sceptical of anything that is lauded as 'best'.

The art of profitability comes from avoiding wasted expenditure on capabilities that deliver little value. Not providing customers with something or accepting only a basic ability in a particular functional activity is tough; wanting the security of scoring at least 4 out of 5 on every dimension is another tendency people are biased towards, and this is compounded by organizational risk aversion and functional self-interest. Nevertheless, the sign of mature strategy development is being able to articulate 'no' as well as 'yes': why something should *not* be offered to customers, why a particular capability should *not* be developed, why some customers should be *not* be served directly. Yet such profit-enhancing prioritization is continually undermined by aspirations to match 'best practice', which typically involves cash expenditure, either in the form of increased operating costs or an up-front investment. In strategic terms, the only practice that is best practice is *appropriate* practice.

In addition, the value of what can be learned from other companies is arguably overestimated (unless the strategy is geared to be a fast follower, where copying is the critical capability), acting as a comfort blanket more than anything else, while the faults that a culture of imitation fosters – dependency, strategic convergence, lagging rather than leading – tend to be ignored. For companies seeking to avoid being perpetual followers, the value of learning from other companies comes when it stimulates creative thinking about specific problems, not when it is seen as a source of pre-packaged best practices.

In addition to its questionable validity and overconfident assertion, management research implicitly elevates imitation above originality. Judicious imitation and experimentation are both necessary to learning, but management science focuses exclusively on imitation, not application or the skills necessary for the fundamental strategic requirement of being different – a capability for originality. Leaders absorb, create and test; followers research, derive and codify.

Yet such research is still very popular and a number of organizations, such as the Corporate Executive Board, have developed to meet it. This raises the question of whether its appeal is again mainly psychological, stemming from the innate human desire to be part of the herd. Behavioural studies have shown how herding distorts behaviour. And the track record of industries where participants behave as a herd – all follow the same path, merely seeking to copy each other – is one of competitive convergence, commoditization and margin erosion. In validating and encouraging any tendency to herd, management research destroys rather than creates value.

The business of business schools

Any challenge to management research immediately raises doubts about the value of business education. MBA studies have become increasingly popular, but behavioural economics challenges whether the value that graduates obtain is due more to a double dose of selection bias than to the education received. First, students who apply to MBA programmes are self-selecting, thereby signalling their ambition and commitment to a career in business. On top of that, the elite schools, where the financial gains are most pronounced, can be highly selective in whom they admit.

Should going to business school be seen as a badge of success or a mark of failure? Rather than value those who gain an MBA, arguably we should value those who have chosen not to – those who are too smart to go to business school because their career is progressing well and they realize that the value of what they will learn there is limited.

If for a moment you set aside the hoped-for financial gains of going to business school (which are a function of selection) and present the issue merely in terms of the competencies developed, how many businesses would invest time and money in a competency development project where 80 per cent of the information acquired is irrelevant and where 80 per cent of the relevant 20 per cent is likely to be forgotten by the time it is able to be used? This fails the critical strategic test of focus.

MBA programmes are a throwback to an era of organizational generalism and technocracy, which are an overhead that few businesses today can carry. Why should that be different for individuals?

Would it not be better to be trained in the specific competencies that will be most valuable to initial career progression, such as a qualification in finance, marketing or supply chain management, and then build on that later as required, rather than trying to do everything up front at significant cost and wastage?

A mismatch between costs and value addition is frequently cited (by business school professors) as a classic sign of opportunity for disruptive innovation. So if the value MBA graduates gain is primarily a function of selection but the costs incurred (both in tuition fees and lost earnings) are driven by the educational component, does that not highlight a great market opportunity for some alternative forms of capability validation and business education? Such an approach would complement the professional qualifications that progression through a functional role demands in order to provide management skills and a broader perspective in small bursts, as and when they are needed. Maybe it is time to put crowd-sourcing to the test and co-create an open-source alternative to the MBA specifically, and the business school generally.

The assumption of uncertainty

It has been estimated that roughly 75 per cent of the MBA curriculum is focused on analysis; the old joke about management by analysis isn't such a joke after all. This emphasis embraces the western intellectual tradition, which has made analysis the default approach to problem solving. And it has proved a powerful tool for improving operational effectiveness, contributing significantly to the productivity gains that have underpinned corporate earnings growth for much of the past 25 years.

Indeed, analysis is highly effective when it is backward facing, built on a solid fact base, informed by high volumes of data. But strategic decisions are about the future, for which facts don't exist. By their very nature they require assumptions. And wherever uncertainty prevails, so does the opportunity for bias, notably the dangerous compounding of overoptimism with overconfidence that is most evident in businesses paying over the odds for acquisitions.

This tendency has long been documented, yet it continues to prevail. At its heart is simple probability blindness. We fatally overestimate the likelihood of a number of necessary events coming to pass. Or perhaps more accurately, we fail even to take a probabilistic view. Research and analysis may suggest that each individual assumption is a reasonable one to make, and that leads us to conclude that the whole model is reasonable when the probability of all of them being met is low. (For example, the compound probability of three independent events, each with a probability of 70 per cent, all occurring is just over 34 per cent.)

In the context of strategy development, analysis will, by definition, be assumptive, therefore it is often simplistic and frequently opaque (if its assumption dependence is not clear). As a result, it serves to increase confidence by more than its accuracy merits. If not a confidence trick as such, this is at least a trick to increase confidence that gives analytical strategy the properties of the proverbial Chinese takeaway: a bloated feeling immediately after consumption before hunger returns within half an hour.

Analysis intoxicates with potential, oversimplifies with its emphasis on 'what' but ultimately disappoints by ignoring 'how' – the most critical element. It is but one part of the value trinity of analysis, design and execution. *Analysis* can locate an opportunity, but *design* is required to unlock the value in that opportunity and *execution* is required to deliver it. The results can then be analysed before the process begins again.

Strategists are quick to criticize marketers for being insufficiently left-brain oriented in their thinking, but are themselves possessors of an arrogance that blinds them to their insufficiencies with regard to right-brain or design thinking. Key elements of strategy – the value proposition to customers, capability prioritization and the operating model used to deliver the desired capability levels – all require trade-offs and therefore do need to be designed.

Right-brain thinking is also necessary for dealing with uncertainty, which for strategists is the final frontier. Managing it effectively requires a different mindset for crafting strategy (certainly compared to the prevailing left-brain approach of making single-scenario assumptions and then treating them as if they were concrete facts), even to the degree of challenging what strategy is, what purpose it performs, who it touches in the organization.

First, strategy needs to provide managers with a frame within which they have the freedom to experiment or make strategy-logical decisions should unforeseen circumstances arise (an unfortunate and all-too-frequent consequence of uncertainty). This requires the corporate strategy department to reinvent its role and become the owner of the organizational middleware necessary to cascade strategy from the CEO to the front line (and back again), ensuring that, both tacitly and explicitly, high-level strategy guides the little decisions that are taken every day by thousands of people across the organization that together add up to success or failure. Such an approach both enables decisions to be delegated to those with the best information and ensures alignment around key principles. The freedom to experiment also yields results that narrow the corridor of uncertainty.

Further big decisions, such as acquisitions, require the focus on analysis to be secondary to a focus on uncertainty management, a process that starts long before the decision clock starts ticking. This involves defining the uncertainties faced and systematically seeking to reduce the degree with regard to the most critical, typically those that will have the greatest impact on the future of the business. Fortunately, the majority of the tools required to do this – scenario and contingency planning, discovery-driven budgeting, likelihood-impact analysis, Monte Carlo simulations and so on – have existed for a long time. Becoming better at uncertainty management simply requires them to be employed in an integrated way.

These theories and contentions will be expanded on in Chapters 4 to 11. I use the term contention deliberately, as the prime aim of this book is to challenge. By that I do not wish to imply that they are hollow statements designed purely to provoke; I believe that there is evidence to justify them, or at least that the evidence does not refute them. That evidence, however, is primarily qualitative. I cannot claim to have a mass of quantitative data to support these views and to refute others, much though I might like to.

In the absence of such conclusive data, I can only appeal to your own experience and observations. If these theories resonate with your experience, then that is great. If you have the insights to expand, extend or sharpen any observations, even better. If they don't – and I'm expecting there to be plenty of times where that's the case – then no problem, but at least let us have the conversation.

My aim with this book is to uncover and subject to scrutiny the assumptions or presuppositions about strategy and marketing (and by implication, management research) that could be limiting businesses' ability to generate that most elusive of factors, profitable organic growth. In the same way that the credit crunch has challenged the Anglo-Saxon–dominated approach to finance, particularly the assumption of rationality, an examination of the period leading up to it suggests an equal need to challenge the presuppositions of management science, particularly those borrowed from neoclassical economics.

So let the debate begin: hopefully we will be able to reach a closer approximation of the truth.

Two

Imprisoned by the Past

Assessing the validity of our presuppositions about strategy, marketing and management science requires an understanding of how they were formed. To do this, we need to examine the forces – political, technological, social, educational, environmental and economic – of the past quarter century and their influence on business thinking.

All these factors have had a significant impact. Social and environmental trends have profoundly influenced the way we think, particularly our attitudes towards science and how we balance ideology and rationalism. More specifically, the rise of management education has shaped how we think about business, particularly how performance can be improved. Economic factors have continually shaped the corporate agenda: which elements of performance should be improved and the timescales within which it must happen. And perhaps most significantly of all, two trends – one political, one technological – have enabled pronounced increases in corporate profitability, moulding much of our thinking about strategy in the process.

The rise of supply-side economics and globalization
The political enabler has been the rise to orthodox status of supply-side economic management, a key feature of the revolutions initiated by Margaret Thatcher and Ronald Reagan in the early 1980s. In contrast to the prevailing Keynesian economic thinking of the postwar era, which focused on managing the demand side of the

economy through government spending while seeking to manage inflation by wage and price controls, Thatcher and Reagan sought economic growth through ensuring that the supply component of the economy was efficient, productive and incentivized to create wealth. Both applied similar levers to achieve this: reducing the growth of government spending and the marginal rates of tax on income and capital; controlling inflation through managing the money supply; limiting union power; privatizing state-owned industries; and increasing competition for monopolies. Of all these, the latter three have had the most direct impact on the business community.

Central to both Reaganomics and Thatcherism was a determination to tame trade union powers. Reagan's defining success came when he broke the air traffic controllers' strike in 1981; and destroying the coal miners' strike in 1984–5 had the same effect for Thatcher. The implications of these triumphs were wider than the specific victories themselves. Economist Irwin Stelzer, writing in 1989, concluded:

> *In both countries the principal gain from taming public sector unions was not the direct saving in wage payments to the affected workers. Rather, it was the successful signaling to the US private sector that the government would not be frightened by the prospect of public inconvenience into intervening in labour disputes, and to the UK private sector that a new, non-inflationary attitude towards wage settlements by private sector employers would receive government support. In America, this contributed to a record stability in unit labour costs; in Britain, it provided an atmosphere and a legal climate ... [to] sweep away Luddite work rule which, until then, had prevented British industry from taking advantage of modern technology, and imprisoned it in a declining spiral.*[1]

In the UK the results were particularly pronounced, with union membership falling from 13m in 1979 to 8m by 1996. In addition to breaking union control, Thatcher sought to reduce the role of the state and replace it with private enterprise, initiating widespread privatizations. This was a double-edged sword for formerly nationalized industries, providing access to capital markets for funding expansion on one side while introducing pressure to reduce costs and grow profits on the other. However, in terms of widening share ownership the initiative was hugely effective: the number of private individuals holding shares rose from 3m when Thatcher took office to over 11m by the time she left. As Stelzer continued:

> *Thatcherism's success in converting state-owned to privately-owned enterprises... [was] a programme so radical in conception, and so successful in operation, as to have won the highest form of flattery from other nations – imitation.*

From a corporate perspective, the supply-side economics revolution created a massive opportunity to cut costs. Among the first to grab this opportunity in the US was GE. As Jack Welch describes it in his autobiography: 'Within five years, one of every four people would leave the GE payroll, 118,000 in all.'[2]

Welch's extensive cuts earned him the nickname Neutron Jack, for removing the people but leaving the buildings standing. Nevertheless, he was soon being imitated by others in increasing numbers. As Gary Hamel has put it,

> *we have seen reengineering, restructuring, downsizing, enterprise resource management and customer relationship management. All focused on how do you take working capital out of your business, how do you take time out of your processes, how do you operate call centres with fewer people. They were a product of global competition and the Thatcher Revolution.*[3]

For those businesses that weren't prepared to perform these unpleasant tasks, there were more than enough potential acquirers willing to do the dirty work: junk bond-fuelled corporate raiders such as Carl Icahn and Ronald Perelman in the US, quoted companies such as Hanson Trust (latterly Hanson) and BTR in the UK. Buoyant economic conditions and falling interest rates created a back drop of booming stock markets, the perfect conditions for quoted companies to fund acquisitions through issuing shares. And for the successful it became a virtuous circle: high earnings growth commanded a high price–earnings ratio, which made acquiring other companies still easier.

These acquisitions generated enhanced earnings growth from a number of sources: price–earnings arbitrage (a mathematical benefit that accrues from issuing shares with a high price–earnings ratio to buy the shares of a company with a much lower price–earnings multiple); the opportunity to increase returns in the acquired company by imposing stricter financial controls; and the latitude granted by accounting rules to create acquisition provisions, effectively meaning that tranches of cost never had to be charged against income. This earnings growth sustained the high price–earnings multiples, thereby reducing the cost of capital and extending the virtuous spiral until these companies had grown to such a size that the acquisitions required to sustain this earnings momentum became too large (at which point the acquiring companies themselves were broken up).

Booming stock markets also led institutional investors to increase their weightings in equities over bonds to boost performance. Increasingly judged on quarterly performance by pension fund trustees, institutional investors reciprocated by subjecting the corporate sector whose pension funds they were managing to much shorter-term scrutiny. And as the opportunity to boost profits through cost savings arose, so too did the need to do so quickly and effectively, with stock market timescales increasingly leading strategic decision making as a result.

However, as most privatized companies were monopolies – either natural (utilities) or strategic (national champions) – a compensating change in the competitive environment became necessary. Without effective competition, these monopolies could exploit their market positions to extract profits from a customer base lacking alternatives to please their new stock market masters, no matter how tightly prices were regulated. As a result, both Reagan and Thatcher sought to introduce competition into what had previously been highly regulated industries. This was more central to Thatcherism than Reaganomics, but that was in part due to reforms already introduced by President Jimmy Carter. As William Niskanen, a member of Reagan's council of Economic Advisers, summarized:

> The reduction in economic regulation that started in the Carter administration continued, but at a slower rate. Reagan eased or eliminated price controls on oil and natural gas, cable TV, long-distance telephone service, interstate bus service, and ocean shipping. Banks were allowed to invest in a somewhat broader set of assets, and the scope of the antitrust laws was reduced.[4]

Within the European Union, this was further enforced by the creation of the Single European Market. Governments sought to (or were forced to) open up previously closed monopolies to new entrants, both domestic and international. For international entrants, often privatized companies themselves, deregulation provided opportunities for growth outside domestic markets as compensation for coming under increased attack at home. Markets that were previously localized and populated with national champions became increasingly dominated by global players.

However, European market deregulation was not the only political factor spurring the internationalization of business. Also important was the collapse of communism in Soviet Bloc countries, symbolized by the tearing down of the Berlin Wall in 1989, which both broadened and deepened trading opportunities. Several rounds of talks from the 1960s through to the mid-1990s increased freedom of trade and reduced protectionism. And after the Uruguay GATT round in 1994, these trade talks started to matter less, with the success of previous rounds given momentum by the private sector, the activities of businesses supplanting in importance the actions of governments.[5]

The combined effect of these factors on international trade has been considerable. Between 1990 and 2008, exports of goods and services more than quadrupled in value from $4.3 trillion to $19.7 trillion.[6] Liberalization on the current account of the global balance of payments has been matched by liberalization of capital account flows and lower trade barriers complemented by reductions in foreign exchange controls. The resulting capital account impact has been huge, with gross global capital flows surging from the equivalent of 6 per cent of world GDP to 15 per cent between 1995 and 2005.[7]

Globalization has created numerous opportunities for businesses to grow profits. On the revenue side it has opened up new markets for international expansion, often via acquisitions. In parallel, it has provided the scope for businesses to reduce costs through transferring activities – initially manufacturing, latterly support functions – to lower wage cost countries, either directly or through outsourcing.

The power of the PC

Supply-side economics and globalization are only part of the reason for the cost savings that have been so important to corporate earnings growth. They created the opportunity to reduce manpower and labour costs, but accessing that opportunity required something that would enable people to be replaced by machines and manual processes by automation. That something was the exponential growth in computing power. As Nicholas Carr put it in his 2004 book *Does IT Matter?*:

> *Along with the rollback of government restrictions on trade, the proliferation of computer hardware and software has been the major*

force shaping business over the past forty years. Today, few would dispute that information technology has become the backbone of commerce in the developed world. It underpins the operations of individual companies, ties together far-flung supply chains, and increasingly links businesses with the customers they serve.

In 1965 Gordon Moore, co-founder of Intel, wrote an article entitled 'Cramming more components onto integrated circuits', in which he outlined why the number of transistors that could be placed inexpensively on an integrated circuit would increase exponentially over the following 10 years. Moore's foresight proved correct and for far longer than he initially anticipated: the cost of corporate data processing has dropped by 99.9 per cent since the 1960s.[8]

Some 20 years on from Moore's original prediction, the costs of computing had fallen sufficiently for personal computers to proliferate across the corporate sector, providing significant processing power to any company that wanted it. The implications were caricatured by Robert Cringely in his 1992 bestseller *Accidental Empires*:

Personal computers came along in the late 1970s and by the mid-1980s had invaded every corporate office and infected many homes. In addition to being the ultimate item of conspicuous consumption for those of us who don't collect fine art, PCs killed the office type-writer, made most secretaries obsolete, and made it possible for a 27-year-old MBA with a PC, a spreadsheet program, and three pieces of questionable data to talk his bosses into looting the company pension fund and doing a leveraged buy-out.

Without personal computers, there would have been – could have been – no Michael Milkens or Ivan Boeskys. Without personal computers, there would have been no supply-side economics. But, with the development of personal computers, for the first time in history, a single person could gather together and get a shaky handle on enough data to cure a disease or destroy a career. Personal com-

puters made it possible for businesses to move further and faster than they ever had before, creating untold wealth.[9]

Computing power enabled businesses to take advantage of the opportunity that supply-side economics had opened up: the automation of what had previously been manual and the replacement of people with hardware and software. As Carr put it,

> *Computers are everywhere, and they seem to be doing almost everything. They have simplified computations of all sorts and have given us easy access to enormous stores of information. Connected through the Internet, they have changed the way we communicate, gather information, and, in some cases, shop and carry out other everyday transactions. Applying their enormous computational power, companies have automated myriad tasks that used to be done manually, speeding up many activities and often reducing costs substantially.*[10]

The continued growth in processing speed has been accompanied by a surge in investment in information technology. Carr goes on:

> *During the last quarter of the twentieth century, the computational power of a microprocessor increased by a factor of 66,000. Spending on software jumped from less than $1 billion in 1970 to $138 billion in 2000. In the dozen years between 1989 and 2001, the number of host computers connected to the Internet grew from 80,000 to more than 125 million. Over the last ten years, the number of sites on the World Wide Web has grown from zero to nearly 40 million.*[11]

This increased expenditure on IT has generated widespread gains in productivity, the momentum increasing in the late 1990s.[12] A study by two economists at the Federal Reserve Board concluded that the use of computers had made a relatively small contribution to the productivity growth achieved during the early 1990s, but that its contribution surged in the second half of the decade, inverting its previous unimportance and becoming the key driver of gains.[13]

The effect of this has continued in the current decade, with Carr concluding:

> *Indeed, the strong continued expansion in U.S. productivity since the turn of the century seems to be, in large part, a product of the IT investments of the 1990s, which have enabled companies to do more with fewer employees.*[14]

The processing power of the personal computer provided the first stage of the productivity revolution; the development of the World Wide Web along with the explosion in bandwidth provided the connectivity to launch the second. Despite the hype of the dot-com era about a new economy comprised of new growth platforms and disruptive business models, the history of Web 1.0 shows that the value it delivered to businesses was akin to old-economy traditions. As Jack Welch, writing in 2001, described it:

> *the sceptics, thinking that we couldn't find any more efficiency at GE, used to ask me if there was any juice left in the lemon. The Net gave us a whole new lemon, a grapefruit, and perhaps even a watermelon – all on a platter.*[15]

Welch highlighted how the internet delivered efficiency savings of 5–10 per cent in buying costs through using online auctions to access more suppliers; savings of $1bn from the digitization of paper in backroom operations; and faster fulfilment for customers without the need for multiple telephone calls (so delivering savings for both GE and its customers).

On top of these gains, the steady increase in bandwidth has provided corporate juice extractors with a pineapple and a papaya by enabling remote access to corporate systems and the wholesale transfer of office-based activities – back-office administration and data entry, middle-office customer support and even front-office customer contact – from higher-cost to lower-cost countries. Corporate functional activities such as HR, finance and procurement can now be performed from offshore locations with information shared digitally across the organization. Application forms can be scanned in the country of origination and the data uploaded automatically, or the digital copies stored so they can be accessed in China and the data entered manually. With digital access to relevant data sets, reconciliations can be completed anywhere in the world. Less complex customer interactions such as simple requests (e.g. for more information) can be transferred to the web, channelled to an offshore location and fulfilled by someone who doesn't need to be able to hold a conversation in the language of the originating country. Lower-value customers can be moved to self-service channels to enable low-cost processing. All customers may have to call a service centre in India, where the operator has access to the enterprise's customer relationship management system and can take orders, resolve account queries or handle complaints.

But as well as replacing lower value-added jobs in economically mature countries, the PC has created them, particularly in the knowledge-intensive services sector. Indeed, a whole new sector – private equity – has grown up on the back of developments in information technology.

As Cringely's comments above suggest, the increasing tide of mergers and acquisitions (M&A), the boom in private equity and hedge funds, and the consequent demands for the services of investment bankers and consultants would never have been possible without the processing power delivered by the personal computer. Spreadsheet programs enabled the creation of detailed cash flow models helping financial acquirers calculate sustainable levels of debt or the value of sophisticated financing techniques. Corporate acquirers could model potential synergies. Bottom-up analysis became easier, so the value of each division or subsidiary could be separately estimated. Hundreds or thousands of simulations could be run, using different assumptions for the key variables, providing a distribution of values for what the target company was worth.

M&A magic

M&A activity surged in the late 1980s, in part due to the advent of leveraged buyouts. It declined due to the economic and interest rate conditions of the early 1990s, before picking up again, with the global value of deals surging to over $3 trillion in both 1999 and 2000.[16] Activity declined once more following the bursting of the internet bubble, but started recovering in 2004 before reaching new highs in 2006 and the first half of 2007. Then the onrushing credit crunch restricted the supply of debt and brought activity almost to a halt.

So why has M&A become the main outlet for corporate investment? Once again, the answer lies in the productivity revolution spawned by supply-side economics and the PC. A conveyor belt of cost-reduction opportunities focused businesses increasingly on operational effectiveness rather than strategic differentiation. For efficiently run companies, their poorly run brethren provided a whole new bag of juicy oranges to squeeze. Even if both were reasonably efficient, there would be opportunities to leverage increased purchasing power into lower raw material costs, access scale economies in production and eliminate duplication in selling, general and administrative costs. In simple mathematics, in revenue terms 1+1 should equal close to 2 (some customers would defect), but on the cost side it should amount to significantly less, maybe 1.5 to 1.7, due to the savings the combined organizations would generate.

M&A also provides a lower-risk route into new geographical or product-service markets. Buying an existing player delivers existing customer relationships and a ready-made organization without building from scratch or risking the creation of overcapacity through investment in additional plant and machinery.

The resulting consolidation can be seen in a McKinsey study into the growth of the mega-company.[17] Over the 20-year period from

1984 to 2004, revenue for the largest 150 companies (measured by market capitalization)[18] grew by 85 per cent in real terms while the number of employees grew by a relatively paltry 29 per cent. Net income grew by 223 per cent, with net income per employee – the best measure of productivity – growing by 151 per cent. As a result, the average market capitalization for this group of companies grew by 558 per cent, by 411 per cent in per employee terms.

The McKinsey study picks the largest companies by market capitalization at three points in time, not the same companies over time. And while it shows how increase in corporate size, driven by M&A, has transformed corporate productivity, this should not be confused with M&A delivering superior financial returns.

The key criterion for assessing the success of M&A as a strategic tool is the price paid by acquiring companies relative to the profits of the target company subsequent to its integration. The consistent findings of study after study over the last 30 years is that most corporate acquirers overpay for acquisitions in anywhere between 65 per cent and 90 per cent of cases.[19] The financial benefits accrue almost wholly to the shareholders of the acquired rather than the acquiring company. This overpayment may arise from competition among bidders leading to the 'winner's curse' (the average of all bids is typically fairly accurate so, by definition, the winner has bid too high), overoptimism about potential synergies, the deal acquiring a momentum of its own or a combination of all three. (These and other behavioural biases will be covered more fully in Chapter 4.) Even if the cost and revenue equations support the logic of acquiring, behavioural factors often mean that the price paid is too high, resulting in an equation of $1 + 1 < 2$ for the acquirer's market capitalization.

While corporate acquirers may not have generated value from M&A, the same cannot be said for financial acquirers, with private equity swelling each tide in M&A activity in the late 1980s,[20] late 1990s and the mid-2000s. Over this period the returns generated have been impressive and the share of private equity as an asset class held by institutional investors such as pension funds has also grown. As a result, private equity firms have been able to raise larger and larger funds and do bigger and bigger deals.

The UK provides a good growth proxy for the industry globally (being less advanced than the US but more developed than Continental Europe). According to the Centre for Management Buyout Research (CMBOR), the total value of UK buyouts grew more than fifteenfold in the 20 years leading up to the most recent peak, from £1.5 bn in 1986 to £25 bn in 2006.[21]

This growth is a result of the superior risk-adjusted returns delivered by private equity investments relative to other asset classes. The BVCA performance measurement survey highlights that private equity generated more than double the return of the FTSE All-Share Index over the five- and ten-year periods to end 2006 and an 82 per cent better return over three years.[22] A CMBOR study of 321 exited buyouts in the UK for the period 1995 to 2004 found an average equity internal rate of return (IRR) of 70.5 per cent.[23]

The spectacular performance of private equity over the 1990s was achieved much in the same way as the stock market-quoted acquisition artists such as Hanson generated excellent returns for their shareholders in the 1970s and 1980s: by buying underperforming businesses and improving their returns (again with some assistance from price–earnings ratio arbitrage, though for private equity purchasers this simply involved buying the company at a low multiple and selling it at a higher one, either due to improving the long-term prospects of the company or general inflation in the multiples paid).

However, the key difference was that divisions rather than whole businesses were typically acquired. A study of the industry found:

In the early years of the current buyout boom, private equity firms prospered mainly by acquiring the non-core business units of large public companies. Under their previous owners, those businesses had suffered from neglect, unsuitable performance targets, or other con-

straints. Even if well managed, such businesses may have lacked an independent track record because the parent company had integrated their operations with those of other units, making the businesses hard to value. Sales by public companies of unwanted business units were the most important category of large private equity buyouts until 2004... and leading firms' widely admired history of high investment returns comes largely from acquisitions of this type.[24]

Such targets provided a significant opportunity for performance improvement with productivity gains at its heart. A study of 4877 manufacturing plants that had experienced a private equity-backed management buyout between 1994 and 1998 revealed that on average these plants were 2 per cent less productive than their peers prior to the buyout, but that productivity increased by 90 per cent post-acquisition.[25]

Personal experience of working with private equity firms confirms this focus on productivity. Of the more than 40 evaluations of potential acquisitions for private equity investors in which I was involved from 1997 to 2004, the vast majority were predicated on returns generated by cost reduction rather than organic growth. As one partner at a leading private equity firm summarized it, 'We give four times the credibility to cost savings than we do to revenue growth.'

This focus also delivers a second benefit. In addition to increased confidence about management's ability to deliver cost savings, timescales for achieving them are shorter. As anyone who has modelled an IRR will attest, the shorter the timeframe, the easier it is to generate a high rate of return. With private equity firms incentivized to deliver a high IRR on investments in order to maximize their share of the returns achieved, a focus on quick wins is understandable.

Nevertheless, there is evidence that this focus may be changing. Latterly, private equity funds have focused on the acquisition of entire public companies, due to a combination of the drying up of opportunities to buy unloved subsidiaries and the need to do larger and larger deals as fund sizes have increased. In addition, the private equity sector has been put on the defensive by increased attacks from the trade unions, in which they have been characterized as asset strippers and job cutters rather than business builders. The combination of these factors is dictating an increased focus on creating businesses with sustainable growth characteristics, not least because exiting the investment will often require an initial public offering on the stock market. Developing a track record of preparing companies for sustained organic growth is becoming increasingly important and creates a more strategic rather than purely operational challenge.

Creative consulting

The exponential growth in computing power has also driven the growth of another professional service sector: the consulting industry. The continuing fall in the cost of data transfer, processing and storage has created wave after wave of investment in enterprise computing – financial control, enterprise resource planning, customer relationship management, e-business and, most recently, business intelligence. The associated requirements for process reengineering, technical design and programme implementation has turned the leading systems integrators into the 800 lb gorillas of the consulting industry.

It has also transformed the strategy consulting industry. First, these consultants have been beneficiaries of the PC-led growth in corporate M&A and private equity transactions, both of which typically require either strategic support or due diligence. In addition, the PC has enabled consultancies to perform more and more detailed analysis – shaping assumptions as to what strategy is in the process – and to operate with a business model that leverages the experienced few at the top of the organization with many relatively inexperienced but bright consultants in the lower tiers.

By the late 1980s the falling costs of microchips made equipping every consultant with a PC increasingly viable. Allying computing power with smart, educated young professionals created a whole new set of activities, built on the collection and analysis of data, for consultancies to sell their clients. This 'intellectualization of business', as former *Harvard Business Review* editor Walter Kiechel describes it in *The Lords of Strategy*,[26] enabled these firms to hire out smart university graduates and freshly minted MBAs at good rates while growing them into the managers and partners that would sustain future growth.

With detailed quantitative analysis increasingly feasible, the consulting industry was able to create offers that leveraged this capability and met managements' ongoing desire for greater understanding of their current situation: cost and service benchmarking studies; plant, product, channel and customer profitability analyses; potential acquisition and capital investment evaluations; statistics-based market research studies such as conjoint analysis and perceptual mapping; purchase and sales data analyses for reducing procurement costs, increasing customer loyalty or improving campaign effectiveness; and many others.

The more analysis that could be done, the more companies wanted done. And whereas historically they might have created internal teams to perform this work, the expertise and experience gained with other clients, a desire to trim fixed cost bases, the need for flexibility and increasingly short time horizons made the option of giving this work to consultants an increasingly attractive one. Also, with key decisions subject to increased external scrutiny, a board of directors could justify key decisions if they were recommended by a prestigious strategy firm.

The value associated with these studies created demand for bright but inexperienced consultants. The supply of willing candidates was plentiful: the high salary more than compensated for the additional employment risk, and the name of a prestigious consultancy on the CV was seen as the first step in a successful business career. This confluence of supply and demand enabled consultancy organizations to become wide-based pyramids, with associate consultants at the bottom and partners at the top, to the financial benefit of all involved.

Despite the inevitable downturns that such an economically geared sector must experience, notably in the early 1990s and 2000s (the almost inevitable consequence of the M&A frenzies of the late 1980s and late 1990s), the consulting industry has grown spectacularly. In the UK, the number of consultants employed by members of the Management Consultancies Association grew by an average annual rate of just under 15 per cent from 1980 to 2006, and at 20 per cent per annum over the 20 years from 1995.[27] Even over longer periods the growth is still impressive, at 8.5 per cent per annum from 1960.

While no such figures are available for the US, the growth appears to be just as impressive. In *The World's Newest Profession: Management Consulting in the 21st Century*,[28] Christopher McKenna describes the growth of two of the industry heavyweights, Booz Allen & Hamilton and McKinsey & Co. In 1960 Booz and McKinsey had consulting staffs of 300 and 165 respectively. By 2003 both had grown to roughly 6000 consultants.[29]

McKenna highlights how prevalent consultancy has become as a career choice for graduates, pointing out that by the middle of the 2000s 'nearly one third of the top MBA graduates and one-sixth of all elite undergraduates (whether at Oxford or Yale) now began their lives as management consultants'. The popularity of consulting was also neatly summarized by Nicholas Lemann in the *New Yorker*, who concluded that the best students were drawn to consulting because these firms offered students 'that odd upper-meritocratic combination of love of competition, herd mentality and aversion to risk' and that the United States had decided 'in effect to devote its top academic talent to the project of streamlining the operations of big business'.[30]

The legacy of this focus on streamlining is that a generation of strategy consultants, including many now ex-consultants in corporate roles, has been brought up on a diet of improving operational effectiveness based around economic analysis and business case development that has been labelled 'Strategy'.

Thinking about thinking

That the PC has brought such growth in well-paid sectors that draw the brightest and the best is no coincidence, as it enables them to do what they enjoy and are good at both faster and more accurately, and on a scale that would not be possible manually. The professions that have benefited most from the fall in data-processing costs are those where the value resides in the approach to collecting and analysing information and turning it into understanding, such as consultancy and investment banking, more than in those where the value lies in innate knowledge developed over years of experience, the foundation of most professions.

Educational beliefs have had a particularly profound impact in this regard. Edward de Bono, inventor of the term lateral thinking and a longstanding proponent of more emphasis on the development of creativity in education, has described how the basic building blocks of our thinking stem from some 2400 years ago and the philosophers of Ancient Greece: Socrates, Plato and Aristotle. From this 'Gang of Three' we have inherited a thinking system based on 'analysis, judgement (and boxes), argument and criticism'.[31] De Bono also highlights the limitations of this approach:

> *While analysis does solve a great many problems, there are other problems where the cause cannot be found and if found cannot be removed. Such problems will not yield to more analysis.*

In *New Thinking for the New Millennium*, he describes the impact this has on how we think about education and academic success:

> *The 'academic game' is a very special game. You are required to take in and remember quite a lot of information. You have to store this. Then, on demand, as in examinations, you are required to sort through the stored information and to give it back. Youngsters who are poor on the input or storage side have no chance at all in the academic game…*

...At university level [analysis] is almost the key theme of intellectual effort: how can we analyze complex situations into their component parts so that we can understand the situation and perhaps apply a poultice of standard remedies. The purpose of analysis is to break things down so that we can judge and identify their causes. A doctor's skill depends on his or her ability to diagnose illnesses. This is a pure judgment process.[32]

The crux of de Bono's argument is that our emphasis on analysis is misplaced, since 90 per cent of errors in thinking derive from errors of perception rather than errors of logic. However, our educational system focuses almost exclusively on using analysis and logic as the means for solving problems. We are taught to think in a certain way and we take that into our business lives, now more than ever given that over the last 30 years there has been a step change in the numbers investing in postgraduate business education. (For anyone who has not studied for an MBA or been on an executive development or advanced management programme, a business school is much like any other school or university. The professors are academics – not business practitioners – with similar beliefs, aspirations and presuppositions as their university brethren.)

This growth in business education can be seen most particularly in Europe. In the UK in the mid-1960s two MBA programmes existed, at Manchester Business School and London Business School. Some 20 years later[33] the choice was still relatively limited, the two original schools being augmented by City University Business School (now known as Cass Business School), Cranfield School of Management and one or two others. On the continent the best regarded were INSEAD in France (Europe's oldest business school, founded in 1958) and IMI and IMEDE in Switzerland (which merged to become IMD in 1990). For those fluent in Spanish there was IESE in Barcelona. Compared to the US, the choice was not extensive. These schools were also relatively new – typically less than 30 years old – compared to the leading US schools, which were founded in the early decades of the twentieth century (or 1881 in the case of the Wharton School of Business).[34]

Nowadays, in contrast, aspiring MBA students are spoilt for choice. In the UK most universities now have a business faculty, the Association of Business Schools boasting approximately 100 members. Britain's three most internationally prestigious universities – Oxford, Cambridge and Imperial College, London – established the Saïd Business School, the Judge School of Business and the Tanaka Business School with endowments from an eponymous trio who create an interesting, if not entirely representative, depiction of great wealth creation during the last quarter of the twentieth century: a businessman with strong connections to the Saudi royal family, a disgraced financier and the leader of one of the first management buyouts in the UK.[35] As well as graduate MBA programmes, business studies has made the leap from being viewed as vocational – and therefore not suitable to be taught as an undergraduate honours degree – to being regarded as academic.

Quantifying questions

These institutions have given weight to the belief that management is a science, that causes and effects are measurable. And one of the side benefits of the growth in enterprise resource planning, customer relationship management and business intelligence solutions that businesses have implemented is the wealth of performance measures they generate. Key performance indicators and metrics have long been a central tenet of operational effectiveness where cause and effect are most easily linked.

However, as important as this laudable empiricism is relativism, an innate desire to measure performance relative to competitors and comparators, often boiled down to a simple number. All performance measures – from reported profits to percentage profit margin and return on capital or stock turn – are simplifications of a complex reality. Yet this doesn't stop these quantifications – particularly relative ones – being hugely powerful.

This became particularly apparent during the few years I spent marketing mutual funds, when I discovered that the most effective advertisements were the ones that had a large number in them. This number could take many forms: screaming out the percentage return of a fund over the past five years ('+104%'), the income yield it would deliver ('over 10%') or simply the number '1' in large type to signify that the fund was the top performer in its sector or in the top quartile (or many 1s to show it had consistently been in the top quartile over many years). You would still always need a story explaining why people should invest, but a great story without a number would yield a lower response than a large number without much of a story. It is our natural tendency to try to transform complexity into something we can easily comprehend and numbers enable us to do this.

In business there is a saying: 'What gets measured gets managed.' Underlying the expression is a basic presupposition that all you need is information to tell you when a problem exists, as the solution will reveal itself in the data.

This is not always the case. A couple of years ago I bought a GPS-enabled golf rangefinder, which provides me with information on carries from tees to fairways, yardages to hazards and exact distances to the front, back or middle of the green. It also helps me calculate how far I hit each ball. However, knowing that I am 157 yards from the pin is a very different matter to hitting the ball that distance and straight. As yet, such data richness – while providing me with the pleasure that precision brings (and an opportunity to faze less quantitative opponents with comments like 'Wow, it is 198 yards to the fairway from this back tee') – has not reduced the only metric that really counts, my handicap. As far as my golf is concerned, errors of judgement regarding distances are minor compared with errors of execution. (Indeed, more accurate distance information removes the possibility of self-cancelling errors.)

I have also recently purchased a solar-powered atomic watch. Its accuracy is a source of great joy to me, though its superiority over my previous watch in this regard has had no impact on my productivity, making no difference to how early or late I am, or others are, for meetings.

Precision, where it can be found, is often a source of comfort for a particular type of business person, especially when all around is uncertain. It is no coincidence that business intelligence initiatives that improve management information thrive in difficult times while other systems initiatives are shelved. The challenge with precision is to prioritize where it is most valuable and not to overinvest when its value is limited; in most cases it is better to be roughly right than precisely wrong.

In business there is a difference between basic operational problems, where quantification may be sufficient for the solution to reveal itself, and more complex strategic ones when it is not; as Einstein noted, 'not everything that counts can be counted, and not everything that can be counted counts'. The significant amount of management effort or consultant time put into counting – specifically analysing and modelling – may improve operational effectiveness. But far more questionable is the impact these processes have on improving the quality of strategic decision making, which by definition is about the future rather than the past, subject to external as well as internal factors and suffers from a high degree of uncertainty with limited hard data on which to build accurate predictions. Our ability to estimate and evaluate probabilities attached to future events has not advanced in line with our ability, courtesy of the lower costs of data processing, to analyse the past.

The problem with probability has been a favourite topic for a number of writers in recent times, including Nassim Nicholas Taleb and Massimo Piattelli-Palmarini, but also the illusionist Derren Brown. All three focus on how cognitive illusions inhibit our ability to make good probability-based decisions.

The following is an example used to illustrate this point. There is a deadly disease that afflicts one in 10,000 people, for which there is a test that is 99 per cent accurate. How worried should you be if you receive a positive test result? The answer of most people asked this question is 'very worried', because they believe that, given the 99 per cent accuracy, there is only a 1 per cent chance that they do not have the deadly disease. In fact the opposite is true: there is a greater than 99 per cent chance that they are disease free, as 100 people (1 per cent of 10,000) will receive false positive results while only 1 person in 10,000 will actually have contracted the disease.

This particular example is merely an intellectual exercise but it highlights a real business problem, as many big decisions that businesses must make require judgements of probability. If we are reviewing the past, we can rely on analysis for illumination. The greater the quantity and quality of relevant data, the more valuable analysis is to support decision making. Decisions on improving efficiency are backward facing and if accurate data on current performance exist, the analytical approaches work well.

However, if we need to make a decision based on how we think a market might evolve, how customers might respond or how competitors might react, we are often stymied by uncertainty. With these forward-looking decisions, data for analysis don't exist, merely a range of different potential outcomes across different dimensions that need to be described, bounded (if a range of outcomes is possible), the impacts assessed and likelihoods attached.

The distinction between what is appropriate for backward-looking as opposed to forward-facing decisions has been lost. Behavioural science has highlighted how we tend to overvalue the study of history in helping us understand the present and the future (the reasons for these historian's fallacies are covered in more detail in Chapter 4). And in business we do the same, projecting into the future using tools, techniques and models that are most effective when describing the past.

This causes problems if we accept numbers at face value and with insufficient scepticism. We are naturally credulous, tending to take what we are told on trust. It is not in the nature of most people when presented with a number to question how it has been calculated so that its credibility can be assessed, or to ask 'How?' and 'Why?' to establish what the number really shows. Percentages are particularly dangerous, especially percentages calculated on a percentage. For example, if the risk of a negative event increases from 0.00001 per cent to 0.00002 per cent, that can be portrayed as either an increase of 0.00001 per cent or one of 100 per cent. We are at the mercy of how the teller wishes to spin the story.

This has given rise to a form of pseudo-empiricism or, as the economist John Kay has described it, 'the age of the bogus survey'.[36] Kay compares real research which 'has the objective of yielding new information' with bogus surveys that 'are designed to generate publicity' through eye-catching statistics. These are now a standard part of the offer that public relations firms make to their clients. Kay cites a headline-grabbing story that 95 per cent of children in the UK had been victims of crime. From a legal perspective, hitting a classmate or stealing a pencil is a crime, so such a high percentage should be expected. Yet the figure was deemed sufficiently newsworthy to be the lead story for a number of newspapers and radio and television channels.

The postmodernist challenge

Bogus surveys, indeed the whole PR industry, have been given momentum by an underlying cultural trend, postmodernism. Postmodernism encompasses both artistic and philosophical dimensions. In its artistic sense, it replaced the minimalist ethos of modernism with an increased emphasis on ornament and representation. While modernism elevated function over form, postmodernism has reversed this.

The rise of the spin doctor is one obvious manifestation that everyone would recognize. Giving a favourable spin to a piece of news is what psychologists call reframing. If you can't change the facts, change the context in which those facts will be judged by the target audience – customers, employees, partners, environmental groups, shareholders, governments or whomever. Failure can be magically transformed into success by selecting a favourable benchmark to compare it against or an advantageous starting point. Or if all else fails, release bad news on a day when no one will notice.

For the most part the transition from modernism to post-modernism has been gradual and barely commented on beyond arts publications. However, in 2004 it attracted newspaper attention when James Dyson, inventor of the eponymous vacuum cleaner, resigned as Chairman of the Design Museum in London over what he felt was the disregard for the 'engineer's creation – the manufactured object'. Dyson summarized his reasons in the BBC's annual Richard Dimbleby Lecture, which he titled 'Engineering the Difference':

There are two sides to the design coin. There is serious design – making sure that the manufactured object performs its task in the best possible way. And there is styling – the essentially superficial task of making sure something looks attractive.

Both are important to me. After all, my wife is a rug designer and an artist. My daughter and son-in-law design clothes.

However, the Design Museum was set up by Terence Conran to champion the manufactured object. There are dozens of places that examine style. The V&A, art galleries, newspapers and style magazines. There are very few places that focus seriously on how and why we make things...

Dyson went on to describe the reactions to his departure:

Meanwhile, in the press, my departure was being deconstructed as a clash between the past and the future. I was told that styling had usurped engineering in the latter half of the twentieth century. And that it went deeper than just a change of fashion. My values of technology and manufacturing were old-fashioned, they said. And if our economy was to succeed, I had to realize something:

the future prosperity of developed nations rested in the hands of stylists.

Yet here I am. Someone whose recipe for success has been to make things that people want to buy. Not because they look better – although of course I hope they do – but because they work better.

What decoration and styling are to the world of design, presentation is to the world of business. In a postmodern society the linkage between image and substance is decoupled – perception is reality. The resulting belief is that you are what you claim to be. If you describe yourself as the best, the leader, the No. 1 choice, then people will believe you, so long as you behave as if you are and repeat the message over and over again. Not surprisingly, the sector that has thrived on the rise of postmodernism more than any other is advertising.

Like the consulting industry, advertising can boast a long track record of growth, most impressively over the last quarter of the twentieth century. During this period global advertising expenditure grew in real terms by an average annual rate of 4.9 per cent, driven by growth in developed countries, expenditures in the US and UK growing at 5.0 and 5.1 per cent respectively.[37] In the case of the UK this was more than double the real rate of economic growth of 2.4 per cent per annum over the same period.[38]

This era culminated in the internet boom when the style-over-substance trend reached its apotheosis, most notably in start-ups blowing millions of dollars on Super Bowl advertising slots, the process of building brand awareness deemed a more valuable use of funds raised from venture capitalists than developing the underlying service. And over the dot-com years, 1995–2000, real expenditure on advertising grew at 6.7 per cent per annum in the US and 7.3 per cent in the UK.

The internet boom was an exceptional period, and it took a further five years or so for expenditure to return to the peak levels of 2000. But the seeds of this excess were sown in the 1970s and 1980s.

These decades are often described as a golden age of advertising, particularly in the UK, spawning the Saatchi brothers, Ridley and Tony Scott, Alan Parker, Adrian Lyne and David Puttnam. The time also saw a marked decline in UK manufacturing in terms of both production efficiency and output quality. Necessity being the mother of invention, the UK was at the forefront of the charge into postmodern marketing, such that it became 'at ease with the idea that its companies were bad at making cars but good at advertising them'.[39]

While things were not so marked in the US, advertising has still become seen as a source of differentiation. At the time of the creation of Omnicom by the three-way merger of DDB, BBDO and Needham Harper in 1986, a *New York Times* article opined that advertising had gained enormous status because it is 'responsible for adding perceived differences in products where actual differences, because of technological advances, often no longer exist'.[40]

Looked at from the perspective of a quarter of a century later, there might be quibbles with the exact wording (technological advances enhance differences, as one company will implement them before others; it is the ability of imitators to copy the innovations of leaders that removes differences). Nevertheless, the perception remains that brand image communicated through advertising provides a true source of differentiation, even in industries where the products are substantive (technological advances play a part) and can be experienced by customers (cars or consumer electronics, for example), not just in sectors where differences in product performance are hard to attest (such as soap powder) or performance is irrelevant as there is no functional definition of better or worse, just taste and preference (e.g. beer and cigarettes). The outward spread of branding from the fast-moving consumer goods sector to most others can be seen in the growth of brand consultancies (now typically part of advertising groups).

As important as the artistic dimension of postmodernism to marketing, its philosophical dimension has had perhaps an even more profound effect, specifically with regard to its impact on rationalism. Given the assumption of rationality that underpins economic and management thinking, this has significant implications. Studies in behavioural economics have shown us to be far more irrational and biased than neoclassical economists have always presumed. And any decline in the value we attribute to rationality and the scientific approach will only increase the gap between convenient assumption and inconvenient reality.

The postmodernist challenge to the scientific approach is that all truth is relative: what we define as truth is simply a product of our value system. When viewed this way, science is simply another belief system based on subjective and personal meanings. We are not as rational as we pretend to be or need to be for the scientific method to yield the truth. All of us, even scientists, are predisposed to certain views and filter evidence so that most weight is attached to that which is supportive (the unsupportive evidence may be acknowledged in the name of the scientific process, but only for it to be dismissed). As such, postmodernists argue that science holds no more or less validity than any other belief system.

Obviously scientists bridle at such a categorization, arguing that collectively science is rational – even if individual scientists are not – with good ideas eventually driving out bad. Also that science, indeed the philosophy of rationalism, has driven the most significant advances of the past two centuries, massively contributing to human well-being in the process. And if scientific developments are used for unethical or immoral purposes, that is because of flawed belief systems – political, religious or philosophical – not flaws in the scientific process. However, such arguments appear increasingly to be falling on deaf ears.

Resurgent religion

The attack on science has been two-pronged: on one side from the resurgence of traditional religious beliefs, on the other from the rise of new age thinking, an umbrella term for everything from alternative therapies to eco-fundamentalism. This has been charted by a number of authors, including Richard Dawkins (*The God Delusion*), Christopher Hitchens (*God Is Not Great*), Dick Taverne[41] (*The March of Unreason*) and Derren Brown[42] (*Tricks of the Mind*), to name but a few.

Beliefs, whether articulated as religious commandments, values, morals or ethics, are fundamental to how we judge right from wrong. In this sense they are critical to social harmony. The conflict with the scientific method arises when such beliefs are used to judge true and false. Scientists argue that judgements of verity and falsity are amoral, best made through the development of hypotheses, the weighing of evidence for and against and a focus on refutation. Such thinking enjoyed increasing acceptance until the latter part of the twentieth century. Alongside learning and democracy, rationalism was a key pillar of the modernist philosophy that originated in the early modern period, gained momentum during the Enlightenment and prevailed for most of the twentieth century.

The recent rise of religion, characterized by the primacy of beliefs derived from holy books when making judgements, is shown by the growth in the proportion of the population attached to the four biggest religions – Christianity, Islam, Buddhism and Hinduism – in the developed world. This has grown from 67 per cent in 1900 to 73 per cent in 2005, the data showing a particularly sharp rise from the 1970s onwards, and is forecast to reach 80 per cent by 2050.[43] John Micklethwait, describing this resurgence in *The Economist*, summarized:

> By the end of the 1970s this counter-revolution [against rationalism] was in full swing. America had elected its first proudly born-again Christian, Jimmy Carter; Jerry Falwell had founded the Moral Majority; Iran had replaced the worldly Shah with Ayatollah Khomeini; Zia ul Haq was busy Islamising Pakistan; Buddhism had been formally granted the foremost place in Sri Lanka's constitution; and an anti-communist Pole had become head of the Catholic Church.

More worryingly from a rationalist point of view, *The Economist* highlighted that growth had been most pronounced at the extreme ends of the different faiths. Christianity has seen an increasing proportion of those believing in Creationism (or a variant called Intelligent Design), which preaches the world is less than 10,000 years old, began with Adam and Eve and could only have been created by an all-powerful supernatural force. Within Islam, fundamentalism, which at its most extreme persuades young men and women to sacrifice their lives in the name of their faith, is growing in strength.

The conflict between the fundamentalist and scientific approaches is summed up by Dawkins as follows:

Fundamentalists know they are right because they have read the truth in a holy book and they know, in advance, that nothing will budge them from their belief. The truth of a holy book is an axiom, not the end product of a process of reasoning. The book is true, and if the evidence seems to contradict it, it is the evidence that must be thrown out, not the book. By contrast, what I, as a scientist, believe (for example, evolution) I believe not because of reading a holy book but because I have studied the evidence.[44]

A new age?

The second pincer in the attack on science comes from what might be loosely described as new age thinking, perhaps best articulated by its unofficial spokesman, Prince Charles. The Prince of Wales has long been at odds with the UK's medical establishment, notably with regard to his lobbying for complementary medicine to be made available on the UK's National Health Service. Similarly, his support of organic farming has led him into conflict with the agricultural establishment regarding genetically modified crops. These differences have resulted in a direct attack on the philosophy of rationalism. In a speech at The Prince's Foundation's Annual Conference in 2010, he remarked, 'I was accused once of being the enemy of the Enlightenment. I felt rather proud.' To his way of thinking, the implication of 'huge challenges all over the world' is that rationalism is not 'really effective in today's conditions'. Warming to his theme, in the following June during a speech to mark the 25th anniversary of the Oxford Centre for Islamic Studies, he took aim at Galileo, blaming his assertion that there is nothing in nature but quantity and motion for the rise of mechanistic thinking, consumerism and the consequent 'de-souling' of the West.

For the rationally inclined, it is fairly easy to take issue with many of Prince Charles' views. Equally, while belief-based interventions may appear a more empathic way to resolve the 'huge challenges' we face, given that many such challenges could be characterized as religious conflicts, validating the primacy of belief risks hardening existing positions. Rationalism has also shown itself to be a powerful engine of economic growth that is more likely to break the poverty trap that typically underlies such conflicts, religious disagreements frequently being the manifestation of tribal disputes over scarce economic resources such as land, education and employment opportunities. Indeed, its success in this regard brings about Prince Charles' second charge. Again though, to the rationalist there appears to be some confusion in his thinking, specifically the conflation of science, as the means of economic development, with social choices, how we decide to enjoy the spoils of prosperity, what he calls consumerism.

It would also be easy to dismiss his views as being accorded more weight than they merit on account of his royal status. But that would be to overlook the fact that his views receive media coverage beyond the traditionally genuflecting conservative press because they reflect those of certain sections of society. One of those constituencies is the environmental movement, which, at its extremes, is as dogmatic as any religion. One example of this is regarding genetically modified (GM) crops. In *The March of Unreason*, Taverne argues:

> *Green lobbies are, if anything, more ready to sacrifice reason for the sake of dogma than politicians are for the sake of party. Weighty*

reports from authoritative sources that have no axe to grind, which show that GM crops can offer substantial potential benefits to the developing world and that there is no special reasons to suppose they are dangerous to human health, are simply ignored. Flimsy evidence from highly partisan sources (seldom if ever peer reviewed), which appeared to support their case against GM crops, is uncritically accepted.[45]

Taverne's fear is that the 'reliance on dogma and ideology instead of evidence is unhealthy for democracy'. He cites the public's increased credulity – its lack of need for evidence – as the main reason dogma can prevail. He also highlights the impact of the media, arguing that it viewed the environmental lobby as a 'sort of collective Mother Theresa', as a result of which the pronouncements of environmental groups were not subjected to the same scrutiny as those of self-serving politicians and company executives. These views were echoed by Mike Moore, the former Prime Minister of New Zealand:

Green ideology is becoming a theology. This new religion has many apostles, especially in the non-profit sector and the soft media... the green agenda... is all too often accepted at face value because it claims to have the planet's interests at heart, unlike grubby politicians and greedy businesspeople.[46]

These, of course, could be dismissed as the biased grumblings of former politicians. Nevertheless, taken from an ethical or moral perspective, their argument that in the court of public opinion the burden of proof lays only lightly on those to whom we attribute good motives makes sense. If conclusions appeal to our sensibilities, we are more likely to take the evidence for them on trust. Equally, those who seek to claim the moral high ground often expect their views to be taken on trust, responding with passion, perhaps even anger and insults, if challenged using rational argument.

Central to the scientific approach is scepticism, a focus on refutation rather than confirmation. The greatest damage done by 'Climategate', the publication of the hacked emails from the Climatic Research Unit at the University of East Anglia, was to the public's perception of climate scientists, specifically that they were biased on the evaluation of climate data. A series of reviews found this not to be the case and the scientific case for climate change remains intact.

In light of this, there has been increasing clamour for science to reclaim the badge of scepticism. In the *New Scientist*, Michael Shermer argued:

> *Scepticism is integral to the scientific process, because most claims turn out to be false. Weeding out the few kernels of wheat from the large pile of chaff requires extensive observation, careful experimentation and cautious inference. Science is scepticism and good scientists are sceptical.*[47]

However, this objective is undermined by the increasing politicization of science. Political affiliations are another expression of intrinsic beliefs. But while the conflict between scientists and religious fundamentalists (as, for example, between those who believe the Earth was created by God less than 10,000 years ago and those who believe in the Big Bang theory and subsequent evolution of all living things) is frequently stark, the politicization of science is less obvious and perhaps more damaging as a result. Rather than thinking best suited to separating right from wrong being applied to making judgements about truth and falsehood, judgements about truth and falsehood are employed to support views of right and wrong. As Shermer goes on:

> *Either evolution and the big bang happened or they did not; both matters can, in principle, be solved with more data and better theory. But the right form of taxation or government cannot be answered with more data and better theory. They are ideological positions that are established by subjective debate.*

The problem is that we find it hard to silence our inner ideologies when evaluating evidence. Writing in *Nature*, Dan Kahan pointed out what a growing body of work suggests:

> *People endorse whichever position reinforces their connection to others with whom they share important commitments. As a result, public debate about science is strikingly polarized. The same groups who disagree on 'cultural issues' – abortion, same-sex marriage and school prayer – also disagree on whether climate change is real and on whether underground disposal of nuclear waste is safe.*[48]

In the absence of being able to evaluate technical data for themselves, most people tend to follow the lead of a credible expert. But 'cultural cognition' as Kahan calls it works here too, with credibility as an expert defined by a perception of shared values rather than academic qualifications.

This can lead to individuals or groups holding contradictory viewpoints on the value of scientific evidence in different areas. Environmental groups are supportive of the scientific consensus on climate change but markedly less enthusiastic about the consensus on GM agriculture. In a blog posting called 'Genetically modified fetishism',[49] environmental campaigner Jonathon Porritt employed language and arguments questioning the science on the safety of GM crops that could have come straight from a climate sceptic's blog:

> *The pro-GM lobby has done a fantastic job in persuading the media and politicians that even the most modest GM-scepticism is tantamount to extreme science-hating emotionalism... To express any reservations about the notional sustainability benefits of current GM crops, let alone about the massively hyped potential benefits of future GM products, is to open oneself up to the charge of debilitating technophobia.*

The most damaging aspect of Climategate from a scientific perspective was how the Climatic Research Unit sought to avoid sharing its data and algorithms, transparency being an overarching principle of science. In the same way that climate sceptics had very significant reservations about the data used as evidence to support the charge of anthropomorphic global warming, Porritt continues:

> One's judgement about 'the balance of the evidence' depends largely on where that evidence comes from, and even pro-GM advocates are very uneasy about the stranglehold that the big biotech companies have over access to data and transparency of the data used by regulators.

Porritt's central point is a perfectly reasonable one – 'there are so many things that can and should be done right now to address issues of food security and increased yields without casting all our eggs in the GM basket'. But his tone raises the question of whether he would be as 'sceptical' about the balance of evidence and the data sources if the results were more supportive of his beliefs and less favourable to GM agriculture.

Beliefs, both religious and political, also mean that uncertainty is insufficiently regarded. In their desire to take actions that they believe to be right, politicians use science to imply certainty when no certainties exist. As *The Economist* has described it:

> the ambiguities of science sit uncomfortably with the demands of politics. Politicians, and the voters who elect them, are more comfortable with certainty. So 'six months to save the planet' is more likely to garner support than 'there is a high probability – though not by any means a certainty – that serious climate change could damage the biosphere, depending on levels of economic growth, population growth and innovation.' Politics, like journalism, tends to simplify and exaggerate.[50]

Equally corrupting of the scientific process is the search for consensus. When Britain's Royal Society sought the termination of funding for academics who were not part of its consensus on climate change, this precipitated a letter from a number of academics highlighting that it betrayed the basic principles of science and the Society's own motto of 'on the word of no one'. The letter went on:

> *The beauty of science is that no issue is ever 'settled', that no question is beyond being more fully understood, that no conclusion is immune to further experimentation... And yet for the first time in history, the Royal Society is shamelessly using the media to say emphatically: 'case closed' on all issues related to climate change.*[51]

Stifling debate in the name of consensus minimizes methodological disagreements, competing interpretations and self-criticism. Hiding dissent also increases confidence in the views and models being promoted. But dissent is central to both the advance of knowledge and good policy development. Writing in the *Financial Times*, Michael Schrage of the Sloan School of Management at MIT argued:

> *History – from Newton to Blackett to Watson and Crick – gives the lie to the notion that excellent public policy is found at the point where excellent scientists agree. The opposite is more faithful to the facts: the most interesting and important public policy debates emerge from where excellent scientists disagree.*[52]

In a follow-up article, John Kay concluded: 'The route to truth is the pluralist expression of conflicting views in which, often not as quickly as we might like, good ideas drive out bad.'

Lack of conflict may make the drafting process easier but that is to the detriment of the quality of conclusions. A genuinely non-partisan working group is necessary because, as Schrage puts it:

> *Science as an enterprise may be objective; scientists as individuals are not. Anyone who has participated in peer reviews or research*

*grant committees knows this. Scientists can be as vulgar, pigheaded
and contemptuously dismissive of contrary evidence as any lawyer,
civil servant, journalist or elite professional.*

Perhaps inevitably, given the postmodern character of debates
where science and politics intersect, the most popular suggested
solution is the personification of postmodernism: scientists need
to become better at PR.

Such efforts have existed for a while concerning climate change.
An Institute of Public Policy and Research publication called
(inevitably) *Warm Words* was subtitled 'How are we telling the climate story and can we tell it better?' It recommends limiting the
effort put into seeking to persuade by rational argument in favour
of seeking to work in a 'more shrewd and contemporary way, using
subtle techniques of engagement'. This includes: 'Simply behaving
as if climate change exists and is real... The "facts" need to be
treated as being so taken-for-granted that they need not be spoken.' The publication concludes: 'It amounts to treating climate-
friendly activity as a brand that can be sold. This is, we believe,
the route to mass behaviour changes.'[53]

The clear implication is that scientists need to recognize that people take into account many factors beyond facts when coming to
conclusions, so in parallel with advancing climate science through
research, there is a need to undertake research into how best to communicate the findings, particularly environmental risks.

A recent *Wired* article quoted one PR expert suggesting a campaign that would inundate the public with the message of science.
This would include:

*two groups of spokespeople, one made up of scientists and the other
of celebrity ambassadors. Then deploy them to reach the public wherever they are, from online social networks to* The Today Show.
*Researchers need to tell personal stories, tug at the heartstrings of
people who don't have PhDs. And the celebrities can go on* Oprah

to describe how climate change is affecting them – and by extension,
Oprah's legions of viewers.[54]

The article acknowledges that such talk unsettles scientists, who hate the idea that they should frame their message and feel that the facts should speak for themselves. In the words of another expert, scientists 'have contempt for the lighthearted fun of communication'.

Such contempt is understandable as the dark arts of PR challenge a basic scientific belief: the presumption that good evidence will win against bad and convince the public through its superiority. Equally, scientists could challenge the assumption that they need to change, but not newspaper editors and journalists. That implicit assumption is instructive, because as damaging to science as its politicization is its dramatization by the popular media. This has two effects. First, good science, which is balanced and nuanced, is often misreported in an attempt to tell a story that engages readers. Secondly, 'bad' or 'pseudo' science, which often makes extravagant claims, receives more coverage (and gains more credibility) than it should. In his book *Bad Science*,[55] Ben Goldacre admits to having collected over 500 foolish media stories about science (dismantling such stories being his *oeuvre*).

He suggests that science is so frequently misleadingly portrayed because it works very badly as a news story, since nowadays 'it does not generally move ahead by sudden, epoch-making break-throughs'. If an experiment is newsworthy, 'it can often be for the same reasons that mean it is probably wrong: it must be new, and unexpected, it must change what we previously thought'. By definition it is 'a single piece of information which contradicts a large amount of pre-existing experimental evidence'.

Goldacre makes a distinction between what is written by specialist science correspondents, who usually have a background in scientific enquiry, with those stories – typically the ones editors perceive to be most newsworthy – that have been passed to generalists. These have what psychologists call 'high availability' – we can relate to them because they are dramatic, emotive and easily visualized. In contrast to stories about miracle cures or scary diseases (particularly if children are involved and distressed parents can be quoted), statistics about risks and recovery rates – the basics of medical science – have very low availability. They seem abstract rather than concrete and are easily forgotten.

The dumbed-down approach to science reporting works because readers are fundamentally credulous – we believe the conclusions as they are posited – and insufficiently sceptical. We are the opposite of scientific in our thought processes. As a result, it is easy for bad science or pseudo-science to gain traction because it is not the rigour of the underlying method that counts or the link between results and conclusions, but how effectively the results can be spun; how psychologically available the findings can be made to be.

This was exactly what happened with the measles, mumps and rubella (MMR) vaccine in the UK, where the scantiest of evidence precipitated a major scare that resulted in immunization rates declining sharply from 91 per cent before 1998 to 79 per cent in 2003, with confirmed cases of measles rising from 57 in 1997 to nearly 1,400 in 2008 and a dozen or so deaths officially linked to the illness. The evidence was derived from a study comprising 12 clinical anecdotes (what is called a case series). It did not compare some children who had been given the MMR with some who hadn't and then compare the rates of autism between the two groups (a cohort study); nor did it compare some children with autism and some without and compare the rates of MMR vaccination between the two groups (a case-control study). As such, a case series cannot demonstrate the relationship between exposure and outcome with any force. At best, it can suggest a clinical hunch.

Despite how unscientific we are – or perhaps because of it – we nevertheless value science. If something has a scientific explanation, it gains credibility in our eyes. We still want science to confirm what we fundamentally want to believe. Goldacre quotes numerous examples of individuals or disciplines that have assumed the mannerisms of science – its language and 'referenciness' – to make claims that mirror the assertions of academics but without the same methodological rigour and supporting evidence. Many disciplines with roots in alternative therapy have successfully cloaked those origins with scientific plausibility to generate mainstream appeal.

Part of the solution may be for scientists to become better at communication, but unless those who are susceptible to the blandishments of PR become more sceptical and less credulous in the evaluation of supposedly scientific claims, the likelihood of cod science increases. Accepting that scientists need to improve their PR skills, if unmatched by any other changes, just increases the likelihood that bad science gains more coverage than good, as the winners will be the most media savvy, those who are smartest at communication rather than best at scientific research.

The science of management

So what relevance does any decline in rationality in general have for management science? Popular management research frequently consists of a series of case studies akin to that used to cast doubt on the MMR vaccine, but focused on successful companies, from which a number of conclusions are drawn that are applied to organizations in general. Since Jim Collins' *Good to Great* there has been greater focus on cohort studies, comparing successful with less successful, yet these still suffer from a number of shortcomings, notably the definition of the sample after the event. *Post hoc*, random fluctuations in performance (driven more by luck than anything else) can appear to be predetermined. The outcomes can be observed in detail, but not the processes that created them. These can only be understood through the distorted lens of personal recollection – typically incomplete and egocentric – on the part of those involved. In hindsight it is difficult to separate what is causal from what is correlated, leaving ample scope for the projection of pet theories onto highly amenable data sets.

That only a low threshold of scientific validity is required for management theories to gain acceptance exhibits itself in a couple of ways. First, there is the frequency with which management fads appear, most disappearing just as rapidly. The success of a particular company, or group of companies, makes any approach that they have used – management by objectives or TQM or whatever – suddenly very fashionable. Our general lack of scepticism regarding attributions of cause to effect means that we are happy to accept that the company's success can be reduced to a single tool or framework without much weight of evidence.

The second manifestation is the subsequent decline of companies held out to be exponents of excellence or greatness. From *In Search of Excellence* to *Good to Great*, inclusion as a positive exemplar has appeared to provide the kiss of death for a number of companies. A 1984 *BusinessWeek* article titled 'Oops. Who's excellent now?' observed that of the 43 'excellent' companies, one third were in financial difficulties within five years of the surveys conducted by the book's authors, Tom Peters and Robert Waterman. The failings were particularly obvious in the high-technology sector, including companies such as Atari, Data General, DEC, Lanier, NCR, Wang Labs and Xerox. Of the 11 companies cited by Jim Collins as 'great', two have found themselves in financial trouble: Fannie Mae (which required special loans from the US Federal Reserve to survive) and Circuit City, which liquidated its stores in 2009 following its bankruptcy filing and failure to find a buyer. And with the exception of Gillette, now part of the much admired P&G, the other nine have rarely been praised as role models subsequently.

The spectacular demise of Enron was all the more ironic since it was frequently cited as an example of best practice when it came to innovation or e-business or any of the other millennium fads. However, in most cases the decline is more mundane – a simple case of regression to the mean. Randomness means that some companies' choices will work out better than others' over a period, but that this will not necessarily be sustained in subsequent periods. This is compounded by risk: higher-risk strategies are rewarded by exceptional performance in good times, but penalized harshly when the bets don't come off. Voltaire suggested that 'the art of medicine consists in amusing the patient while nature cures the disease'. In business, for companies in rude health – and those that seek to codify their success – it is more a case of making hay while the sun shines, maximizing profile until the performance cycle turns down (most vengefully against the hubristic).

Notwithstanding the problems with the case-study approach, the adjective 'scientific' is often appended to management, typically as a signifier of merit – the right way to manage. Scientific management has been around for over a century, its father being Frederick Winslow Taylor, who set up a consulting practice to spread his ideas about manufacturing efficiency in the last decade of the nineteenth century.

Since Taylor's time, the idea that scientific management is better than 'gut instinct' decision making has gained momentum. In *The Lords of Strategy*,[56] Kiechel describes this as the coming of 'Greater Taylorism, the corporation's application of sharp-penciled analytics... to the totality of its functions and processes.' But given how frequently 'science' is incorrectly cited as validation for a proposed course of action by those with no appreciation of what the scientific approach actually entails, the purported superiority of scientific management does raise a couple of questions. First, how genuinely scientific is it? And secondly, how scientific is the justification for it?

Regarding the first question, the origins of scientific management do not provide an auspicious start for a positive response. When Taylor was contracted to Bethlehem Steel Company, he conducted experiments to estimate how much iron could be loaded onto rail trucks. The figure he landed on was 47.5 pig tons per day. However, the biggest factor in calculating this target was the 40 per cent 'adjustment' applied to the figure he had calculated by extrapolating a sample period of 14 minutes to a full work day. Some time obviously needed to be allowed for lavatory breaks, rests and meals, but the only justification he could provide, when asked, for this 40 per cent adjustment consisted in his judgement and experience – exactly the sort of intuitions that scientific management was meant to replace. As Matthew Stewart, author of *The Management Myth*, has argued: 'Why time a bunch of Hungarians down to the second if you're going to daub the results with such a great blob of fudge?'

Taylor wrote a complete book on the principles of scientific management and much of what he advocated is now standard rather than scientific practice. In modern parlance, scientific management has come to mean fact-based or data-driven (algorithmic, even) decision making based on the information and performance measures culled from the enterprise systems of a business. While evidence is obviously necessary to the scientific method, it is not sufficient. There needs also to be the systematic creation of new hypotheses and their testing, the results of which add to an ever-increasing body of understanding. However, this test seldom seems to be applied to scientific management.

In part, this omission stems from science and management having fundamentally different objectives: scientists seek to increase knowledge while managers seek to increase profits. The two are not incompatible: increased knowledge often leads to increased profitability. And if a business were focused on systematically increasing insight with the intention of translating this into higher revenues and higher profit margins – increased insight is the objective with increased profits being the outcome – the 'scientific' tag would be genuinely merited.

This may seem a minor distinction but it requires a fundamental change in attitude, particularly towards experimentation. Experiments test what works and, more critically, what doesn't. When strictly applied, the scientific approach focuses on refutation, on the basis that it is easier to prove a negative than a positive. In this way knowledge advances through the elimination of bad theories and ideas. Such an attitude does not come naturally to most people; we are programmed to seek confirmation rather than the opposite.

Experimentation requires us to do something in a way that is not optimal according to our current understanding. That does not sit well with a business ethos that is focused on short-term maximization. It also requires us to accept that our current assumptions may be incorrect; never easy for people who have invested heavily in beliefs based on those assumptions. Equally, it will require us to treat people – staff, customers, suppliers – differently, so that a proposition can be tested with a sample population against a control group. This contravenes our natural sense of fairness: some people will be treated worse than they might otherwise have been. In advance we don't know which group that will be (though a hypothesis should exist), though we do know that, by definition, some people will be disadvantaged relative to others. And while it is easy to pay lip service to the idea that in the long term everyone should benefit from the knowledge gained, these benefits appear distant and abstract compared to the short-term and concrete discomfort that comes from violating accepted norms.

Ultimately, what is called scientific management is, though not cod science, at least a low-calorie or diet version – science lite, perhaps. That leads to the second question: how scientific is the basis for asserting the superiority of scientific management over intuition? Have companies been assessed and split into two (or more) groups and their performance assessed? If so, how have they been split? How has relative performance been assessed – over what periods; as part of a live study or retrospectively? There is no doubt that some companies that have been run on what would be described as a highly scientific basis have suffered a marked decline in fortunes or failed completely, while some that have been run intuitively have been highly successful. How is this accounted for? Is the failure of the first seen as poor execution of the scientific principle (rather than a reflection on the principle itself) while the latter companies are just lucky?

Studies that purport to measure the benefits of scientific management generally compare whether certain metrics are tracked and the performance against those metrics. To obtain a statistically significant sample, these studies are heavily reliant on self-assessment. This, unfortunately, introduces huge scope for bias, calling the validity of any such findings into question.

The reason for such scepticism is that by definition, it is not possible to be scientific about some of the decisions a business must make, specifically the long-term strategic ones. With operational decisions, there is a wealth of relevant data and it is reasonable to assume that the period over which the data is collected accurately depicts the future period over which the decision's impact will be felt. In such a context, it is possible to make 'fact-based' decisions; and it is likely that those decisions will be superior to those that rely merely on instinct and experience.

The problem is that as already noted, there are no facts about the future, only predictions based on assumptions or intuitions. These predictions may be dressed up in the finery of a complicated model and comport themselves as if they were facts, but ultimately they are just formalized intuitions. Any decision about the medium- to long-term future, by definition, involves intuition. The danger with scientific management is that this is not recognized, that the structured and systematic approaches used to make predictions and decisions based on those predictions ignore how fundamentally assumptive the whole process is. Models help, but they need to be treated with caution as they provide the appearance of methodological rigour while being built on foundations that are rarely scrutinized as closely as they should be. Any model that fails to take a probabilistic view of all the assumptions being proved correct risks increasing confidence by more than its accuracy merits.

Wherever assumptions exist, so does the possibility for bias. Yet our belief that we are using scientific approaches shields us from the ugly reflection of our possible irrationality, the business implications of which (and indeed of any decline in how much we aspire to rationalism) are very significant given that frameworks and tools are developed with the convenient assumption, inherited from neo-classical economics, of rational implementation. Once the potential – even likelihood – of irrational implementation is considered, the susceptibility to flawed implementation becomes important. Rather than simply assessing the value created by effective execution, the value destroyed by flawed execution needs to be included in the evaluation of approaches. Frameworks that have psychological appeal need to be treated with particular scepticism, as they are likely to compound rather than counteract innate biases. We need frameworks that force us to play devil's advocate with ourselves, not accentuate our natural inclinations.

This is not to say that all belief-based thinking is damaging. Belief – be it spiritual, environmental or economic – is a more powerful motivator than balanced evaluation of facts. It has great force, both good – people giving time or money to support charities due to religious beliefs, recycling waste and reducing carbon emissions because of environmental ones – and terrible, when extreme belief transcends into hate. Great changes in society are wrought when the convictions of a few spread to become the beliefs of many. Equally, great companies are also built on beliefs, a shared set of values.

As is often the case, it boils down to using the right system of thinking in the right situation. Beliefs are the best means to separate right from wrong, science the best way to assess true or false. Given their important role in society, businesses need to make ethical and moral judgements. In that respect, beliefs are important, now more than ever. And the creation of a vision, a mission, a purpose, big hairy audacious goals and corporate values should be the realm of belief-based thinking.

However, the danger comes when beliefs start to colour our assessments of true and false. If we believe something to be true, we inevitably become less scientific in our appraisal, seeking only confirmatory evidence. We may acknowledge the value of rationalism and wish to appear scientific in our appraisal; but if we are fundamentally driven by belief, that is merely a veneer, because the underlying approach has been compromised. The challenge is separating the two decision-making approaches and it is the inability to do so that leads us to be irrational.

So where does this brief sweep through the major political, regulatory, economic, technological and cultural trends of the last quarter century leave us?

To summarize, over the past 25 years, the combination of supply-side economic policies, Moore's Law and globalization has created a stream of opportunities for businesses to grow profits through boosting productivity in their operations. In part because these gains could be delivered in short order, the timeframes for achieving results have become compressed. Companies have either cut costs or have been taken over; something of a Hobson's choice, but one that drove stock markets higher during the 1980s and 1990s on the back of strong growth in earnings, the expansion in price–earnings multiples and surges in M&A activity.

Contributing to the last element has been the growth of the private equity industry, also enabled by the continuing slide in the cost of computing power. Private equity funds and hedge funds have provided alternative investment opportunities to traditional quoted equity or bond ownership, with even the average capable of generating high returns over relatively short time periods.

One consequence of the growth of the alternative investment industry has been the creation of great individual wealth. And as European universities have sought to add business schools, there have been enough multimillionaires willing to follow the well-worn philanthropic route to immortality through endowing a business faculty in return for their name above the entrance. These new business schools have readily grasped traditional ideas about scholarship and intellect, and their freshly minted MBAs have provided investment banks and consultancies with the analytical fire power to help their clients edge productivity ever higher through consolidation and rationalization, offshoring and outsourcing, and acquisitions and divestments.

While strategists have concentrated their attention on the supply side of the value chain and the cost side of the income statement, the challenge of growing the demand and revenue sides has been left to marketers. They have willingly responded, causing the spend on marketing communications to surge. As our sensory perceptions have become dulled by the volume of messages to which we are subjected, so have marketers shouted louder and louder for their brand to stand out. In the name of branding, marketing has become more and more communication based, lending itself to the belief that creating clever advertising is more important than creating great products and experiences and pricing them profitably. Or if not more important, certainly easier.

As a backdrop to this, rationalism appears to be on the decline, the principles of scientific thinking being challenged by religious fundamentalists or corrupted by the intrusion of belief into decisions where evidence should prevail, and there should be a focus on confirmation rather than refutation. As a result, we have seen a rise in pseudo-empiricism, cod science and the like. Rationalism remains a comfort blanket. We wish to portray what we want to believe as having scientific justification. We have never been as rational as we would like to think or models of economic behaviour and management decision making have liked to assume, and if anything we are becoming less so.

And why do the trends of the last 25 years matter? Simply because like generals, we have a tendency to fight the last war – we are imprisoned by the past. Our mindsets and models are shaped by what has worked in recent history. And like the metaphorical boiled frog, we fail to recognize the extent of change when it is continuous. Or if we do, we fail to recognize the fundamental causes and attempt to rectify problems by employing the same thinking that created them.

If that is the case, the result is a set of approaches, frameworks and tools that are no longer fit for purpose, that are inappropriate for the biggest challenges businesses face, particularly when trying to generate growth. The question is whether that is genuinely the case now. To understand that, we need to look at what the stock markets were telling us, even before the onset of the credit crunch and the global recession.

Three
Concealed by the Shadow of Recession

G overnment bailouts prevented a widespread banking collapse in 2008, but they could not save developed economies from tipping into a deep recession, plunging stock markets into turmoil as a consequence. In some mature economies, notably those with a high dependence on financial services such as the US and the UK, the downturn was the worst in over 70 years. And the ugly metamorphosis from liquidity crisis into economic crisis into government funding crisis will cast a long shadow for many years over issues perceived as peripheral to the central problem.

Given present preoccupations, it would be understandable if commentators – economic, financial and corporate – limited their efforts to identifying the causes of the meltdown. But for corporate commentators there are other insights to be gleaned from this interlude, notably regarding the limited impact that the 'growth revolution', spawned in the late 1990s and a focus for many a management guru, had both on financial performance during that period and on judgements about future growth prospects. Investors went from believing that organic growth was an easy consequence of the internet revolution to believing it was the province of very few, the majority remaining reliant on squeezing further rounds of efficiency savings from a productivity revolution entering its third decade.

Research by the Corporate Executive Board (CEB) into the financial performance of the Fortune 100 group of companies over a 50-year period highlights how important productivity gains have become in driving earnings growth. For the first part of the period, income or profit growth lagged revenue growth; but on the back of the productivity gains made possible by Thatcherism and Reaganomics, in the late 1980s income growth exceeded revenue growth for the first time.[1] This reversal of the previous trend has become the new norm, with wave after wave of cost-saving opportunities breaking across the corporate landscape, typically as a result of advances in information technology enabling process automation and organizational dispersion.

Income growth continued to exceed revenue growth into the early 1990s, after which the two tracked each other until the later part of the decade, when the rate of income growth surged ahead again. Fears about the sustainability of productivity-led income growth have been around for a number of years, leading institutions such as the CEB, business schools and strategy consultancies to focus their research effort on resolving the enigma of organic growth for large companies. Such research has proved popular (as evidenced by a number of bestselling books), since it purported to provide a solution to a well-recognized management problem. Since the turn of the millennium, the elusiveness of organic growth was consistently cited in yearly surveys of CEOs as their most pressing challenge until the recession and liquidity crisis refocused attention on survival rather than growth.

The judgement of investors on these growth efforts has not been glowing, as shown by an unexpected dichotomy in the period from the end of the twentieth century to the onset of the recession. The spread of both high-bandwidth internet access and globalization made this an extremely buoyant period in economic terms, global GDP growing by over 75 per cent[2] from its 1999 level in the years to 2008 (before flattening off in 2009). But despite this positive backdrop, stock market returns approximated more closely those of the economically disastrous 1970s than the more economically comparable 1980s and 1990s.

Highs and lows

On 30 May 2007, the S&P500 closed at 1530.23, beating its previous all-time closing high of 1527.46 set on 24 March 2000. Similarly the DAX, which comprises the 30 largest quoted companies in Germany, closed higher than its peak of 7 March 2000 for the first time on 20 June 2007. Such rescaling of previous peaks was not achieved by the major British and French indices, the FTSE 100 and CAC 40, which only managed to come within 3 per cent and 11 per cent respectively of their previous highs during 2007, not surpass them.

The new high for the S&P500 was marked by much comment in the financial press, but it went relatively unnoticed in the business pages, the implicit assumption being that the seven-year hiatus was due to an inflated starting point (coming at the height of dot-com mania) rather than business fallibility.

Yet by the standards of recent history, seven years is long time for an old high to stand. In the bull market of the 1980s and 1990s, equities became overvalued on a number of occasions, most notably in 1987. And in the crash of October that year, the S&P500 declined by 30 per cent, but recovered those losses within two years. Similarly, declines of 20 per cent in 1990 and 1998 were made back within 12 months. The experience with the major European indices was pretty similar. (The exception to this, of course, is Japan. The closest parallel to its financial crisis of the 1990s and persistent deflation is the Great Depression that followed the 1929 Wall Street crash, from which the Dow Jones Industrial Index took 25 years to recover. It was with an eye to the economic and financial consequences in both the US in the 1930s and Japan in the 1990s that western governments were desperate to avert a full-scale banking collapse in 2008.) So a gap of such magnitude merits exploration and more explanation than simply blaming the starting point.

If we go back further we can find a hiatus of similar magnitude. It took ten years for the Dow Jones Industrial Average to return to the 1000 level that it briefly topped towards the end of 1972. And in the UK, the FTSE All-Share Index fell by some 70 per cent from its peak in May 1972 and only recovered those levels in August 1978.

Superficially there are some economic and political parallels between the mid-to-late 1970s and the first years of the new millennium, notably an unpopular war and sky-rocketing oil prices. However, these similarities are more coincidental than correlative. The last couple of years of the Vietnam War accompanied the start of the 1970s bear market, whereas the stock market malaise was already well established before the war with Iraq was pursued. And even if the magnitude of the oil price rise is similar – a fivefold increase in the inflation-adjusted average annual crude oil price between 1971 and 1980 versus a fourfold increase between 1998 and 2007[3] – the causes are very different. In the 1970s OPEC applied a tourniquet to the supply of oil, whereas in the decade to 2007 the rise was driven by global economic growth and surging demand, particularly due to the industrialization of highly populous countries such as China and India.

More significantly, the fundamental economic situations of the two periods were very different. The 1970s was the decade of economic disputes and 'stagflation' (stagnant economic growth and high inflation); something that briefly threatened in the early stages of the credit crunch before a halving of the oil price and similar declines in other commodities turned concerns about inflation into fears about the more painful consequences of deflation.

The UK was the poster child for the ills of developed countries in the 1970s. For the seven years following then Prime Minister Edward Heath's dash for growth in 1973, the UK economy averaged growth of a paltry 1 per cent per annum, inflation of 16 per cent and over 12,000 days lost to industrial disputes each year. The seven-year period from 2000 showed a very different picture: annual economic growth averaging 2.7 per cent per annum, annual inflation of only 2.6 per cent per annum and fewer than 700 days lost yearly to industrial disputes on average.[4] The differences are less marked in the US. However, inflation in 2000–06 still averaged less than a third of what it was in 1974–80, and days lost in industrial disputes less than a quarter.[5]

The early 2000s were not without their own ills. The ambition and effective execution of Al-Qaeda's 9/11 attacks raised the spectre that terrorism could damage economic stability and therefore corporate earnings. The initial panic, arising from a dramatic increase in the perception of risk, resulted in future earnings being discounted at a higher rate and sharp share price falls.

Over time this has been replaced by measured risk analysis: the likely frequency of such events recurring multiplied by their potential impact on corporate earnings. The vigour with which the war on terror has been pursued over the subsequent period has produced a less pessimistic assessment of the risk of repetition. There has been a cost to governments in pursuing wars in Iraq and Afghanistan, but the drag on economic growth created by 9/11 was relatively brief, reducing output by an estimated 0.5 per cent in 2001 with the economy returning to growth in the last quarter of that year. As a result, the impact on both earnings and price–earnings multiples was short-lived.

However, stock markets beginning to recover from the shock of 9/11 were then hit by the whirlwind of two major corporate scandals, both involving fraudulent accounting: Enron in November 2001 and WorldCom in June of the following year. These struck at the heart of a basic stock market presupposition – that reported financial performance reflects real financial performance – thereby undermining confidence in the denominator against which share price multiples can be applied for valuation purposes. These were not the first organizations to be caught out. In 2000 two software companies, Unify Corporation and MicroStrategy, reported accounting irregularities and restated sales and earnings, having been premature in revenue recognition. Nevertheless, the size of Enron and WorldCom and the complicity of their auditors created a fear that all reported earnings should be mistrusted, with shares marked down as a consequence.

Scandals of this type are typically lagging (rather than leading) indicators of corporate downturns. The underlying driver of fraudulent accounting in these cases was the need to demonstrate sustainable, organic growth of revenue and profit in order to sustain share price valuations and facilitate further issues of equity and debt. Typically, the need for creative accounting only arises once difficulties have already hit and the predicated growth is not being achieved. And with Wall Street analysts rescrutinizing the companies they followed, auditors tightening up their rules, authorities introducing tougher regulation and no further miscreants coming to light, the perceived risk of repetition is much lower. The principal economic legacy of these scandals is increased compliance costs due to the Sarbanes-Oxley accounting reform, a heavy burden for some of NASDAQ's smaller quoted companies, but not a significant drag on earnings for most in the S&P500.

In purely economic terms, better parallels to 2000–07 are the equivalent periods in the 1980s and 1990s. In all three cases, the decade started with economic difficulties. In the early 1980s there was recession brought on by the monetary tightening of the Reagan administration. In 1991 there was stagnation in the US and decline in the UK, again produced by high interest rates in the preceding two years (a response to the overloosening of monetary policy following the stock market crash of 1987). And in 2001–02 there was a sharp slowdown due to the bursting of the dot-com bubble. Of all three, the early 2000s saw the least pain in economic terms: growth slowed rather than stopped or reversed.

The parallel continues with corporate earnings trends, earnings per share of the S&P500 (based on bottom-up weighted aggregation of its constituent companies) showing declines of 7 per cent and 15 per cent in 1990 and 1991, compared with a one-off but sharper decline in 2001 of 31 per cent.[6] Any boom contains the seeds of its own destruction. High share price valuations create a low cost of equity capital, which encourages companies to raise funds and invest in new plant and equipment. The result is excess capacity, leading to fierce competition and resulting in a sharp decline in earnings. So even though the overall economic situation was better in 2001 than in 1990–91, the preceding boom meant that the subsequent decline in earnings was greater.

When looked at on a compound basis, EPS growth from the beginning of 1990 through to the end of 1997 for the S&P500 was 8 per cent per annum, whereas over the same period from 2000 it was 6 per cent.[7] This was lower, but certainly not sufficiently so to explain the vastly different stock market returns: 13 per cent per annum for the eight years through to the end of 1997 versus 0 per cent for the same timeframe to the end of 2007.[8]

For the 1990s as a whole, the return on the S&P500 index was 15 per cent per annum. In the UK over the same period, the total return of the FTSE All Share Index was also 15 per cent per annum, a decline on the returns of the 1980s, which were 24 per cent per annum on a compound basis.[9]

The internet illusion

All of this begs the question: why did stock market performance over 2000–07 (that is, prior to the havoc wreaked by the credit boom and bust) approximate that of the less economically analogous 1970s, while not even coming close to that of the 1980s and 1990s with which the parallels are far stronger?

The answer looks simple: the 1990s ended with the dot-com boom and a stock market bubble. This both inflated returns for that decade and created a high base from which returns in the 2000s would struggle to move into positive territory. A simple examination of average stock market price–earnings (P/E) ratios provides some evidence to support this theory.[10] For the S&P500 the P/E ratio doubled from 15 at end March 1995 to 30 at end March 2000.[11]

The S&P500's P/E ratio also doubled in the five years to end September 1987, just prior to Black Monday, from which stock markets recovered in just a couple of years. However, more important than the absolute increase is the degree of overvaluation at the end point. At the end of September 1987, the S&P500 P/E ratio was just over 20, having been under 9 five years before – a starting point of undervaluation, the P/E ratio being half what it was 10 years before and less than two-thirds of its average for the preceding 20 years. An increase is also more justifiable given the decline in inflation over that period.[12] Inflation rates and stock market P/E ratios are inversely correlated: the lower the rate of inflation, the lower the discount rate that should be applied to future earnings, so the higher the multiple of future and current earnings share prices will be at.[13]

There should thus be no doubt that the internet bubble led to a severe overvaluation of share prices. But to attribute all of the seven-year hiatus to an inflated starting point, merely leaving the analysis at the aggregate level, misses a couple of key factors, in particular the underlying cause for the near-halving of the P/E ratio for the S&P500 from its peak of around 30 to around 18 in mid-2007 when the 2000 index high was briefly surpassed.

First, the most egregious examples of overinflated valuations were those attributed to start-ups and funded by venture capitalists. In terms of companies quoted on stock exchanges, only the technology, media and telecommunications sectors of the quoted market shared this excess. Technology stocks rose from comprising less than 10 per cent of the valuation of the S&P500 for the first five years of the 1990s to over 25 per cent of the index by the end of the decade, while their share of earnings was roughly half that. And old-economy sectors certainly lagged in comparison.

Secondly, accepting that even old-economy companies had their valuations inflated, why was that the case? Isolating the underlying cause requires an understanding of the context that encouraged such irrational exuberance.

When looked at from this angle, one answer presents itself. The internet appeared to provide the answer to the big question that companies were asking themselves: after 15 years or so of reaping the benefits of cost cutting, how do we generate new revenue streams to maintain our growth in profits?

Excitement among investors about how the internet would enable the development of new business models was obviously excessive and misplaced. However, this enthusiasm reflected the scale of the problem that the internet appeared to solve: the need to replace productivity-led earnings growth with organic, revenue-led growth. The internet was the *deus ex machina* for sustained corporate growth.

Except that of course it wasn't. And neither were the subsequent initiatives. As mentioned above, earnings growth in the 2000s pre-credit crunch period was 6 per cent per annum versus 8 per cent in the 1990s. In the light of decelerating earnings growth – not the acceleration that was hoped for – the near halving in the P/E ratio becomes understandable. But it raises the question, why did the growth revolution fail to materialize?

The growth challenge

By the turn of the millennium, for almost two decades businesses had enjoyed the low-hanging fruits of the supply-side economic revolution, notably reduced regulation enabling labour costs to be cut and industries to consolidate both nationally and internationally. The bandwagon had started rolling in the early to mid-1980s, but momentum really picked up in the 1990s, creating exceptional opportunities for profit growth. As Gary Hamel put it with characteristic élan:

> *One hundred years from now people will look back at the last decade, especially the last half of the decade, as an economic aberration. It was time when a variety of forces conspired together positively to create a buoyant economic climate.*[14]

Notable among these forces was significant expenditure on technology and IT, enabling in Hamel's words, 'an unprecedented attack on inefficiency'. Driving this was a generation of management heroes who were 'dealmakers and efficiency addicts', the result of which was an 'orgy of mergers and acquisitions'. Hamel concludes:

> *There's a lot of data that says that companies have reached the point of diminishing returns in their efficiency programmes... Retrenchment doesn't buy you growth; it doesn't buy you a future, at best it buys you time.*

This vivid description of the growth challenge facing businesses was manifested in the new millennium zeitgeist; no surprise as he was one of its leading proponents, *Leading the Revolution* being one of the iconic books of that era. It sought to provide a road map for how old-economy whales could reinvent themselves as new-economy sharks – Enron being the prime example – and indeed needed to, or else they would themselves be devoured. The underlying message of most books in this vein was that growth was within the reach of any company if it embraced new-economy thinking and new ways of working.

After a diet of consolidation and cost cutting, with the consensus view that the productivity lemon had pretty much been squeezed dry, suddenly there was a feast of opportunities for businesses to grow courtesy of the new economy. The prospect of revenue-led earnings growth, perceived as more sustainable, therefore better quality and rated more highly, encouraged share price valuations to spiral upwards. But once it was clear that the internet would not lead businesses to the sunlit uplands of effortless organic growth, merely extend the plain of productivity gains, it was the pressure to justify these valuations that led the likes of Enron and WorldCom to switch to fraudulent accounting practices.

An article in the July–August 2004 *Harvard Business Review* (a special double edition focused on top-line growth) by Pankaj Ghemawat[15] tracked the number of new books focused specifically on growth. This doubled from 200 in 1994 to nearly 400 in 1998, then remained in the 300–400 range. Over the same period, the total number of new business titles showed significantly lower growth.

Ghemawat also notes how the proposed solution to the 'growth crisis' (as those with a tendency to hyperbole described it at the time) changed, with a watershed appearing around 2000:

Earlier books, presumably written during the internet bubble, tended to take the availability and attractiveness of growth opportunities for granted: they simply mentioned network economies or winner-take-all effects in passing before getting on with their primary tasks of discussing which opportunities to pursue and how.

Later books, written against a less exuberant backdrop, spend more time making the case for growth strategies. They argue that managers must pay more attention to business growth right now for one of two reasons: either because the paths to profitable new growth are less obvious than in the boom years or because cost-cutting has run its course, making growth the best option.

In terms of corporate activity, this change was manifest in the rise and fall of corporate venturing as the favoured solution for growth-seeking companies over the period. The logic of corporate venturing runs something like this: the only way to generate significant new growth is through the development of new businesses; if the new business cannibalizes an existing one, those with a vested interest in the existing business will seek to strangle it before it succeeds; as a result, new businesses cannot be started from within existing ones and need the special support of a central team with the specialist skills required to identify opportunities and nurture these new ventures through their early development. Once they are strong enough, they can be transferred into an existing business or, ideally, spun off in a lucrative IPO.

The problem is that it's a bit like launching some prototype speedboats from a supertanker with the intention that they will tow the mother ship along and accelerate its progress; generally it doesn't work. A study of corporate venture units in large companies found that, in the 1970s and 1980s, 44 per cent of internally generated start-ups and 50 per cent of joint ventures were divested or closed in the first six years, not much better than the 60 per cent failure rate of small business start-ups over the same period.[16] The study concluded:

> Many [corporate venturing] units were launched with gusto in the second half of the 1990s to mimic the processes and methods of the venture capital industry. Corporate financing and third-party venture funds were available for all promising projects; in other words, normal rules of corporate risk aversion were suspended. Yet only a handful of the more than 100 such units in our survey developed any new business... Corporate venturing units do have their uses, but they don't solve the problems of mature companies.

The result was that many of the newly created venturing units or innovation teams were quietly closed down, the limited number of successes not material enough to have an impact on the performance of the overall business. As another article put it:

> Interest in the new ventures tends to be cyclical. Brief surges of enthusiasm, triggered by abundant resources and the need to diversify, are followed by sharp declines. The life spans of both internal venture units and corporate venture capital funds, therefore tend to be short – on average, only four to five years.[17]

Even if the corporate venturing cycle has turned down, judging by the huge number of hits it generates on HBR Online, innovation remains as popular as ever, particularly the idea of breakthrough innovation. Yet it remains prone to many of the same challenges that limit the impact of innovation units. To quote Michael Treacy, co-author of The Discipline of Market Leaders:

> Like swinging for the grand slam in baseball or betting on the trifecta in horse racing, going for broke with innovation is glamorous.

Breakthrough innovations, whether the next blockbuster product or a next-generation business model, create a buzz in the boardroom while lesser forms of innovation go unnoticed. Yet a body of evidence in recent years makes a strong case that breakthrough innovation should be the growth strategy of last resort...

First, don't forget the point of innovation is growth. Since all innovation incurs risk, managers should ask, 'can I increase revenues without innovation?' The answer is usually yes. Simply retaining existing customers and improving the targeting and coverage of new ones can yield significant revenue growth, especially in inefficient markets, where innovation isn't required to keep customers. [18]

The point Treacy is making is that the time to launch big innovations is not when they are necessary for your business, but when they are essential to your marketplace. The overriding problem with innovation is that it is a means to growth, not an end in itself. Yet because it is fun and exciting, people fall in love with the process and lose sight of the purpose to the detriment of the desired outcome.

Despite this focus on innovation and growth over the last ten years; despite the increase in business schools, business school professors and MBA graduates; and despite the growth in management consultants and ex-consultants in corporate roles, the organic growth conundrum remains unresolved. Most growth initiatives continue to fail and organic growth has stubbornly remained the top priority for senior management. At the end of 2007, 'sustained and steady top line growth' remained the biggest concern and top priority for North American CEOs according to the Conference Board Survey, as it had been in 2004; in both surveys, more of a challenge than growing profits. This category did not exist in the 2001 Survey, but the top management challenge – customer loyalty/retention – was similarly revenue related and ranked as a bigger challenge than cutting costs. [19]

Fortunately, new sources of productivity gains have appeared, with outsourcing and offshoring replacing reengineering and rationalization. The predictions of pessimists about the limits to productivity enhancements have not proved true so far. And while CEOs may fret about achieving organic growth, they are not going to be sentimental about it – last year's failed growth initiative becomes this year's cost-reduction opportunity.

'So what?' you might ask. Who is to say that continuing advances will not yield further cost-cutting opportunities? Maybe organic growth at any significant rate is not possible for large companies, so what is wrong with using mergers and acquisitions as the primary engines of growth?

It is unlikely that we have come to the end of the opportunities that technological advances and geopolitical trends will create for businesses to reduce their costs of manufacturing products and serving customers. Yet fears about the sustainability of productivity-led profits growth were again raised when corporate profits in 2006 accounted for a higher share of US GDP than at any time since 1950. As *The Economist* warned:

> *Perhaps globalisation has shifted the balance of power firmly in favour of the corporate sector and away from labour. But workers have votes and may demand the balance be shifted back, either through taxes or trade barriers.*[20]

In all probability, further drivers of productivity gains will be marginal and will not generate more than single-digit percentage earnings growth. As Jeff Immelt put it when outlining the rationale behind the development of GE's growth toolkit: 'After I came in as CEO, I looked at the world post 9/11 and realized that over the next ten to 20 years, there was not going to be much tailwind.'[21]

As to whether large companies can generate organic growth at any significant rate, of course it would take an economic miracle (or much higher inflation) for all companies in the Fortune 100 to grow revenue at 10 per cent annually through internally generated means. However, not many CEOs of Fortune 100 companies will be prepared to stand up in front of analysts and sketch out a future that will deliver only 5 per cent earnings per share growth per annum, not least for fear of losing their job. Even if there will always be outperformers and underperformers, we need to broaden the pool of those achieving significant growth beyond the isolated examples that crop up in case studies in a more effective way than the current default approach; that is, attempting to codify the success of these companies for others to copy, thereby encouraging imitation rather than invention and perpetuating risk aversion and followership. Courage blended with experimentation – and a dose of luck – is necessary to leapfrog current leaders.

What about the earnings boost that acquisitions can provide? The problem with this argument is that study after study has found that corporate acquirers generally pay too much, destroying rather than enhancing value for their own shareholders. Ultimately, many of the human biases (described in the next chapter) that afflict organic growth initiatives – most notably overestimation and overconfidence – are writ even larger in acquisitions. Industry consolidation has also reduced the supply of potential acquisitions and for those that exist there is increased competition, notably from private equity purchasers. When faced with such competition, the risk of the winner's curse increases – whoever wins the auction has inevitably overpaid.

Wondering about wisdom

Once economies start to recover and growth again becomes the focus for strategic intent, we should not forget to ask the uncomfortable question: did prevailing wisdoms serve companies well prior to the bursting of the credit bubble? It would be understandable if once released from the shackles of a sluggish economy, the desire to take action prevails over any inclinations towards reflection. But any failure to grow revenue profitably is a failure of strategy and, to a lesser degree, marketing. If the objective is to make a step change in growth versus what was achieved previously, wouldn't we be advised at a minimum to examine, challenge and be prepared to throw out some of the most dearly held assumptions of strategy and marketing? And also to question whether the approach to knowledge development in these disciplines, and management research in general, embeds error, distortion and bias?

A starting point for such deliberation is investigating whether the approach has been driven by historical factors and whether those conditions still prevail. It is my contention that the 1980s and 1990s saw the coincidence of three factors that generated surging profitability, profits and returns for shareholders: the supply-side economics revolution, the explosion in personal computing and the primacy of analysis in western intellectual thought. As a result of its role in this perfect storm, strategy has come to be seen as an analytical discipline. If strategy were purely about opportunity identification, then analysis would be more than sufficient; and indeed it has been for much of the last 25 years. But once strategy becomes about opportunity creation and revenue growth – the biggest challenge facing large businesses – analysis is necessary but not sufficient, with any failure to recognize this creating a millstone around the corporate neck.

The second point requiring investigation is the presupposition that the purpose of business strategy is to beat the competition. Getting one over on the competition boosts testosterone-fuelled egos, but correlating psychological appeal with economic benefit risks any victories being Pyrrhic. The subtle difference between an outcome and an objective is lost. If beating competition is seen as an objective, the risk of behavioural distortion increases relative to when it is seen as an outcome of achieving other objectives, notably serving customers in a superior way. As John Kay points out in his book *Obliquity*, sometimes our goals are best achieved indirectly.

Equally appealing in psychological terms is the allure of the quick win and the idea that strategy is about big decisions. In part it is, of course; but the track record on mergers and acquisitions does not provide much support for the success of prevailing approaches in dealing with the uncertainty inherent in strategic decision making. Furthermore, sustained growth is not only about senior managers getting the big decisions right, it also about getting the little decisions right: the choices made ten times every day by hundreds of middle managers or front-line stuff that add up to thousands of decisions and millions in revenue. If strategy is to play a role in guiding these choices, providing a frame for decision making and thereby ensuring that it can be delegated to the person with the most relevant, specific information, a different definition and manifestation are required to the analysis-driven preoccupation with big decision making.

In the same way, we need to reappraise some of our fundamental assumptions about marketing. These were shaped by the environment of the last 50 years of the twentieth century, a period when supply constraints prevailed and competition was predominantly limited to national boundaries. It was a case of build it and they will come, so long as you tell them about it. In his book *The New Law of Supply and Demand*, Rick Kash describes it thus:

> *With few exceptions, and with only a cursory glance in the direction of the customer, businesses could sell virtually all they produced... Given their limited choices, consumers were frequently willing to pay whatever their desired goods cost... Of course, there was competition within mass markets, resulting in lowered prices, but production efficiencies made it possible to drop prices and remain profitable. Moreover, lower prices attracted more customers.*

Perhaps this is no surprise, as the word 'marketing' – derived from the idea of a traditional market, transformed into a verb and then nominalized back to a noun – implies supplier power. Businesses simply need to display their products, set a competitive price and they will find customers.

However, the success of supply-side economics and the rise of the internet fundamentally changed that. As Kash goes on, 'in the early 1990s, the tectonic plates underpinning the world economy shifted. The supply economy was dead, killed by the producers themselves.' The combination of technological advance, productivity gains, availability of capital and globalization generated over-supply. Reverse engineering, white-label manufacturing, online purchase aggregation, purchasing consortia, the possibility of buying from anywhere at any time have all shifted power from suppliers to buyers. Suppliers now suffer from excess capacity, increased competition and competitive convergence; buyers benefit from reduced search costs, greater product and price transparency and a wider choice of what to buy and where to buy it from.

The question is whether marketing has adjusted to the new reality or remained stuck in an egocentric way of thinking, where the solution to any decline in market share is to shout louder.

Ultimately, if there is a problem with both marketing and strategy, there must also a problem with their foundations: management research. Here again, some of the basic presuppositions are worthy of challenge. At the root of most management science is the presupposition that decisions are made rationally, despite increasing evidence to the contrary. Such an assumption makes the creation of models and frameworks easy, but the effectiveness and value of their implementation questionable.

Equally, studying successful companies continues to be perceived as the most valuable way to expand management knowledge. But increased behavioural understanding also leads us to question how scientific such studies are: how sample selection introduces bias; how the complexity of business systems correlates many variables with success, enabling pet theories fuelled by confirmation bias to flourish; and how easily causality can be misattributed. It also leads us to question, even if there is validity in the findings, the value in the prescriptions offered. How transferable are they? What hidden costs lie in their implementation?

Finally, such questions lead inevitably to others about the value of business school education. The MBA remains the favoured choice of many wannabe entrepreneurs, high rollers, consultants and investment bankers. It is the default choice for anyone seeking advanced management education, because its perceived value is high. What creates that value has over the past couple of years come under increasing scrutiny from those within the much expanded boundaries of business education. These accept that most, if not all, of the value gained by participants in such programmes stems from the selection rather than the education process. Yet all have stopped short of the Innovation 101 conclusion: that any industry where there is a mismatch between what elements contribute most to costs (salaries of professors, opportunity cost of time spent studying) and what contributes value (how difficult it is to gain entry to the programme) is at risk of suffering disruptive innovation.

The book is structured with these questions in mind. The next three chapters cover the implications of behavioural economics for management science and management education. Next are the chapters challenging the presuppositions of strategy: the value of the analytical approach, the bias introduced by the focus on competition and the failures in decision making. Finally, there is a section on marketing, challenging the primacy of branding, the reduction of marketing to marketing communications, and the blinkered definition of who the customer is.

Four

Adoption, Adaption and Corruption

One is tempted to define man as a rational animal who always loses his temper when he is called upon to act in accordance with the dictates of reason.

Oscar Wilde

U nderpinning classical economics – and its offspring, management science – is the assumption that we act rationally. Not only is all relevant information available, but we use it to calculate the value of different options, selecting whichever is in our economic best interest, with no cognitive or psychological factors disrupting the decision-making process. Decisions are therefore logical and predictable, because a rational individual will perform a unique set of actions in any specified circumstance. This has the advantage of making theorizing and modelling easier. As Nassim Nicholas Taleb argues in *The Black Swan*, 'there is a strong link between rationality, predictability and mathematical tractability'. The latter, in the form of optimization and maximization techniques, is the cornerstone of traditional economics.

However, ambiguity is more normal than predictability. The arguments may be elegant and the theorems logical, but fitting perfect maths to an imperfect world demands unreasonable assumptions, bringing to mind the philosopher John Locke's definition of madness: reasoning correctly from erroneous premises.

The assumption of rationality dismisses any idea that people may wish to do something other than maximize their economic benefits.

It goes so far as to refute the possible existence of other benefits that are not economically computable; psychological benefits, for example. Yet research in the area of behavioural economics shows this not to be the case. At the beginning of his book *Predictably Irrational*, Dan Ariely summarizes: 'the results presented in this book (and others) show, we are all far less rational in our decision making than standard economic theory assumes'. In contrast to their classical brethren, behavioural economists believe that people are influenced by their immediate environment, that they are susceptible to 'irrelevant emotions, short sightedness, and other forms of irrationality', to quote Ariely again.

Balancing bias

The subject of bias in decision making has received increasing attention over the past four decades, culminating in one of the subject's pioneers, Daniel Kahneman, winning the Nobel Prize for Economics in 2002. Over that time, some three dozen cognitive biases have been identified (an inventive and musical high school psychology teacher in Maryland has even defined some of them in song as a study aid for his students). Kahneman began his research in the early 1970s and published many articles with his long-time collaborator Amos Tversky, with whom he developed Prospect Theory for which he received the Nobel Prize.[1] Kahneman, Tversky and their associates created what we know today as behavioural economics.

In recent years, appreciation of behavioural economics has become more mainstream. Taleb's bestselling *The Black Swan* described many of the biases that behavioural research has uncovered, outlining how they can distort financial markets, something the credit boom and bust made apparent. Equally, Richard Thaler and Cass Sunstein highlight how an understanding of behavioural factors can enable policy makers, indeed any architects of choice, to 'nudge' people into making better decisions.

The behavioural approach has also made some inroads into management science. In July 2003 the *Harvard Business Review* published an article by Dan Lovallo and Kahneman called 'Delusions of success: How optimism undermines executives' decisions'. At the same time, and identifying many of the same factors, Charles Roxburgh wrote an article in the *McKinsey Quarterly* called 'Hidden flaws in strategy'. Yet for the most part management scientists have parked behavioural influences in a box marked 'inconvenient truths'. Models, frameworks and approaches are developed in the Panglossian belief that they will be implemented rationally. Susceptibility to bias is ignored; as is the usage cycle, which in all likelihood will follow a pattern of adoption, adaption and corruption. Even if a model is adopted in its purest form in the first instance, zealotry declines with time or breadth of implementation so that it is adapted to fit with the quirks of the situation before becoming corrupted by the mindsets of those who use it – a means and justification for what they wanted to do.

In management science these frameworks are usually derived from attempts to codify the secrets of fast-growing and highly profitable companies. A presumption of success pervades their design. Irrational implementation – and the potential damage it would cause – is not even considered. Behavioural economics also raises the spectre that the popularity of certain frameworks may owe more to their psychological appeal than the value they deliver (the justification for which is management research that is cod science masquerading as the real thing, as the following chapter will explain); and in pandering to human fallibility these approaches further accentuate it.

So where is the risk greatest? As bias rides on the back of uncertainty, it is externally focused strategy and marketing decisions that are most susceptible to its distortions. (With internally oriented, more operational initiatives, there is typically far more hard data to inform the decisions that need to be made, so the scope for bias and error is significantly reduced.) Until behavioural understanding becomes the foundation of management science, not merely a decorative addition that provides techniques to review and adjust decisions made within traditional models, the development, evaluation and selection of strategic initiatives will continue to be biased by our fallibility in the face of uncertainty. In turn, companies will continue to invest more in improving operational effectiveness – where the greater certainty involved has resulted in a strong track record of improved profit levels (at least in the short term) – than in growth initiatives and sources of differentiation, to the detriment of long-term profitability.

The first step towards making behavioural factors the foundation of management science is the acknowledgement of innate bias. Understanding the susceptibility to bias of the decision-making approaches employed, particular those that drive the allocation of corporate resources, is the next. Greater appreciation of inherent bias and scrutinizing for it will reduce the number of damaging decisions.

Not all decisions will work out, of course, nor should they: experimentation is critical for reducing uncertainty and with this approach comes the certainty that some decisions will not result in the desired outcomes. But keeping the failures small and learning from them will ensure that big decisions have a better chance of success. It is big bets that wreak most damage and value destruction when they are based on flawed assumptions. To improve the quality of their assumptions, businesses must improve their capability for uncertainty management and weave it into their strategy development processes, not simply rely on the backward-facing analytical approach to decision support typically used for due diligence on large investments. While the value of risk management is appreciated (especially after the financial crisis), uncertainty management has yet to enter the management lexicon.

Reducing poor decisions on big bets does not accelerate growth directly, though it does remove the braking effect on earnings from wasting corporate time, energy and resources on flawed initiatives. The first step towards growth is plugging resource leakage or, as a senior manager from one of the UK's leading insurance companies put it, 'The secret of growth? Simple, just stop doing stupid things.' To do that we need to understand how cognitive biases cause us to be stupid.

Much of Kahneman and Tversky's research focused on uncertainty and flawed application of probabilistic thinking, thereby illustrating our susceptibility to cognitive bias. As described in Chapter 2, we have become increasingly adept, thanks to increases in computing power, at slicing and dicing vast quantities of historical data. Yet the research has shown that our ability to look forwards rather than backwards is hampered by blindness and inconsistency when it comes to making probability-based decisions. Given that strategic choices are made against either implicit or explicit probability assignment, any such flaws are very costly.

Typicality vs likelihood

One of the most commonplace biases when it comes to assessing probability is confusing typicality with likelihood: confusing what we perceive to be most typical with what is most likely to happen. The easier we find something to imagine, the more normal we think it is, the more frequent we assume it will be. This is shown in an experiment where participants are offered the opportunity to bet on which of the following sequences represents the actual results from tossing a coin seven times:

1 HHHHTTT
2 THHTHTT
3 TTTTTTT

The findings of Kahneman, Tversky and others have shown that sequence 2 is strongly preferred to the others. Basic probability theory tells us that in seven tosses of a coin the probability of any one sequence is exactly the same as any other, so our preference for each sequence should be the same. But typicality deludes us into believing that one sequence is more likely than the others. Alternating heads and tails is more frequently selected, not because it is more probable, but because it appears more normal.[2]

The same tendency has been shown in another Kahneman and Tversky experiment. Imagine a die that has been painted so that it has four green faces and two red. The die is shaken and thrown onto a table and you are invited to bet on which of the following sequences represents the actual one:

1   RGRRR
2   GRGRRR
3   GRRRRR

In experiments when subjects were invited to bet on the sequence that resulted, the expressed preference is 2 followed by 1 then 3. Furthermore, a majority of subjects continued to bet on the second sequence, even when it is highlighted that sequence 1 is the same as sequence 2 with the first throw removed so, by definition, more likely. (The chance of the longer sequence being correct is two thirds that of the shorter sequence – the probability of the additional throw coming up green.) The problem is that the second sequence is perceived to be more balanced and therefore more typical.

This delusion is also known as the gambler's fallacy, the presumption that chance is a self-correcting process in which a deviation in one direction induces a counterbalancing one in the other direction. If we are playing roulette and red has come up 20 times in a row, we are instinctively drawn to bet on black, even though the chance remains 50:50 and the outcome is independent of what has occurred before. The gambler who believes that sooner or later the equilibrium between red and black will be reestablished at about 50 per cent has fallen prone to this fallacy. As Massimo Piattelli-Palmarini, author of *Inevitable Illusions*,[3] summarizes it: 'Statistically, we believe something to be true for short sequences that is only approximately true for very long sequences, and rigorously true only for sequences near to infinity.'

Framing

Bias is also introduced by how choices are framed. This is demonstrated by two examples with the same backdrop: a deadly disease that has put 600 people at risk. In the first experiment, subjects have to choose between Programme A, which will definitely save 200 out of the 600, and Programme B, where there is a one third probability that all 600 people will be saved and a two-thirds probability that no one will be saved.

The same test is given in a slightly different form to another set of subjects. Again, 600 people are at risk from the deadly disease, but this time the two options are Programme C, in which case 400 people will certainly die, and Programme D, where there is a one third probability that no one will die and a two-thirds probability that all 600 people will die.

In probability terms the two tests are the same: Programme A in the first equates to C in the second and B equates to D. But the first describes the potential outcomes in terms of lives saved and the second in terms of lives lost.

Not surprisingly, the results of these experiments show that the stated preference is for Programme A over Programme B. Even though statistically the expected value is the same (200 lives saved), psychologically we derive greater expected utility from the certainty attached to the 200 lives saved. In the second experiment the expected value of each option is again 200 lives saved. However, in this case subjects prefer D. As the choices are framed in terms of lives lost (as opposed to lives saved), the lower degree of certainty that D offers delivers greater psychological benefit. On average, the research findings were that 72 per cent of respondents prefer A and 28 per cent prefer B, while 22 per cent favour C and 78 per cent favour D.[4]

There is nothing irrational in expected utility to trump expected value. But what is irrational is that preferences (based on expected utilities) conflict when the expected outcomes remain the same but the frame of reference is changed. Certainty is preferable when the outcome is expressed in terms of lives saved but not when the same outcome is expressed in terms of lives lost. It is not the final result that matters but how it deviates from our mental starting point.

When we change our initial reference, conflicting preferences arise for the same outcome.

While the above example is contrived, research has also high-lighted inconsistencies in real-world examples due to framing, even with highly trained professionals in their own area of expertise. One example from the medical world was described in a 1982 study in the *New England Journal of Medicine*. In this study a sample of 421 doctors was presented with data summarizing the results of surgery and radiation therapy for lung cancer. The doctors were asked to imagine that they had lung cancer and to choose between the two therapies on the basis of the data provided. Different groups of respondents received data that only differed in whether the out-comes were framed in terms of the probability of living or dying. The preference for surgery, relative to radiation therapy, was substan-tially greater when the problem was framed in terms of the proba-bility of living rather than in terms of the probability of dying.[5]

A similar distortion in preference for certain versus uncertain out-comes (of the same expected value in probability terms) arises when choices are framed as winning or losing. Results show that we tend to be risk averse when it comes to winning – when faced with a choice between two bets with the same expected value, our expected utility is higher for the one with greater certainty attached – but we become more adventurous when facing a loss.

For example, in another Kahneman and Tversky experiment the subject is asked to choose between two outcomes: A, a certain gain of $75, and B, a lottery with a 75 per cent probability of winning $100 and a 25 per cent probability of winning nothing at all. The results were that a substantial majority choose A over B. However, the expected utility changes dramatically when people are offered a choice between C, a sure loss of $75, and D, a lottery in which there is a 75 per cent probability that they will lose $100 and a 25 per cent probability of not losing anything at all. Now the uncertainty of D is preferable to the certainty of C. Again, if true economic rationality prevailed, those choosing A should choose C, but that is clearly not the case. What Kahneman, Tversky and their collaborators have shown is that there is considerable psychological asymmetry between the prospect of winning and losing. This will be obvious to most people who went through the process of determining their own choices above, but such asymmetry is not accounted for in models of decision making employed by economists or management scientists.

As a further example of this, imagine you are taking two different investment proposals requiring significant funding to your company's executive committee to approve the expenditure. They offer equivalent economic returns in terms of net present value, internal rate of return and payback period for the same capital outlay. However, one is an investment to protect existing business: the returns are predicated on an assumption that revenue and profits will decline unless the investment is made. The other is an opportunity to expand into a new or adjacent market. If there were only funds for one, which do you think the investment committee would prefer (indeed, which would you prefer to present to the committee)? Which potential decision error would be more psychologically costly: spending money unnecessarily to protect existing business and forgoing a growth opportunity, or going for growth and losing existing sales as a result?

An investment to maintain the status quo is generally a hard sell, as anyone who has built a business case for 'licence-to-operate' investments will attest. You need to persuade key executives that the business's baseline is deteriorating financial performance, not flat as might be seen as reasonable, or increasing due to natural momentum as most people would prefer to believe. The risk with such executive reluctance is that potential upsides – cost savings or revenue increases from new business won – are invented to gain approval. The investment is consequently seen as a failure when it fails to deliver the promised upside, even though it was critical for the business to continue functioning.

At the heart of this asymmetry are our love of owning and fear of losing. We are so desperate to avoid any loss or perceived failure that we are prepared to take more risks than we otherwise would to win back what we once had. Fear of loss is why free offers are so attractive to us. Any transaction entails potential loss if what we buy doesn't perform as we would like or expect. But if something is free, to our psyche there appears to be no such risk.

This fear is so strong as to cause myopia, particularly regarding what we own. As Ariely points out, we fall in love with what we already have, tending to focus on what we may lose rather than what we may gain and to assume that others will see transactions from the same perspective as us. This also applies to points of view:

Once we take ownership of an idea… We love it perhaps more than we should. We prize it more than it is worth. And most frequently, we have trouble letting go of it because we can't stand the idea of its loss.[6]

The result is irrational stubbornness. Humphrey Neill, author of *The Art of Contrary Thinking*, highlights the strength of such emotions:

If one relies stubbornly on his own opinion he is likely to 'stand on his opinion,' right or wrong. No trait is stronger, perhaps, than of defending one's own opinion and of being unwilling to admit error in judgment.[7]

In business the costs of intransigence are high, for example retaining for reasons of emotional attachment a business that should be divested on economic considerations. Successful entrepreneurs are often reluctant to sell the original business from which everything else has sprung, believing that if it is removed the whole edifice will collapse. Another example is pouring good money after bad into a business or programme in an attempt to raise the returns it is generating to those forecast in the original proposal. Pride, a desire for self-justification or an unwillingness to admit mistakes all result in damaging decisions being made.

Less obviously, the desire to avoid loss extends to an unwilling-ness to limit our choices. As Ariely puts it:

> *Normally, we cannot stand the idea of closing the doors on our alter-natives… In the context of today's world, we work just as feverishly to keep all our options open… We might not always be aware of it, but in every case we give something up for those options.*[8]

Retaining optionality has strategic appeal, yet at the core of strategic intent is the ability to define what a business will *not* do as articu-lately as what it *will* do. This means saying 'no' to entering certain markets; serving certain segments and customers; offering certain product features; excelling in certain capabilities; and funding certain investments. In our hearts we want to do everything *and* do every-thing well; psychologically we are the antithesis of strategic. Making genuine strategic choices does not come naturally to us, which is perhaps why we tend to confuse strategy with one of its subcompo-nents, strategic analysis. Analysis does come relatively easy, at least to those who obtain MBAs or work in strategy consultancies or in the strategic planning functions of large companies. Analysis allows us to quantify and rank. It is only in the act of design that we are forced to choose, to make trade-offs, to say 'no'. Unfortunately, design has become the forgotten competency, rarely taught in busi-ness schools and seldom mentioned in strategy conversations (a sub-ject that will be discussed in more detail in Chapter 7).

Framing also limits the way we approach problems, seeking to solve them in the way they are presented. We can become imprisoned by the frame we are given. This limits our ability to generate a range of potential solutions and arrive at a better decision. Compounding this acquiescence is what Tversky and Kahneman call segregation: isolating the problem from its wider context so that it becomes the immediate and exclusive centre of our attention. One manifestation is setting goals or targets that distort behaviour because they are too narrow. A unilateral volume-based target will encourage sales reps to offer large discounts to customers; a focus on speed will cause quality to slip (and vice versa); overarching revenue targets risk a decline in satisfaction if customers perceive they are being fleeced. Yet such damaging goal setting is common.[9]

The conjunction fallacy

Framing and typicality effects are not mutually exclusive and often compound each other. One example is the conjunction fallacy, again first identified by Kahneman and Tversky. In their study, subjects were given a sheet describing the attitudes and characteristics of Bill. He is 34 years old and intelligent, but unimaginative, compulsive and generally apathetic. In school he was strong in mathematics but weak in social studies and humanities.

On the basis of this skeletal description, subjects were asked to assess the likelihood of Bill having a certain trade or profession and enjoying different pastimes, specifically by ranking in order of decreasing probability the following list of jobs and hobbies:

Bill is a doctor, and his hobby is playing poker
Bill is an architect
Bill is an accountant (A)
Bill plays jazz for a hobby (J)
Bill surfs for a hobby
Bill is a reporter
Bill is an accountant who plays jazz for a hobby (A&J)
Bill climbs mountains for a hobby

Subjects were also given a description of Linda. She is 31 years old, single, outspoken and very bright. She majored in philosophy. As a student she was deeply concerned with issues of discrimination and social justice, and also participated in antinuclear demonstrations.

As with Bill, we have to rank in descending order of likelihood the following professions or hobbies:

Linda is a teacher in elementary school
Linda works in a bookstore and takes a yoga classes
Linda is active in the feminist movement (F)
Linda is a psychiatric social worker
Linda is a member of the League of Women Voters
Linda is a bank teller (T)
Linda is an insurance salesperson
Linda is a bank teller and active in the feminist movement (T&F)

As you will most probably have recognized, the descriptions of Bill and Linda were deliberately constructed to be representative of an accountant and a feminist. The effect of this is to blind us to all other considerations. In the case of Bill, we almost all pick A (Bill being an accountant) as the most likely and allow this to colour our assessments, so that we pick A&J (an accountant who plays jazz for a hobby) ahead of J (just playing jazz for a hobby). The same applies with Linda: we pick T&F (a bank teller who is active in the feminist movement) ahead of T (a bank teller).

However, by definition the probability of any conjunction – two characteristics being simultaneously true – has to be lower than the probability of either of the two characteristics taken alone. It must be more likely that Bill enjoys playing jazz (while working at whatever or nothing at all) than it is for him to both play jazz and work as an accountant. The accountants who play jazz are by definition a subset of all those who play jazz. Equally, it has to be more likely that Linda is a bank teller than it is that Linda is both a bank teller and active in the feminist movement.

Nonetheless, the vast majority of people submitted to tests like this believed that the conjunction was more likely than one of the paired activities individually. In the case of Bill, 85 per cent of all respondents thought the conjunction of accountancy and jazz more likely than jazz alone (i.e. the probability of A > A&J > J). And with Linda, 85 per cent assessed the combination of bank teller and active feminist as being more likely than her simply being a bank teller (i.e. the probability of F > T&F > T).[10] Surprisingly, the research found no great difference in the average responses of uninformed subjects and those of statistical experts. Kahneman and Tversky also found that the conjunction fallacy extended to doctors, generals and engineers in their specific areas of expertise. For example, a study of doctors found that they considered the simultaneous presence of two normally associated symptoms to be more probable than the presence of either separately.

The conjunction fallacy exists because we are blinded to the probabilities by what we find easiest to imagine – what we find most typical or stereotypical. Of the professions offered, Bill's profile most stereotypically suggests accountancy. In the same way, Linda's activism suggests feminism. In both cases the impressions are so strong that they dominate every other characteristic in our ranking of probabilities. Some elements in the profiles suggest Bill's interest in jazz or Linda's working in a bank as being unlikely. We pay no attention to the objective (i.e. demographic, statistically based) probabilities about professions or hobbies. And because the two conjunctions resonate more tunefully with the information provided, we select them over the one subcomponent that feels like a less good fit.

Our blindness to conjunct probabilities is linked to one of the most frequently observed biases when faced with uncertainty: the tendency to be overoptimistic. Thaler and Sunstein cite a number of studies highlighting that over 90 per cent of people believe they are above average, whether it be MBA students taking Thaler's class in managerial decision making, car drivers or simply people judging the quality of their sense of humour. Equally, despite half of marriages ending in divorce, those getting married typically rate the risk as being close to zero in their specific case. We systematically underestimate the risks of something bad happening to us: losing our job, getting cancer from smoking, getting a sexually transmitted disease. We may understand the risks at the aggregate level, but assume it will happen to someone else; this explains some irrational risk taking with regard to health and life. As captured in the percipient lyrics of the Go West hit, we tend towards being Kings (or Queens) of Wishful Thinking. The problem is that unrealistic optimism results in increased risk taking.

In a business context, the conjunction effect heightens this natural tendency. It is most obvious in forecasts made of revenues from new product launches and new ventures or of synergies from acquired companies. As highlighted previously, research over the past four decades has shown that the vast majority of new ventures fail (and of those that survive, the majority probably did not achieve their financial projections) and most acquisitions fail to deliver the expected returns.

The reason for this is simple: any significant business activity such as launching a new product or acquiring a competitor is a complex process with conjunctive characteristics – a sequence of interconnected tasks must be successfully completed for the undertaking as a whole to be successful. Even if each one is likely, the overall probability of success is low if the number of events is high. We are likely to overestimate the overall probability of success if we use the probability of a single event as the starting point in our estimation. We note that the average event likelihood is high and this blinds us to the compound likelihood being low. Even if we acknowledge the compound effect and mentally correct for it, because adjustments tend to be insufficient (for reasons described later) the final estimates remain overoptimistic. This bias is hard-wired by organizational factors which reward overoptimism, as projects with the most positive forecasts are prioritized in the resource-allocation process.

Nevertheless, it is also important to note that overoptimism can cut both ways – both the new and the status quo are prone to exaggeration. The statement 'the only constant in business is change' has become clichéd, but it still runs counter to human nature. The first step in any successful transformation programme is creating a sense of urgency to shake people out of their belief that it will all work out OK in the end, that nothing dramatic is required. Or in the words of Rahm Emanuel, President Obama's White House Chief of

Staff: 'You don't ever want a crisis to go to waste; it's an opportunity to do important things that you would otherwise avoid.' With difficult and painful decisions – managers requiring people to change what they have become comfortable doing or making redundant people they have known and worked with for many years – over-optimism about the current state (i.e. how things will pan out without the change being implemented) becomes the more likely error.

The need for narrative

So how can this have an effect in the real world? At the heart of these distortions is a need for a narrative; and at the heart of narrative is simplification – a reduction in the complexity of the world as we see it. What appears typical to us is a reflection of how we understand the world to work. If something does not fit with our existing simplified understanding of the world, or does not present a new narrative that we can quickly grasp, we reject it. Our need for narrative has a particular impact on how we interpret the past; how this distorts the development of management knowledge will be tackled in the next chapter. However, its impact is more direct than that.

Any significant investment opportunity will require a compelling story to accompany the economic evaluation. The risk, of course, is that the story becomes so compelling that it outweighs or biases the supposedly objective financial assessment. As highlighted above, studies have repeatedly shown that value is destroyed for the acquiring company in the vast majority of cases, yet acquisitions continue to be the favoured means of corporate expansion, to the confusion of economic rationalists. However, when looked at in the context of narrative trumping objective assessments, it is no longer surprising. All it takes is an investment banker spinning a story about corporate necessity (if you don't buy them your number one rival will), the legacy the CEO will leave (a reshaped, more profitable landscape) and wealth for all stakeholders (profits will double, the share price will go through the roof and your options will be worth millions). What chance does objectivity have when pitted against such a compelling cocktail of self-interest? (And if you're nodding at this point, it's a narrative with a stereotype based on popular prejudice that has caused you to do so!)

Causality

In addition to blinkers created by framing and typicality, we also struggle with causality. The inferences we draw from two sets of information are frequently asymmetrical when, if a relationship exists, it has to exist in both directions. Here is another problem that Tversky and Kahneman asked students at the University of Oregon, with the number choosing each answer in brackets:[12]

> Problem 1: Which of the following events is more probable?
> (a) that a girl has blue eyes if her mother has blue eyes? (N=69)
> (b) that the mother has blue eyes if her daughter has blue eyes (N=21)
> (c) equal confidence (N=75)

By definition, a statistical correlation has to be symmetrical. The probability of a mother and daughter having blue eyes is absolutely the same whether one starts with the mother or the daughter. And the laws of genetics make this perfectly symmetrical calculation of probability true. Kahneman and Tversky asked similar questions about predicting the height of a son from the father's height and vice versa and found essentially the same distribution of answers: approximately three times as many had confidence in predicting the son's height from the father's than the opposite way round. There was a similar asymmetry in the confidence of predicting a man's weight from his height (N=78) compared to the prediction of a man's height from his weight. The asymmetry of inference extends to when there is no direct causal link, provided that one of them (e.g. height) is more naturally viewed as explaining the other. Again typicality plays a part in this bias: the prototypical tall man is quite heavy while the prototypical heavy man is not tall.

If we add in framing, then we have the classic Ralph and Joan case. Joan complains that Ralph is forever stepping on her feet when they dance. Ralph says he's an experienced dancer and does no such thing. How do we verify which of them is correct? One obvious way is to see whether Ralph steps on the feet of other dance partners. However, given the way the problem has been framed – Jane is the one doing the complaining so Ralph's guilt is presumed – fewer people think to test whether other dancers step on Joan's feet.

One result of this misperception concerning the symmetry of causality is our tendency when reviewing the past to judge favourable outcomes as being due to our actions, unfavourable ones as the result of factors beyond our control. When successful we exaggerate causality and ignore luck, when unsuccessful our perception of the cause is inverted. When looking forward a similar misperception exists, however in this instance it is due to exaggerating what we know versus what is uncertain. There is a significant (negative) difference between what we know and what we think we know. Taleb calls this epistemic arrogance, a form of hubris that arises from focusing on the extent of our knowledge, thereby resulting in its exaggeration, rather than its limits. (If our natural inclination was to frame the problem in terms of limits rather than extent, the imbalance would be smaller.)

Misunderstanding causality has profound implications in both economic and business policy when models infer causation from correlation. Anyone who has taken a course in statistics will have been taught that correlation can be measured but causation cannot and to assume that the former implies the latter would be erroneous. But that is the first trap that those seeking to justify pet theories fall into. The pressure to deliver something perceived as useful creates a bias towards determinism, whether the relationship justifies such a stance or not, and the distillation of the real world into a model that states, if only implicitly, that if you do this, then you will get that.

The most famous example of where such a relationship proved fallacious was identified by Charles Goodhart, an economist at the

Bank of England. He noted how attempts by the government to control inflation by relying on its statistical relationship with a particular measurement of the money supply (such as M3) were thwarted. As soon as the particular measure of money supply was targeted, the relationship fell apart. This observation has become known as Goodhart's Law: 'When a measure becomes a target, it ceases to be a good measure.' In business an analogous example is the relationship between profitability and market share, which has influenced strategic thinking since the 1970s (the flaws in which will be discussed in Chapter 8).

Assumptions about cause and effect are also widespread in management literature, namely that superior financial performance can be definitively traced to key decisions or actions and that the key to great performance is studying greatness. This assumed relationship is one of the foundations of traditional business school research. But, as will be explained in the next chapter, this presupposition and other assumptions that pervade management research become far less robust when viewed through a behavioural lens.

Confirmation bias

Exacerbating overoptimism and overconfidence is confirmation bias, the tendency to weight only evidence that supports our beliefs, ignoring any that refutes them. This presents a major barrier to change, manifesting itself in selective recall: managers only noting evidence that supports the current strategy, citing the views of favoured customers and not a representative sample, even an unwillingness to undertake research into questions that may challenge the approach as 'we know the answer already'. Research can be equally flawed, only seeking out supportive evidence or leading the witness. In both cases, supposedly rational evaluations can be easily biased by the way questions are framed or answers interpreted.

Confirmation bias was noted as far back as the earliest years of the seventeenth century by Sir Francis Bacon:

The human understanding when it has once adopted an opinion draws all things else to support and agree with it. And though there be a greater number and weight of instances to be found on the other side, yet these it either neglects and despises, or else by some distinction sets aside and rejects, in order that by this great and pernicious predetermination the authority of its former conclusion remain inviolable.

Bacon is synonymous with the inductive methodology of scientific enquiry based on planned procedures for investigation that became known as the Baconian or scientific method. The philosophy underlying this approach was the pursuit of rationality. Bacon is often described as the father of modern science and his approach underpins much of what we have learnt about the world over the last 300 years. Yet even if the modern scientific approach, with its emphasis on peer review, ensures that science is rational, at an individual level we remain as prone to confirmation bias as in Bacon's time. In the words of the philosopher and Nobel Laureate Bertrand Russell:

If a man is offered a fact which goes against his instincts, he will scrutinize it closely, and unless the evidence is overwhelming, he will refuse to believe it. If, on the other hand, he is offered something which affords a reason for acting in accordance to his instincts, he will accept it even on the slightest evidence.

Such thinking applies equally in business, as the twentieth century's most famous investor, Warren Buffett, has dryly noted: 'Any business craving of the leader, however foolish, will quickly be supported by... studies prepared by his troops.' Buffett's long time business partner, Charlie Munger, put their shared viewpoint across this way at the 1995 Berkshire Hathaway annual meeting. Referring to financial projections, he commented:

they are put together by people with an interest in a particular out-
come, have a subconscious bias, and [their] apparent precision
makes them fallacious… Projections in America are often lies,
although not intentional ones, but the worst kind because the fore-
caster often believes them himself.

We are so discomforted by uncertainty that we are prone to lie to ourselves by pretending the world is more certain than it possibly can be.

Underlying this is the patterning system that imprints itself in our
brains to simplify the hundreds of decisions we need to make each
day. We fall into patterns of belief based on our experiences, influences or social needs. It is not necessary to make a conscious decision
to believe something, merely to end up believing it is sufficient. In
either case that belief is only ever surrendered reluctantly. And the
more convinced we are of a correlation between two variables, the
more refutations spur us on to discover new confirmations.

It was an understanding of this that led the philosopher and scientist Karl Popper to his theory that scientific hypotheses can be fal-
sified, but not verified. Popper's method begins with the formulation
of a bold conjecture followed by the search for the observation that
would prove this wrong – the focus is on seeking refutation rather
than confirmation. The philosophy underpinning this approach is
that we know what is wrong with more confidence than we know
what is right. However, this flies counter to our intuition, which is to
seek out truth rather than uncover falsehood. We may acknowledge
learning more from mistakes than successes, but subconsciously and
spontaneously we are drawn towards verification, not falsification.
But problems arise if we apply our instinctive, intuitive approach to
momentous decisions that require more effective scrutiny. We need
to be able to be flexible in our approach to evaluation.

The certainty effect

Imagine there is a lottery with multiple winning tickets, each granting its holder a luxury £5000 holiday. You have a 50 per cent chance

of winning, but you have the opportunity to increase that to 55 per cent. How much would you be prepared to pay for this? Now for the same prize, how much would you be prepared pay to increase your chance of winning from 94 per cent to 99 per cent? Is it the same as in the previous example, more or less? Typically the response is more. Even though the economic value of a 5 per cent increase in probability is the same, the latter is more valuable due to the disproportionate allure of certainty. At the other end of the spectrum, we are indifferent between a 9 in 10,000 probability of winning the lottery versus a 5 in 1,000 one – both appear extremely unlikely and our ability to evaluate the difference or willingness to put a financial value on that difference is minimal. Below a certain threshold, probabilities come at the same price.

The same effect occurs if we move from benefit to loss. Experiments show that we are prepared to pay more for reducing the risk of contracting a deadly disease from 1 in 1000 to 0 than we are for reducing it from 2 in 1000 to 1 in 1000, even though in each case the reduction of risk in probability terms is the same. Piattelli-Palmarini describes this effect as probability blindness: 'we are impressed by nothing less than *big* [his emphasis] differences in probability, and only when those occur at either pole (certainty and near-certainty not)'.

The certainty effect, magnified by the fear of regret, drives the whole concept of insurance. A test for this is to calculate how much we are prepared to pay for an insurance policy that provides cover only if the loss occurs on a Tuesday, Thursday or Saturday. If we were economically rational, we would be prepared to pay 3/7 of the premium for seven-day coverage. But experiments show that such a policy does not appeal, with subjects only willing to pay significantly less than the economically fair value. The fear of suffering a loss on one of the days not covered by the policy – regret, having to explain to family members and so on – outweighs the benefits of the lower financial cost. It is our desire for certainty and our willingness to pay an incremental premium for it that drives the profits of insurance companies.

The insurance industry also profits from our tendency to link the likelihood of something happening with how easily it is recalled; and in turn by how our ability to recall is influenced by a combination of the media's determination of newsworthiness, personal experience and salience. If a disaster is reported on the news, we become more conscious of the risk and increase our estimate of its likelihood. Equally, if we experience something directly, such as an earthquake or a tornado, our assessment of the risks of such events increases as well. We also correlate how easily and vividly an event is imagined with the chance of it happening; awareness of and the perceived risks associated with global warming have been increased through its being linked to any natural disaster that occurs. The consequence of this is the overestimation of some risks, to the gain of the insurance industry, and the underestimation of others, to the loss of good health. The danger for businesses is that the strategic planning process develops contingency plans and mitigations for the risks that are not the most likely or the most damaging, like generals preparing to fight the last war rather than the next one.

The uncertainty effect

There is another distortion known as the uncertainty effect or irrational prudence. As well as distorting the decisions we make, uncertainty also acts as a brake on our willingness actually to make a decision. This occurs when an event will result in one of two possible situations arising that, when taken separately, would lead us to the same course of action. Logically we would be able to make that decision prior to the event taking place. But before we know with certainty which eventuality will prevail, our decision-making faculties become paralysed. When there is true uncertainty, delaying a decision would be prudent and entirely rational. But when all the necessary information is available to conclude that we would make the same decision whichever situation arises, to fail to do so is irrational prudence.

Amos Tversky found himself caught in such a situation when his department was about to offer two new professorships, but didn't want to offer the second until they knew whether the first had been accepted, even though it would have no impact on who was offered the second. Realizing that this could be a generalized phenomenon, Tversky with Eldar Shafir created the following test.

Imagine you have agreed to bet on the toss of a coin in which you have an equal chance of winning or losing $100. Suppose that the coin has been tossed but you don't know the outcome. Would you gamble again? If you had lost on the first gamble, what would you decide? Finally, if you had won $200 on the first bet, how would that influence your decision whether to bet a second time? Tversky and Shafir found that the majority of students agreed to the second bet when they knew that they had either won or lost the first bet, but a majority rejected the second bet when the outcome of the first was unknown.[11]

The same results occurred when Tversky and Shafir tested students at Stanford on whether they would take up a cheap vacation to Hawaii if they had passed an exam, failed or didn't know the result. Many decided to take the holiday if they knew they had passed (as a reward) or knew they had failed (as a consolation), but decided to postpone – and pay a premium for doing so – when the outcome was uncertain.

It appears from this that psychologically we need a good reason to make a choice. If we don't know what has happened – passed or failed the exam, won or lost the bet – we have insufficient reason to act.

It is not hard to see how this could be translated into the business world, for example seeking further information about what customers are saying or competitors are doing before making a decision that will be the same whatever insights are revealed. Spending money to know more if the decision will not be changed by the findings is obviously irrational, but if we blend irrational prudence with confirmation bias (and remember Buffett's words above on studies supporting the cravings of business leaders), it appears a genuine risk. How many due diligence studies fall into this category, having been shaped more to confirm a preordained decision than genuinely to challenge it?

Anchoring

Uncertainty also requires us to make estimates. Frequently we are not making a choice between discrete options but needing to select a point along a spectrum. In such situations we are susceptible to bias from anchoring: our final estimate is anchored by our starting point, as the mental process we follow is to define an initial value and adjust from it. The initial value may be given directly, suggested by the framing or formulation of the problem or derived from a partial computation. In each case adjustments are rarely sufficient.

Somewhat surprisingly, the anchor does not even have to be related to have an impact. Ariely conducted an experiment with MIT students, asking them to write down the last two digits of their social security number and then bid for a selection of products – a bottle of fine wine, some Belgian chocolates and a cordless keyboard and mouse, among others – to see whether this arbitrary anchor would have any impact on what they were prepared to pay. What he found was:

> the students with the highest ending social security digits (from 80 to 99) bid highest, while those with the lowest ending numbers (1 to 20) bid lowest. The top 20 percent, for instance, bid an average of $56 for the cordless keyboard; the bottom 20 percent bid an average of $16. In the end, we could see that students with social security numbers ending in the upper 20 percent place bids that were 216 to 346 percent higher than those of the students with social security numbers ending in the lowest 20 percent.[13]

The most common form of anchoring is pricing. As Ariely notes, price tags are not definitively anchors in themselves, but they become anchors when we contemplate buying a product or service at that particular price. This imprints a benchmark from which we assess what is good value or overpriced.

This has very significant implications for economic policy, as it completely undermines the central assumption of traditional economics that prices rise or fall to the level that balances supply and demand. This idea depends on the two forces being independent and together producing a market price. However, the anchoring effect makes them dependent: what people are willing to pay can easily be manipulated. Preferences and utility derived from different products or experiences are subjugated by our expectations of what we need to pay to receive that product or experience; and these expectations are derived from manufacturers' suggested retail prices, advertised prices or retail promotions, all of which are supply-side variables. Demand is not independent of supply but strongly influenced by it. Instead of our willingness to pay influencing market prices, the causality is reversed, with market prices influencing our willingness to pay.

This effect also influences the outcome of negotiations: the opening gambit often anchors the final price agreed. Equally, the perception of the price needed to win can become a magnet for the value that is believed to be fair. When making an acquisition, a company will be advised by its investment bankers of the likely price required to persuade shareholders to sell. This price becomes an anchor, which can become the target as far as valuations are concerned.

Anchors that are self-imposed are equally powerful. Twenty years ago, my first project as a consultant was supporting the application by our client, an international telecoms company, for a second-generation mobile telephony licence in the UK. The first-generation companies, Vodafone and Cellnet, had proved to be extremely profitable for their owners (Racal and BT) and the British government wanted to increase competition by releasing radio spectrum for the operation of mobile services by four new providers. Central to the application was a financial model to prove the economic viability of our client's proposal.

The revenue side of this model was fed by inputs derived from sophisticated analytical market research techniques to estimate the saturation point for mobile telephony as a percentage of the UK population; the rate at which it would penetrate and the years before saturation level was reached; and the likely market share of first-generation providers versus second-generation solutions (which were at that time expected to offer slightly different features and benefits) and versus other telephony solutions. The cost side of the model was equally detailed.

Yet for all this sophistication, the output of the financial model was never in doubt. On an almost daily basis the partner leading the project would pronounce 'this is a £1 billion opportunity'. The joke in the team was that everything in the model could change except for the NPV – the Net Present Value of the opportunity, the worth of all the future cash flows the new business would generate if discounted back to the present at an appropriate rate. My recollection is that the NPV in the base case submitted to the telecoms regulator was £1050 million.

The application was successful, indeed to such a degree that our client's consortium was granted its licence before any of the others, so in that respect the partner's intuition was spot on. The figure of £1 billion suggested that the proposal was economically viable, but not so profitable that licences should be sold rather than granted for free. History would suggest that the latter was more of a risk. The two winning companies, One-2-One and Orange, were sold for around £10 billion and £20 billion respectively some ten years later. Still, the government did not want to risk another similar giveaway and auctioned third-generation licences the following year, netting billions in the process.

However, even if in this case the valuation error was on the conservative side, the corporate track record on acquisitions would suggest erring on the low side to be the exception rather than the rule. This is something to which anchoring will have contributed, along with other biases such as the conjunction effect and misplaced causality.

Finally, the effect of anchoring extends beyond what is quantifiable, to the extent of existing subconsciously in our own behaviour. Ariely describes this as happening:

when we believe something is good (or bad) on the basis of our own previous behaviour. Essentially, once we become the first person in line at the restaurant, we begin to line up behind ourself in subsequent experiences.[14]

The implications of this are profound, both in terms of marketing but also change management. Managing change in any organization is notoriously difficult. As individuals we have patterns of behaviour that make us change averse – including a tendency to overvalue anything we ourselves have created – and in a corporate environment, when these patterns are imprinted across hundreds or thousands of people, this resistance is compounded. The culture of a company anchors it to the past, and the culture itself is formed of multiple anchors that need to be identified and hauled up or repositioned for change to occur. The result of this anchoring is to make change more difficult.

Herding

When we become anchored on the behaviour of others it is called herding. This happens when we assume that something is good or bad on the basis of other people's behaviour and follow suit (an apocryphal example being tourists joining a queue outside a building and ending up in a soup kitchen).

We are influenced by others in both our behaviour and our opinions more than we probably appreciate or would readily admit. This has been tested in conformity experiments, starting with Solomon Asch in the 1950s. Asch asked people to match a line to one of three comparison lines that are identical in length. Subjects would state their selection aloud in sequence. For the first three rounds this would all proceed smoothly, everyone stating the obvious choice. But on the fourth round something odd would happen: the first five people (all stooges) would make an obviously incorrect choice. The result was that the next person made the same incorrect selection more than a third of the time, preferring the safety of the crowd to trusting their own senses. If everyone else sees something a certain way, we are inclined to believe that they are right. And agreeing with them creates a psychological reward. Recent experiments involving brain scanning have shown that conformity triggers more reward-related brain activity.[15]

In part this is due to primal instincts – loners are more easily picked off by predators – and may result in social safety. But in finance such conformity generates bubbles. Bankers are notorious for their herding instincts, the subprime crash being just the latest in a long line of examples. While the macroeconomic impacts of herding are highly noticeable, as the recession induced by the bursting of the credit bubble proved, they also less obviously exist in smaller, homogeneous groupings, the result of which is bias from groupthink.

The theory of groupthink was first posited by psychologist Irving Janis following a study of American foreign policy fiascos, from the failure to predict Pearl Harbor to the misguided invasion of the Bay of Pigs. Janis argued that when decision makers are too alike in view and mindset, they become more convinced that the group's judgement on important issues must be right. Homogenous groups cohere more easily than diverse groups, but internal dependency and insulation from external opinions both increase with the degree of cohesion. Such groups, Janis suggested, develop an illusion of invulnerability, a tendency to quickly dismiss counterarguments to the group's position, and a conviction that dissent is unhelpful. As James Surowiecki commented in *The Wisdom of Crowds*, 'small groups can exacerbate our tendency to prefer the illusion of certainty to the reality of doubt'. Groupthink is a good friend to overconfidence.

Relativity

Linked to the distortions introduced by herding are those induced by relativity: we judge our success relative to others in our herd. In the words of economist Charles Kindleberger, 'there is nothing so disturbing to one's well-being and judgment as to see a friend getting richer'.

This tendency was confirmed in a study by Sara Solnick and David Hemenway of more than 250 faculty, staff and students at the Harvard School of Public Health.[16] Participants were given a choice between two worlds: in the first they would have a lower income in absolute terms but one that was higher than that of others in society; in the second they would have a below-average income, but one that was twice what they would receive in the first (with purchasing power held constant so they could enjoy double the amount of goods and services). The majority of respondents preferred the income that was lower in amount but high in relative terms. When given the choice of earning $150,000 when our peers are earning $100,000 on average or earning $300,000 when our peers are earning $500,000, relativism predisposes us to the former, even though it means half the income.[17] Conversely, we are susceptible to *Schadenfreude*. In extremis, this becomes a need for someone else to be the loser. We are always comparing, whether it be ourselves to other people, or our company to other organizations.

Relativity has a profound impact on behaviour, most disturbingly in a willingness to make decisions that will be self-damaging if we think we will harm someone else (a pain-deserving party) in the process. This behaviour is contrary to the classical assumption of behaviour being driven by rational analysis of what is in our best economic interests. This can be seen in experiments involving the 'ultimatum game'. One player proposes a division of a sum of money, say $10, between himself and a second player. The other player must either accept or reject the offer, but if he rejects it, neither person gets a penny. *The Economist* described the result in the following terms:

> *According to standard economic theory, as long as the first player offers the second any money at all, his proposal will be accepted, because the second player prefers something to nothing. In experiments, however, behavioural economists found that the second player often turned down low offers – perhaps, they suggested, to punish the first player for proposing an unfair split.*[18]

Most people would prefer to have nothing than let the other player walk off with an unfair share. They will punish perceived greed, even if it means personal loss. Unsurprisingly, most proposers anticipate rejection of low offers on the basis that they would do the same if roles were reversed. The most common offer in the ultimatum game is a 50:50 split.

However, when the rules are changed so that, rather than luck determining the allocation of roles – that is, one of the two players is perceived to have earned the right to propose, for example by doing better in a test – behaviour changes accordingly. In the original version of the ultimatum game, luck determines who gets to be the proposer and who the respondent. So the split, people feel, should be fairly equal. But people's behaviour in the game changes quite dramatically when the rules are changed:

In those experiments, proposers offered significantly less money, yet not a single offer was rejected. People apparently thought that a proposer who merited his position deserved to keep more of the wealth.[19]

These experiments show rejection to be linked to perceived fairness. According to research by Terence Burnham of Harvard University, rejection of unfair offers is also correlated with testosterone levels. Burnham asked a group of men to play a game of ultimatum. In this experiment, the subjects had a pot of $40. The only options available were to offer to split the money $15/$25 or $35/$5. The participant chosen to make the offer had to decide whether to offer the other player $25 (more than half the pot) or just $5. (As the focus of the experiment was on rejection behaviour, the constrained choice was designed to make the low offer the more likely proposal.)

The testosterone levels for all subjects were collected and related to acceptance or rejection of the $5 offer. The men who rejected the $5 offer had, on average, a testosterone level more than 50 per cent higher than those who accepted the offer.[20]

That high-testosterone alpha males strive for relative rather than absolute prosperity is no great surprise, since that hormone is correlated with social dominance in many species. The resulting behaviour, while irrational in pure economic terms, is entirely rational when viewed biologically. What money can buy is merely a means to an end: social status and the reproductive opportunities that brings. But a willingness to accept less in order to prevent a rival getting ahead has profound implications for business decision making, given the preponderance of alpha males in senior executive positions and the widespread belief in 'competitive strategy'.

In microeconomic thought – from which much thinking about strategy has emerged – the purpose of a firm is to compete against its rivals, with the most efficient gaining the spoils so that spare resources flow to where they will be used most optimally and to the benefit of the economy as a whole. Such a presupposition gives licence to the natural instincts of high-testosterone executives, the risk being that the resulting behaviour is suboptimal if deals are rejected on the basis of fairness, a concept rooted in self and riven with bias.

Egocentricity

Relativity requires a reference point for comparison and for most individuals it is themselves, while for most employees it is their company, since a close relation of relativity is egocentricity. I was educated in how innately egocentric we are on a consulting assignment in the 1990s. Halfway through our first conversation the client company CEO posed me the following question: 'When you get your holiday photos back, what is the first thing you do?' In those days films were sent off to be developed and printed photos were received in batches. All the joy or disappointment of several days, weeks or months of pictures – in many cases the taking of which had long been forgotten – was condensed into a period of a minute or so.

Without a sheaf of newly printed pictures in front of me and the specific patterns buried deep in my subconscious, I had no idea what I did. The CEO enlightened me: 'Well, if you are like the vast majority of people, you will quickly look through the lot for the pictures of you.' He was right, of course, both in my case and generally; my recounting this episode has generally induced wry smiles and nodding heads.[21] It neatly captures how unconsciously egocentric we are, but we do not have to look far for other examples, the rise of diary-style blogging and the thousands applying for slots on reality television shows being just a couple.

Our pre-Copernican reflex – the presumption that everything revolves around us, rather than vice versa – was also encapsulated by Wittgenstein in a conversation with a friend.

'Tell me,' Wittgenstein asked, 'why do people always say it was natural for man to assume that the sun went round the earth rather than that the earth was rotating?'

'Obviously because it just looks as though the sun is going round the earth,' responded his friend.

'Well, what would it have looked like if it had seemed as though the earth was rotating?' responded Wittgenstein.

I was told the 'pictures of me' story in the context of the company's approach to customization: seeking to build a core that was standardized across customers but with an outer layer that gave each customer their desired reflection. When understood, this insight becomes an additional means to create value for customers. But if our innate tendency to default to self-absorption is unchecked, the opposite occurs.

One example of this is the increased importance attributed to corporate 'pictures of me' in the shape of branding. Brands provide customers with short cuts in the decision-making process, so they are valuable assets. But the process of branding also serves to legitimize and accentuate corporate egocentricity. It roots marketing inside the organization as its mouthpiece to the world. In the process, the more valuable role, that of being the eyes of the outside world looking in, both receives less attention and becomes harder. It is more difficult to see clear-sightedly if you are peering through the lens that branding introduces. Both roles are important, of course, but innate egocentricity leads us to overweight the internal orientation versus the external and branding accentuates that. It would not have become so prevalent in such a relatively short time if it conflicted with our natural inclinations, inclinations that do not always serve us well.

Egocentricity can also distort strategic decision making, providing another set of blinkers when we are faced with uncertainty. Typically this takes two forms. First, individuals weigh personal experience more highly than the experience of others, the risk being that the interactions of key decision makers are unrepresentative of the norm and their judgement is shaped by atypical circumstances. Secondly, egocentricity contributes to overoptimism, increasing the perceived attraction of our own offerings while reducing the perceived threat of competitive reaction. Strategic planning consistently underestimates the response of competitors to strategic moves while discounting competitors making moves of their own.

Equally, egocentricity can colour other growth processes, such as innovation. As highlighted in Chapter 2, innovation has been the hottest topic in management science since the turn of the millennium. Despite this attention, businesses have struggled to generate organic growth and remain reliant on productivity gains to generate earnings growth. So the emphasis on innovation has failed to deliver the desired results.

One explanation is that innovation, like branding, is a concept rooted in self – it is what the business does, it is an organizational process that creates excitement for those involved. As a result, it can becomes an end in itself – companies want to be seen as being innovative, people want to be seen as innovators – rather than a way to achieve an overarching purpose. In the context of companies trying to grow, that purpose should be the creation of enhanced value for customers. This externally oriented objective, focusing on the end rather than the means, subtly changes the emphasis.

Interestingly, the expression 'customer value' is also a litmus test for orientation. Ask people 'How do you aim to increase customer value?' and note their response. In this context, customer value could either mean 'value for our customers' or 'value of customers to us'. The first interpretation is externally oriented while the second is the internal perspective. My guess is that nine out of ten people you ask will assume the latter.

A prerequisite to extracting value from customer relationships is creating value for customers. And until companies systematically overweight the external perspective and become first obsessed about creating value for customers and only then about extracting it, growth initiatives will struggle to overcome the hidden barrier that innate egocentricity provides. Of all the biases described in this chapter, egocentricity is probably the least recognized, but among the most damaging.

Acknowledging our flaws

So where does this leave us? If there is one thing we can know with certainty, it is that when faced with uncertainty we are subject to a multiplicity of biases. We are blinkered by what we believe to be typical and by how problems are framed; we are irrationally asymmetrical in the way we look at winning versus losing and living versus dying; we miscalculate the probabilities of conjoined events, typically resulting in overoptimism; we compound this with confirmation bias and overconfidence; we prefer the comfortable decision making that homogeneity offers to the challenges posed by heterogeneity; we misjudge correlation and causality in events; we overvalue certainty; we are irrationally prudent, preventing us from making decisions when we have all the information necessary to do so; we are misled to certain conclusions by anchoring and herding; we judge outcomes on a relative basis so that we don't always maximize our economic best interests; and we view the world from an innately egocentric perspective.

That is a long list of biases, but the starting point in addressing them is to acknowledge our flaws. There has been increasing focus on the potential for bias in decision making in publications such as *Harvard Business Review*,[22] but these articles tend to be checklist driven – these are the most damaging biases, make sure you review any key decisions with these in mind. Effectively such thinking tries to adjust existing approaches so that they fit with our new understanding, in effect post-rationalizing the belief that they are still appropriate.

A notable exception to this is an article, not surprisingly by Ariely, focusing on the need for a different approach in the shape of more experimentation.[23] The underlying insight is that our understanding of behavioural influences should lead us to challenge the validity of existing practices, not merely alter them. Rather than simply trying to compensate for potential bias, we need to redesign decision-making processes where borderline rationality is the starting point, not an inconvenient variation. We need to recognize that human nature is such that companies will adopt frameworks, adapt them to their specific needs and corrupt them by both individual and collective bias. Rather than focusing simply on how successful specific models have been, we need to consider how damaging they can be when not implemented in the rational way their devisers have assumed.

It is this risk that is often missing in the recommendations for different approaches emanating from the management literature or consultants, not least because the suggested approach has been derived from attempted deconstruction of successful companies; the downside has never been considered. Rather than an exclusive diet of success-based case studies, we need more that focus on failure, even mediocrity, to understand how approaches that work in some companies don't in others, and the scale of potential damage that irrational implementation incurs. This damage would include consuming extensive funds and time for limited benefit as much as the more obvious signs of failure (such as bankruptcy). Any golfer will attest that it is your bad shots that rack up the damage – no one can hit the ball well all the time and it is the relative quality of their worst shots that distinguishes the best players from the average.

Such an argument will stick in the throats of purists, who would respond that we exist to help companies succeed, not just avoid failure; we must focus on learning from top performers if we are to raise standards; we do need to understand why approaches fail sometimes, but we should do this to establish the preconditions to ensure that they deliver to their potential. Such arguments can also be justified by market demand. Success is what businesses want to hear about: that there is an approach, or a few combined, that will create the magic formula for superior performance.

Nevertheless, that desire to discover easily transferable, performance-enhancing tools that competitors will not also embrace in itself betrays a number of inherent biases. And if behavioural insights lead us to challenge anything, it should be the validity of a purist approach. We need to acknowledge the tendency to be kings of wishful thinking, only seeing things from our own perspective and seeking only confirming evidence; all of which are embodied in the purist justification.

Making behavioural factors a foundation stone of management science requires us to examine the presuppositions that underpin traditional thinking through a lens that elucidates bias and distortion, rather than one that seeks to shade them into the background. The biases highlighted in this chapter call a number of these fundamental assumptions into question. The starting point is to raise them from the collective subconscious in which they are so deeply ingrained as to never be discussed, before subjecting them to debate.

Five
A Health Warning for Management Research

Man is a credulous animal, and must believe something; in the absence of good grounds for belief, he will be satisfied with bad ones.
Bertrand Russell

When we consider uncertainty, it is normally because we are seeking to peer into the future. We rarely consciously think about it when reviewing the past. But for anyone who believes that history affords us a clear view of how events unfolded, consider the following experiment, developed by Aaron Brown and Paul Wilmott and described by Nassim Nicholas Taleb in *The Black Swan*.

Operation 1: imagine an ice cube and try to envision the shape of the puddle it will make as it melts over the next two hours; Operation 2: consider a puddle on the floor and try to reconstruct the shape of the ice cube it may once have been.

As Taleb points out, the first operation, the forward process, is a specific physics or engineering problem and how the ice cube will melt can be predicted with great precision. But the backward process, which by its nature is non-repeatable and non-experimental, is much more complicated. From the pool of water you can conceive of infinite ice cube shapes; assuming, of course, that melting ice was the source. As Taleb concludes: 'the limitations that prevent us from unfrying an egg also prevent us from reverse engineering history'.

What is the relevance of this to management science? Simply that the development of management knowledge involves historical study. Management research is, in effect, attempting to reconstruct the ice cube from a pool of water; or, from a pool of companies, attempting to reconstruct the specific actions that contributed most to their success.

As the ice cube example shows, the backward process opens the door to uncertainty and therefore distortion. But even if behavioural economics has raised questions about management decision making, it has yet to do so as far as management research is concerned. And once it is considered, a number of uncomfortable questions raise their heads.

First, is popular management research just cod science? The typical approach of working backwards lays itself open to bias from sample selectivity, misplaced causality, misguided generalization and other historians' fallacies, the recognition of which has yet to spread from history to business faculties.

The *Financial Times* columnist Gideon Rachman neatly captured the distinction between historians and economists (for which you can also read management scientists) in a piece entitled 'Sweep economists off their throne'.[1] Rachman contrasts the humility of historians, as defined by their appreciation of the limitations of what can be learnt from history, with the pretensions of social scientists who seek to derive general, predictive laws from studying the past:

> *History can suggest lessons and parallels and provide wisdom – but what it cannot do is provide a sociological equivalent of the laws of physics. Yet this seems to be the aspiration of many economists, who notoriously suffer from 'physics envy'.*

The deterministic models developed by management theorists based on historical research into successful businesses can be cast in a similar light to the models of economists that, as Rachman highlights, failed to predict the financial crisis.

Secondly, to what degree is the impact of any one factor overestimated and therefore its importance overconfidently asserted?

Given the multiplicity of factors involved (both within and beyond the boundaries of a business), diagnosing the real drivers of superior performance is difficult and far harder than the causes of failure. Yet you would not think so from how the universal 'best' is frequently and inaccurately employed. Any description of a practice as best is more a measure of research arrogance than accuracy.

Thirdly, even if the findings have scientific validity, how much value do they add to a business seeking to implement the associated recommendations, and do they even destroy it, through elevating imitation over originality? Even if the correct drivers of superior performance are identified, the benefits will be short term – if you can imitate, so can others. Elevating imitation over originality increases the likelihood of excessive risk aversion, companies becoming too fearful to act unless a competitor or comparator has already done so. The result is constantly having to play catch-up – often copying competitors' initiatives but having to execute them at excessive speed (one set of risks is substituted by another) to bridge an identified performance gap – and becoming locked into followership. In so doing the capability and courage to be original and develop the practices that others will aspire to imitate is lost.

Defenders of current practices will understandably highlight the popularity of success-focused research, as shown by a number of bestsellers over the past 25 years that have taken such an approach. How can something so popular be wrong? But behavioural economics also highlights how such popularity could stem from human factors – the satiation of psychological need – more than economic ones. In the case of management research, the psychological draw is the human desire to conform, the herding instinct. And by pandering to it, the distortions introduced are accentuated.

Equally, they could challenge the contentions above by asking what evidence there is to suggest that management research does not add value. There is some, notably that collected by Jeffrey Pfeffer and Christina Fong, which led them to conclude that business school scholarship had a relatively limited impact on management practice.[2] However, the converse question is equally true: what evidence is there that management research *does* add economic value? Where is the research that shows that companies implementing research-generated management ideas perform better than those that don't? Where are the case studies on those who read case studies?

Research by Nick Bloom and John van Reenen for the Centre of Economic Performance at LSE did find that better management practices are significantly associated with better financial performance. The eighteen management practices measured were limited in breadth, covering operations, monitoring, targets and incentives, but this study does highlight that not all components of the management curriculum should be tarred with the same critical brush. There are certain areas – operations management in particular, but also some elements of finance and the harder end of marketing – that do lend themselves to genuinely scientific evaluation. Here experimentation and statistical analysis have advanced knowledge, the application of which has contributed to the significant productivity gains that have been the primary driver of corporate earnings growth over the past quarter century. The issue arises when a similarly deterministic mindset is applied to softer data and a broader context.

The one thing case-study companies typically have in common is that they did something different: they were original. By definition, they didn't wait for another company's innovative practice to be written up and then copy it. Does it not seem more likely that this commonality is a more likely cause of superior performance than what each specifically did?

Making management research more scientific and less susceptible to bias will require a very different approach. Science has long recognized that creativity is critical to the expansion of knowledge through the generation of alternative ideas to received wisdom. These ideas are then tested and either eliminated or become the standing hypothesis. Unlike management research, which focuses on confirmation, seeking to explain the drivers of superior performance, the scientific approach focuses on refutation. To refute the criticism of being cod science, the focus of research must switch from confirmation to elimination. Different perspectives need to be taken so that multiple hypotheses can be generated that are then tested over an extensive period with a critical eye using real-time data collection, ideally incorporating experimentation so that genuinely new knowledge is developed.

This would be a big change, and any change would take time. Changing how the research is perceived by those who read it will be far quicker. One way would be for published management research to come with a health warning. Such a warning would hopefully encourage authors to be more humble in their assertions. It should emphasize that the insights are imperfect, that they should be seen as a starting point for further thought, a provocation for idea generation and experimentation, a stimulus for divergent as opposed to convergent thinking. And as covered in the next chapter, ideally there would be increased emphasis on creative thinking processes in management education courses, to give managers the tools necessary to build from these conclusions rather than simply absorb them.

Research or practice?

The primary engines of management knowledge are the business schools. Anyone who has not studied at one of these institutions may be under the impression that their focus on 'business' would make them less academic, more practical and vocational than traditional universities. As any MBA graduate will attest, this is not the case. Academics, not practitioners, take the vast majority of professorial roles. Their primary objective is expanding the body of knowledge, not educating, with a resulting ethos that research is the best use of time, not teaching – publish or die, in the language of academia. All of which was brought home to me when the professor my classmates and I had voted best core course professor was sacked for not undertaking enough research. Expanding knowledge sounds quite a worthy objective until you are spending significant sums of money to be taught marketing by someone who has never marketed anything in his life.

Such criticism has been recognized by a number of leading lights of the business school world. In an article in the *Harvard Business Review*, Warren Bennis and James O'Toole argued: 'During the past several decades, many leading B schools have widely adopted an inappropriate – and ultimately self-defeating-model – of academic excellence.'[3] In answer to the question of why business schools have embraced the scientific model of physicists and economists rather than the professional model of doctors and lawyers, they conclude:

> *Although few B-school faculty members would admit it, professors like it that way. This model gives a scientific respectability to the research they enjoy doing and eliminates the vocational stigma that business school professors once bore. In short, the model advances the careers and satisfies the egos of the professoriat.*

Henry Mintzberg has been equally disparaging, arguing that as far as research is concerned, clear thinking or intellectual rigour comes second to methodological rigour, the result of which is a decline in relevance. 'People too concerned about doing their research correctly often fail to do it insightfully', he comments.[4] He argues that there is a conflict between inductive and deductive thinking; the latter being what business school academics enjoy practising. Inductive thinking is about generating ideas, concepts and theories for investigation. By contrast, deduction involves testing any findings to define how explanatory they are. The preference for deductive thinking draws research towards what can be easily measured rather than what is most valuable, what Bennis and O'Toole call 'methodolatry'. Both are valuable, when applied in tandem. Behavioural economics is a great example of a field in which new knowledge and understanding of the world we live in has been developed through inductive idea generation, with the ideas then tested in deductive experiments.

The difficulty is that many business problems do not lend themselves to deductive thinking – there is simply not enough data to test rigorously the explanatory nature of different factors on relative business performance. Rather than thinking inductively with the modest ambition of hypothesis generation to stimulate experimentation, the deductive mindset is determinedly deterministic, seeking to draw conclusions from information that is often subjective and always incomplete, with the resulting findings being falsely definitive and overconfident.

Marketing and strategy represent disciplines where the application of deductive thinking in the first instance is flawed. In part this is because for business school professors there is no second instance in which they can test via experimentation hypotheses generated inductively in the first instance, though for companies such opportunities do exist. As a result, academic research embraces the backward process of investigating successful companies in an attempt to determine which factors have contributed most to their superior performance.

This is partly to feed the hunger generated by the case-based approach that dominates teaching, but there is also an inherent presupposition that success can be deconstructed into lessons that students can learn and apply elsewhere. In this respect research is probably a rather grand title, since it does not so much expand knowledge but merely redistribute what some companies already know and have put into practice. Codification would be a more accurate description.

Management academics would rarely admit to such a description, notable exceptions being Marcus Alexander and Harry Korine in a *Harvard Business Review* article in December 2008.[5] In a sidebar to the main article (on the merits of globalizing), the authors caricature how widely held and unquestioned assumptions, such as the need for companies to become more global, can undermine rational behaviour, with the management trends or fads that grow out of these assumptions resulting in dangerously sloppy thinking:

Company X, with talented people at the helm, pioneers a new management approach. The firm does well, and others take notice. Maybe one or two experiment with similar innovations. Then stockmarket analysts and journalists spot the new approach. They view it as part of a broader pattern, and someone comes up with a clever sounding label. The word 'paradigm' may even get tossed around. As the phenomenon gains visibility – often in publications like this one – academics develop 'frameworks' to help companies understand it. Their codification, intended simply to explain the phenomenon, further validates it.

The key point of using the term codification[6] rather than the somewhat grander sounding research or analysis (even synthesis) is not to score points against self-important management academics (though that is a pleasant side effect), but to ensure that the value of the insights, indeed the value of management research *per se*, is kept in perspective. It does not actually expand knowledge, merely redistributes that which already exists – it is derivative rather than inventive. It encapsulates a clear message for readers: others are already doing this and probably have been for a while. (Next time you read an article where the author trumpets his or her research findings, substitute the word codification for research and see what effect this reframing has on your perception of the conclusions.)

To be fair, this approach to marketing and strategy research can be justified as customer focused. Anyone who has worked as a consultant knows how much clients like case studies. And out of this understanding a new segment has emerged, encompassing companies like the Corporate Executive Board, purely focusing on providing best-practice case studies to their client base. If you read the advice that the *Harvard Business Review* provides to authors submitting articles, the same emphasis on research appears. Conference speakers are also provided with guidance that what delegates want to hear about is case studies, 'and lots of them'. All this is a natural consequence of the herding effect, the desire to conform and avoid risks, not to try something unless someone else has proved it can work, justified in clichés such as 'we don't want to reinvent the wheel', 'stealing with pride' or 'pioneers get shot'.

However, what customers request and what delivers value often diverge, as anyone with market research experience will understand. Ask customers for an outcome and you will get an accurate picture of what they require, but ask them what they want in a product or service and the result will be features that are not necessarily the best way to deliver the outcome desired. They are not experts in their suppliers' business, only their own. In the case of management research, if the objective is position of advantage, the imitation of what others have done is hardly going to achieve it.

More important than deflating the self-importance attached to such a research approach is highlighting the flaws inherent in the findings achieved by concluding deductively from incomplete and ambiguous information. The one-stage deductive approach seeks to link often immeasurable drivers to objective performance outcomes. This is fraught with problems. At what level do you measure the performance outcome – revenue, profit or cost; product, segment or business unit? Are the accounting treatments consistent across the sample of companies? How are the input factors measured? Are all possible causes of performance accurately measurable? Again, how consistent is this across the sample?

The answer is that it is practically impossible to do the above in the deterministic way implied. As a result, the level of investigation is highly qualitative: it relies on interviews with interested parties to develop the insights into superior performance. Consequently, actions or activities can only be intuitively – and therefore loosely – linked to outcomes. Fine if you are generating hypotheses for future testing, not so fine if deductive determination causes findings to be labelled as conclusions.

Banality and bias

Here's a question for you: when was the last time you read some management research that was counterintuitive and original in its findings (genuinely so, not just the authors branding their conclusions as such)? My experience is that the published management research that meets this description is rare. The problem with the conventional approach is that, by definition, it traps conclusions inside existing frames of reference – it does not engender creativity and the search for alternatives, it does not seek to source data that provides conviction to counterintuitive conclusions. Without hard data to provide any challenge, the information can be weighted to support existing preconceptions. As a consequence, the findings are frequently mind-numbingly banal.

As an experiment, the next few times you read some published management research, try scoring it on the Levitt–Fawlty scale. Imagine that at one end of this scale sits Steven Levitt, one of the co-authors of *Freakonomics* and the master of blending inductive and deductive thinking to expand our understanding with rigorously supported and often counterintuitive findings. Then please suspend rationality for a second and imagine that enthroned at the other end is the fictional Sybil Fawlty, whose specialist subject was the 'bleeding obvious', according to her husband Basil, the proprietor of the eponymous Fawlty Towers hotel in Torquay.[7]

Scoring on this scale is totally subjective: it is a measure of opinion more than truth, designed both to raise awareness and to prompt questioning. Any article in which the author self-importantly parades findings from 'my research' can be awarded up to three Stevens, for originality, and up to three Sybils for banality. (An article can receive both Stevens and Sybils if the insight quality is variable.) At the end of the review period, compare the number of Stevens and Sybils you have awarded. My guess is you will have more of the latter.

Worse than banality is bias, which enters the equation both from those performing the research and those they interview. In the case of the former, bias stems from the authors seeking to find something new and original that will merit publication in esteemed journals. Such bias is natural; as was noted in Chapter 2, science is rational, but individual scientists are not. Science can make the claim to be rational through the process of peer review, with the original article providing sufficient information on the approach taken to enable other scientists to reconstruct the experiments and test the findings. A similar process exists in the world of management academia since any quantitative analysis can be reviewed for its rigour, but the process of drawing conclusions from qualitative data is sufficiently judgement based for peer review to be merely another opinion.

If we turn to bias on the part of interviewees, the first distortion is created by their selection. How many people in a company do you need to interview to get an accurate view of the reasons for success over a given period? Only the CEO(s)? All those holding C-Suite positions during the period? What about below that? How do you balance front-line knowledge of what really happened with a strategic helicopter view? Different people will bring different angles to the collective recollection shaped by the role they or their department played in the success. As a result, the findings are very much dependent on what researchers are looking for and who they select to interview.

A further consequence is that the same companies are trotted out again and again as exemplars of range of different practices. Remember how frequently Enron was cited in business books published around the turn of the millennium? This was brought home to me when two articles in the same edition of the *Harvard Business Review* cited the same three companies (Toyota, Dell and Wal-Mart) to celebrate the success derived from hardball strategy and operational innovation respectively.[8] It is likely, of course, that successful companies have multiple practices that are good. As such, it is easy to take a successful company and project onto it pet theories, then interview people who will support it; a double dose of confirmation bias. That still leaves the small problem of selecting which factors have had the greatest impact and for which the causality between profitability and capability is reversed – success and greater profitability has enabled higher levels of investment in certain areas, rather than vice versa.

The problem is that unless a wide range of people at multiple layers are interviewed, the findings will be missing the full breadth of viewpoints. However, those doing research into marketing practices are most likely to interview marketing executives. Even if they wanted to interview more broadly, people in other functions are less likely to cede some of their valuable time to a marketing professor than are marketers (whose career prospects would be advanced should their name appear in a marketing text as part of a eulogistic case study).

Then there is the company angle. Have you ever noticed that despite boasting about 'research into over 40 companies', the vast majority of lessons cited in any management article tend to be derived from perhaps three or four? It could be that these were the companies from which there was most to learn. Alternatively, it could be the case that these companies were the ones to which the researchers had greatest access. Having been involved in many research programmes for consulting projects, I can assure you that access is by no means equal. Indeed, those that you wish to spend most time talking to are frequently those that have least to spare, the two aspects being intertwined.

Access bias is further compounded by a tendency to exaggerate, particularly when it comes to self-assessed scoring, frequently used when seeking to determine whether a particular capability is stronger in more successful companies than average, the implication being that such a capability is causal.

The validity of any self-assessed scoring has been called into question by a couple of recent studies on the subject of lying. Dana Carney and her research colleagues at Columbia University divided research subjects into two groups, employees and bosses (the latter were given larger offices and power to decide employees' pay). Half of all subjects were asked to steal a $100 bill, which they would be allowed to keep if they could convince an interviewer they had not taken it. Those who had not stolen the money were questioned as well to provide a reference point. During these interviews, the thieves in the boss group showed fewer involuntary signs of dishonesty when trying to convince the interviewer of their innocence than the thieves in the employee group. Indeed, liars with power were almost indistinguishable from those telling the truth, their feelings of power buffering them from the stress of lying, thereby increasing their ability to deceive.[9] These findings were confirmed in another study by Joris Lammers and Diederik Stapel of Tilburg University and Adam Galinsky of Northwestern University.[10]

These studies raise the likelihood that employees of successful companies feel that corporate success gives them licence to exaggerate and score their businesses higher on assessment criteria than they genuinely are. This would mean that you could give out 20 different assessment questionnaires, each seeking to measure a different supposed driver of superior corporate performance, and the more successful would score themselves higher on each one than the less successful – and higher than an independent judge would score them – simply because they felt that high scores were deserved. At best, finding that success is magically correlated with whatever is being assessed would confirm the presence of multiple confounding variables and that genuine causality cannot be established. At worst, such a finding would suggest that any study involving subjective self-assessment is completely valueless.

Then there is the bias introduced by interviewees' recollections. Memory is more subject to cognitive distortions than we would like to think. As eminent psychologist John Medina has put it:

Bona fide memory is a very rare thing on this planet. The reason is that the brain isn't interested in reality, it's interested in survival. So it will change the perception of reality to stay in survival mode. Unfortunately a lot of people still believe that the brain is a lot like a recording device – that learning is something like pushing the 'record' button and remembering is simply pushing 'playback'. In the real world of the brain, however, that metaphor is an anachronism. The fact is that the actual moment of learning – the moment of fixing a memory – is so complex that we have little understanding of what happens in our brains in those first fleeting seconds. Long-term memory is even worse. That's because, much like cement, memory takes a long time to settle into its permanent form. While it's busy hardening, human memory can very easily be modified, as traces of earlier memories leave their imprint on it. All of which is to say that our understanding of reality is approximate at best. [11]

Behavioural scientists have identified four biases that call into question the veracity of such recollections: the belief that they knew all along what they know now (hindsight bias) or that what they think now is what they thought then (self-consistency bias); remembering things as they expected them to be and not necessarily as they actually were (expectancy bias); and attributing success to what was in their control but failure to things outside their control (self-serving bias). The last is particularly important. The recollection of events is biased to portraying ourselves in the best possible light. We overstate both our contribution and capabilities because, as Medina highlights, we have a primal need to survive, even if only economically speaking (managers included).

Fallacy failings

The susceptibility of retrospection to distortion was first highlighted by David Hackett Fischer, whose historians' fallacies we encountered in Chapter 1. We may perceive historical study to be like diving in the clear waters of the Great Barrier Reef, examining the coral with a trained eye to ascertain how it has been formed, when the reality is more akin to diving on wrecks off the South Coast of England in bad weather. George Santayana's epigram 'Those who cannot remember the past are condemned to repeat it' is often quoted. Less frequently cited is Georg Hegel's: 'What experience and history teach is this – that nations and governments have never learned anything from history.' Seeking to interpret the past is one thing, but using that interpretation to forecast the future and make recommendations based on that is a different matter altogether. How many historians do you see making predictions of what will happen in the next one, five, ten or twenty years?

The past is a far easier place to be right and this gives rise to what is known as the historians' fallacy: assuming that decision makers of the past viewed events from the same perspective and with the same information as those subsequently analysing the decision. The reasons can appear very clear after the fact when you know how events have panned out. We enjoy 20/20 hindsight, but our confidence in our foresight is pretty limited. In anything except driving, the view from the rear-view mirror is much clearer than the view through the windscreen.

The historians' fallacy has major implications for the case-based method of teaching that most business schools practise. This is supposed to provide MBA students with a breadth of notional experience to arm them against challenges that their later careers will throw at them. The problem is that history, especially commercial history, never repeats itself precisely. The similarities and differences only become clearly apparent after the event. The required analytical approaches may remain the same, but you don't need a simulation of reality in the form of highly edited case studies with carefully selected data tables to practise those techniques. What the case study embodies is an assumption that studying business history is valuable, that it will provide students with the skills to classify situations and the expertise to respond appropriately. Such an assumption may be worth revisiting.

A number of Fischer's fallacies also have significant relevance for management research. The fallacy of many questions involves framing a complex question but demanding a simple answer. A business example is seeking to determine from the multiplicity of causes that exist both externally and internally in the business system which has had the most effect on superior performance. The fallacy of prevalent proof makes mass opinion into a method of verification; linking a theory to a company that is widely perceived to be great is a popular approach to gaining traction for ideas.

Under fallacies of generalization, Fischer starts with the fallacy of sampling: generalizations that rest on an insufficient body of data, a sample that misrepresents the composition of the object in question. This is something to which management science is highly susceptible given its *post hoc* selection of successful companies as the sample for investigation. An extension of this that, in Fischer's words, 'deserves special condemnation', is the fallacy of the lonely fact, a statistical generalization from a single case (or case study).

The focus on success also falls into the trap of the prodigious fallacy, 'the erroneous idea that it is the historian's task to describe portents and prodigies, and events marvellous, stupendous, fantastic, extraordinary, wonderful, superlative etc., and the more wonderful, the more historic and significant it is'; and the aesthetic fallacy, the selection of beautiful facts or facts that can be built into a beautiful story, the attempt to create an *objet d'art* by an empirical method. Related to these are the fallacies of composition, either that of difference, the tendency to conceptualize a group in terms of its special characteristics to the exclusion of its generic characteristics; or more likely the fallacy of non-difference, rendering a special judgement on a group for a quality that is not special to it.

Under fallacies of narration, Fischer states: 'A historian must distinguish between the analysis of the becoming of an object and an analysis of the object it has become.' Research can fall into the trap of describing a great company as it is now, not how it achieved greatness. In this category Fischer also includes the fallacy of false periodization, false conclusions being drawn because the period under review is not a true representation; and the didactic fallacy, attempting to extract specific lessons from history and apply them literally as policies to present problems, without regard for intervening changes. Sound familiar? Also familiar is the quantitative

fallacy, which assumes that importance is in proportion to susceptibility to quantification; that is, facts that can best be counted count
most. This is an easy trap to fall into when highly analytical, deductive reasoning is the default approach.

Probably the most significance for management researchers
comes in the fallacies of causation. These include the *post hoc, propter
hoc* fallacy. This translates as 'after this, therefore on account of this',
and it is the fallacy of believing that because one event follows
another, the second has been caused by the first. This introduces
the bias of misplaced causality, as there is no way of knowing
whether the second event would have occurred even without the
first.

Related to this is *cum hoc, propter hoc* – mistaking correlation for
causation, an example of which is the idea that profitability
increases with relative market share. As Richard Miniter has pointed
out, the latter could also fall into the category of putting the cause
before the effect (high profitability causing high relative market
share rather than vice versa, as is generally assumed). Other fallacies
of causation that are relevant to business include the reductive fallacy, reducing complexity to simplicity and diversity to uniformity;
and the related mechanistic fallacy, treating the various components
of a system as if they were detachable, isolable, homogenous, inde-
pendently operable and therefore capable of being added or sub-
tracted from the causal complex.

The above presents a selection of the hundred plus fallacies that
Fischer mentions, some of which we will return to in more detail
below. What all of them support is the idea that history is far
murkier than we might like to think. We see the outcomes clearly,
but what we don't see clearly are the patterns that create them. The
study of history has been likened to reading Macbeth by lightning
flashes: tiny extracts are brilliantly illuminated while most of the
plot is unreadable due to the lengthy, intervening periods of dark-
ness. The result is an illusion of understanding – thinking we know
what is going on in a world that is more random and complicated

than we would like to believe – and a tendency towards over-confidence when drawing our conclusions.

The seduction of success

Probably the greatest degree of distortion stems from the success-based approach, most notably bias brought about by sample selection, the focus of research having been only on those that have survived, not those who have been average or failed. Without a control group of failures, it is difficult to determine with any degree of accuracy the truly distinguishing factors in superior performance. As Jerker Denrell has put it:

> *Here's the problem about learning by good example: Anyone who tries to make generalizations about business success by studying existing companies or managers falls into the classic statistical trap of selection bias – that is, of relying on samples that are not representative of the whole population they're studying. So if business researchers study only successful companies, any relationships they infer between management practice and success will be necessarily misleading.* [12]

Taleb calls this the reference point argument:

> *You should not compute odds from the reference point of the winning gambler but from the relevant population of all gamblers. If you take a population of new gamblers, one of them will almost certainly win handsomely, though it will not be possible to tell in advance which one. From the reference point of the starting population, this is not extraordinary. But for the winner (who does not take the rest of the starting population into account), his continuing success appears too extraordinary an occurrence to be explained by luck.*

Denrell highlights that the consequent mistake, as far as business success is concerned, is the overvaluation of risky business practices.

In the same way that investment funds with a high risk profile tend to be either at the top or bottom of the performance rankings and only rarely in the middle, businesses that take high risks will follow the same pattern. The ones at the bottom may go bust, as a result of which they are soon forgotten and the lessons from their experience are never learned. The successes, on the other hand, can confidently expound on what exactly it was that made them what they are today, without ever getting close to the fact that luck and randomness played as much a part as skill, if not more. Denrell also makes the point that performance can feed on itself, for example through reinvestment of exceptional profits, the result of which is current accomplishments being unfairly magnified by past achievements and vice versa.

In addition to higher-risk practices receiving too much adulation, random ones may also be attributed more importance than they merit. Over the past couple of years, the success of behemoths in emerging markets such as India and China has brought them to the attention of management researchers and there has been a torrent of articles attempting to codify their success. Is this genuinely a new paradigm, equivalent to the advent of mass production in America or the advent of total quality and lean approaches to manufacturing in Japan? In all likelihood that is the case. But how much can be learnt from these companies is a different matter, for two principal reasons.

First, critical to success have been some long-appreciated concepts. A study by Adrian Wooldridge in *The Economist*[13] concluded that 'this new management paradigm pushes two familiar ideas beyond their previous limits: that the customer is king and that economies of scale can produce reduction in unit costs'. In terms of the latter, these businesses are helped by having huge home markets that have often been protected from international competition.

Secondly, lessons should be learned from the overhyping of Japanese management practices. Rather than simply celebrating total quality management or lean manufacturing, management researchers raved about all things Japanese: the focus on consensus, the submission of self to a collective identity, a way of doing business that typically took years to master, respect for age and experience, the tendency of managers to work for one business for an entire career. All these factors are now cited as contributing to the stultification of Japanese businesses, most clearly expressed in the problems suffered by the poster child of the previous paradigm, Toyota.

Ironically, there is perhaps more to learn from Toyota now than previously. Both Denrell and others have suggested a need to study failure as much as success. In the words of Henry Petroski,

> *Successes give us confidence that we are doing something right, but they do not necessarily tell us what or why. Failures, on the other hand, provide incontrovertible proof that we have done something wrong. That is invaluable information... Unfortunately, what makes things work is often hard to express and harder to extract from the design as a whole. Things work because they work in a particular configuration, at a particular scale, and in a particular culture.*[14]

Petroski also points out that when complex systems succeed, the proximity to failure is masked. He cites this example:

> *Imagine that the* Titanic *had not struck the iceberg on her maiden voyage. The example of that 'unsinkable' ship would have emboldened success-based ship-builders to model larger and larger ocean liners after her. Eventually the* Titanic *or one of those derivative vessels would probably have encountered an iceberg with obvious consequences.*

That is not to say that failures are never studied. But those that are tend to be the more spectacular – failure only sells books when either public outrage or *Schadenfreude* makes it front-page news. These melodramas may provide cautionary guidance on ethics and governance. However, it is the more mundane failures that hold more useful lessons for most executives. The problem is that such tales of failure are far less welcome than stories of success; managers that read the management literature are after sure-fire strategies and role models more than cautionary words.

Doubts about the value of success-based management research have also been cast in a 2009 paper written by Deloitte consultants Michael Raynor and Mumtaz Ahmed with Andrew Henderson. Its key conclusion is:

> *researchers who think they are studying successful companies are usually studying the winners of a random walk. What does this mean for the soundness of some of the most popular and influential management research? The bottom line: you can't trust it.*

The authors conclude that superior performance is more a result of luck than anything else; and that management research fails to distinguish between the roles played by systematic variability (what they call common causes) and individual skill (specific causes).

In essence, the bar for determining excellence or greatness has been set too low. Greatness in these studies is the corporate equivalent to tossing a coin and getting seven heads: someone will do it given a large enough starting population. As a result, the studies are not sufficiently scientific to give confidence in their findings and managers cannot hope to achieve reliably the results they are told to expect. The authors acknowledge that managers may have found the prescriptions in these studies helpful, but attribute this to the placebo effect, the association of improvement with the prescription, even if there is no causal link; or the Hawthorne effect, where the mere effort of focusing on something improves performance.

Not the best

Bias is understandable, of course, and the damage it causes can be limited so long as its presence is recognized. But rather than admit the possibility and couch findings accordingly, if anything management science has gone the other way, becoming more definitive, liberally using universal terms such as classifying practices as best. It has chosen to compound the flaw of bias with the sin of arrogance.

The term 'best practice' is probably the most misleading and damaging expression in the world of business. It presumes that there is one way – and only one way – of doing things right; any other way is by definition suboptimal. There are multiple problems with this idea.

First, we have the problem discussed above of cause and effect. It is possible, though not as easy as might be assumed, to define best-in-class results – the effect side of the equation. The ease of comparison depends on the complexity of the measure. For simple operational metrics, there are many organizations that collect data from a variety of companies and present the findings in a benchmark survey, such as Merchants' *Global Contact Centre Benchmarking Report*.

At the other end of the quantification spectrum, it is possible to compare quoted companies on measures such as profit margin and revenue growth, so we can ascertain whether Procter & Gamble is performing better than Unilever on the overall measures that contribute to shareholder value. The problem is drawing a line between the two when group profitability is influenced by factors of far greater magnitude than front-line operational metrics.

At a lower level, the financial performance of different business units is not usually available and even if it were, comparing across businesses would be difficult given different accounting practices, different treatment of group charges and so on. Even on the effect side of the equation, determining best in a meaningful way is thus difficult.

However, those problems are compounded when we start to look at the cause side of the equation – the specific practices that generate results. For example, the practices that reduce average call handling time in a service centre are likely to conflict with those that increase first call resolution. If a company has the lowest average call handling time, can that be categorized as best practice? What if a high proportion of customers need to call back? Linking a specific practice to overall business profitability and growth is nigh on impossible, especially across a sample of companies.

This brings us to the question of what 'best' actually means. In business there are relatively few absolutes. And even where there are, such as with health and safety, businesses still have choices about how much they will impose on employees above the statutory minimum to reduce the risk of personal injury. The vast majority of business decisions involve a trade-off between reducing costs and increasing revenue (albeit indirectly through improving customer experience).

To be classified as best, a practice needs to be contextualized with answers to the following questions:

1　According to whom is this best practice? What particular authority has set itself up to be the judge on this matter and what credentials does it have?
2　What is the comparison base? What is the range of practices it was compared against across what population of organizations?
3　What is the strategic context in which this has been described as best? Is the overriding objective increasing growth or reducing costs? Can the practice be a differentiator in terms of the experience delivered to customers or is it simply a cost to be minimized?
4　In what organizational context can it be described as best? What is the purpose of the organization? What is best will differ with different organizational designs, cultures and purposes, also with the significance of the part to the overall whole and whether it is seen as an area of opportunity or not.
5　At what scale of activity is this best practice? What is right for large and small businesses or large and small volumes of activity is undoubtedly different.
6　For what level of investment is it best, or what average staff cost? You would expect that a multimillion investment in

process automation will improve efficiency and probably effectiveness as well, but some businesses may not have the funds to do this or believe that there is a sufficient return on the investment in doing so (or have other opportunities where they expect to get a better return for their money). Equally what is best when you have high-quality, more expensive staff will differ from that when you have relatively untrained staff.

There are probably many other qualifications that need to be applied, but the above should be sufficient to highlight that most descriptions of best practice are at best lazy and at worst misleadingly dangerous.

That said, internal determination of best practice can be valuable. One instance would be across a multibusiness company where it is possible to distil best-in-class performance into its component drivers, so long as there are sufficient similarities in the businesses being compared – culture, type of business, capital intensity, strategic objective and accounting policy. As part of a group it should be possible to dig deeply enough, experiment even, to understand cause and effect. Equally, knowledge-based companies will learn from experience how to do things more efficiently and effectively and the codification of this is both reasonable and valuable. Consultancies, for example, will learn from their experience of multiple previous projects how to implement in the most time- or cost-efficient way. Such a claim of (internal) best practice is justified, though in legal documents, for instance contracts, consultancies are moving away from these claims, preferring to use the more reasonable claim of good practice for the reasons cited above. Proving something to be best in a court of law would not be easy; in the court of public opinion the burden of proof is lighter and acceptance more readily forthcoming.

What the above brings to life is two debates: experience versus research and good versus best practice. In the consultancy example cited above, the practice is valuable because it has been derived from deep experience and developed over time. Most designations of best practice are a product of research rather than experience, the universal being added by the researcher to accentuate importance and mask both its notional nature and their lack of direct experience. As a colleague of mine has noted (let's call it Hicks' Dictum), best practice citation and experience tend to be inversely proportional – the more frequently someone invokes best practice, the less real-world experience they typically have of that practice. Someone with extensive experience is far more likely to say 'in my ten years of working on these types of projects I have found that...'[15] as supporting evidence for what they suggest than to use the more priggish and hectoring 'best practice states that...'

The distinction between best and good is also important: good suggests a starting point, best implies that it is the only way to do something. But even more valuable than 'good' practice is 'good enough' practice. Businesses cannot, and should not try to, excel on all dimensions. Good strategy is as much about specifying which customers will not be served as those that will, what will not be offered to those customers as much as what will, and the capabilities that will not be developed as it much as those that will.

Strategic choices require managers to say that we will settle for having a basic capability in this area, perhaps even that we will have no capability in this area. This is incredibly hard to do – it requires clear thinking and the confidence to be laser-like in focus. Without that level of understanding and self-belief, it is easy to fall into the trap of trying to be good at everything for which there is inherent organizational pressure.

For one client we developed a tool covering all customer management activities across marketing, sales and service, the capability defined according to levels of customer intimacy. This tool was then used in workshops across the different businesses, with workshop attendees from each function scoring the current and desired activity capability in their area: marketers for the marketing activities and so on. Typically we found that the current capability level on most activities was around 2 out of 5, but unless clear prioritization guidelines were given, attendees aspired to be at least 4 out of 5 on every dimension.

On one level such aspirations of excellence are great, but the problem is that they would be far too costly to implement. The idea that they should only aspire to a level of 1 or 2 on most activities, complemented by a few at 4 and 5, does not sit comfortably with many people. Show someone a scale and they are scared if they score low and even more scared to *aim* low. Trying to convince them that scoring low on some aspects is the essence of strategy is difficult. As stated in the previous chapter, strategy does not come easily to us. We hate the idea of making trade-offs – we want everything.

This trait is more accentuated by numerical than qualitative scales, but it still applies in the latter instance. Ask whether someone wants to be basic, fair, good or excellent on different activities and the same clustering at the higher capability levels will occur. Start invoking a practice as best and it will become an anchor towards which people will aspire, whether it is relevant to their strategy or not. In this regard, the greatest damage wreaked by the concept of best practice is that it is the antithesis of good strategic thinking – it seeks to draw everyone to the same level, when strategy is in fact about being different.

If best was always countered with basic practice and it was emphasized that basic practice was OK, then this would not be a problem. However, this isn't typically the case. Here, for example, is an extract from a recent article:

> *Rather than simply comparing yourself with your top competitor, figure out which firm (including yours) is the best in each area… You can then construct a hypothetical competitor representing the best of the best, or what we call best demonstrated practices.* **That hypothetical company will have lower costs and better performance than any real-world company; you can use it as a benchmark for improvement, striving to leapfrog your competitors instead of just trying to catch up.**[16]

The subeditors even thought the element in bold sufficiently insightful for it to be repeated as highlighted, floating text.

That this thinking should be propagated by employees from a leading strategy consultancy is quite scary. The idea that a company could – should even aspire to – match the best of the best of its competitors across all areas is both egocentrically arrogant and extremely foolhardy. It implies that all competitors are either resource constrained or bumbling idiots if they can collectively be matched by one company.

The idea that this will lead to leapfrogging is similarly laughable for two reasons. First, it contains the classic bias that competitors will stay still while 'we' progress. Secondly, leapfrogging is not achieved by matching across all dimensions but by taking perform-ance in one area – one that is critical either to delivering value to customers or to company profitability – and making a step-change improvement, taking it to a level that other competitors do not con-ceive possible and find hard to emulate. It is more likely to be deliv-ered by narrow, discontinuous change than by broad-scale performance matching. The latter, even if it delivers short-term gains, will not be sustainable over longer periods as chastened com-petitors invest to regain their leadership in their areas of particular expertise, extending so-called best demonstrated practices to levels that the resources of one company cannot match.

Such thinking can be called the fallacy of full potential, particu-larly when it is used to develop strategic plans with audacious finan-cial goals. It is beloved by analysts, as it enables them to showcase quantitative wizardry to highlight what the business could achieve. Unfortunately, this wizardry is much easier in spreadsheets than it is in the real world of day-to-day operations. Any manager presented with such a report should quietly ask 'Do I get free prawn crackers with this?' (for reasons that will be explained in Chapter 7).

To counteract this tendency, management science needs to eulo-gize more about basic practice, whether that be settling for using the basic out-of-the-box processes embedded in enterprise IT systems in most cases and only customizing on the selected processes that differentiate; or only training staff in specific, critical competencies rather than across a broad range; or focusing performance measurement on selected metrics rather than trying to monitor a whole raft, losing all sense of prioritization in the process.

More than anything, management science needs to get away from the idea that there is only one optimal way of doing something and replace it with the idea that the only best practice is *appropriate* practice which, by definition, should differ from business to business. Companies thrive by offering something different to customers, developing different capabilities. To state the obvious, being different is the basis of differentiation. The concept of best practice inevitably leads to competitive convergence, with companies providing similar offers to customers meaning that price becomes the deciding factor, resulting in commoditization and margin erosion.

Don't imitate, originate

The greatest economic loss that management science has cost society may well be its elevation of imitation over originality. As Jeffrey Pfeffer and Robert Sutton have pointed out,[17] the most obvious, and therefore most imitable, practices can be the least important ones. It may be possible to deconstruct a success story and find a set of techniques that can be imitated. However, if the value is not in the techniques *per se* but in their integration with an underlying philosophy or culture – far less obvious and transportable – similar results will not be achieved. In such cases, the seemingly easy short cut that imitation offers will incur valuable time and resources only to underachieve on aspirations.

More worrying is the impact that replacement of conception by imitation has on corporate health and the economy as a whole. In part this has arisen because technological advances have made imitation easier, the explosion of different media enabling us to know what others are doing or thinking. Equally, there is no stigma attached. At a management conference recently, one speaker's talk was entirely about all the ideas and practices 'borrowed' from other companies. Fears about reinventing wheels and wasting resources in unnecessary experimentation trump concerns about the loss of such a capability on long-term financial health.

Imitation has its virtues, of course, as Eric Bonabeau has pointed out, being the basis for learning, language and social cohesion.[18] However, the key is *selective* imitation. In *The Wisdom of Crowds*, James Surowiecki cites the work of scientists Robert Boyd and Peter J Richerson, who have pioneered the study of the transmission of social norms. Boyd and Richerson found that everyone benefits when a sizeable percentage of the population imitates, but that this is only true if some are willing to originate. In other words, if people just keep following the lead of others regardless of what happens, the well-being of the group suffers. While intelligent imitation can help the group, by making it easier for good ideas to spread quickly, slavish imitation hurts. The prerequisites for intelligent imitation involve both access to a wide array of options and information and the willingness of some people to put their own judgement ahead of the group's, even when it does not appear sensible to do so. In a business context, this means stealing with pride in some areas while seeking to originate in others.

The problem is that slavish imitation is more the norm. Describing what he calls institutional imperatives, the forces that indelibly shape business behaviour, Buffett put it this way: 'The behaviour of peer companies, whether they are expanding, acquiring, setting executive compensation or whatever, will be mindlessly imitated.'[19] Such actions should be monitored and should prompt focused discussion on how current operations can be improved – and at times imitation will be necessary to regain competitive parity. But at the very least, these initiatives need to be justified by a strategic direction and modified for specific sources of differentiation. Ideally, the aspiration would be to leapfrog a competitor's actions – broaden or extend them – to avoid the margin erosion that perpetually following brings. And as Bonabeau, among others, has pointed out, industries where companies continually ape each others' moves are prime candidates for plummeting profitability.

Getting better

Becoming more genuinely scientific requires a different approach to management research. It requires the application of Popper's approach of hypothesis and refutation, with much greater emphasis on refutation – seeking to prove that factors have had no effect on superior performance rather than the other way round. As such, it also requires a better blend of inductive hypothesis generation with deductive determinism. Once hypotheses have been generated and selected for testing, the sample must also be selected, but in advance of the review period, not after it, with studies set up for extended periods into the future, not into the past. Consequently, patience will be necessary as results will take time to reveal themselves – possibly five, maybe ten years after the review period has begun. The research needs to be viewed as a continuing process with stage gates where performance is evaluated, rather than as something with a clearly defined start and end period.

Deductive quality should be improved by greater incorporation of experimentation. This would have the additional benefit of genuinely expanding knowledge, rather than simply repackaging and redistributing existing practices (whether value generating or not). Experimentation demands a closer working relationship between researchers and their sample companies. It will necessitate a clear exposition by the researchers of the benefits to the company of being part of the research programme and the benefits it will enjoy from experimentation – unique insights that only it will have.

Further, it will require ongoing collation of qualitative and quantitative data from a range of sources, both external and internal. External sources would include industry blogs, trade publications, industry associations and the like. Internal qualitative information should be drawn from across functions and levels, potentially via the form of employee blogs to which the researchers have access, providing a diary form that captures actions as they take place and events as they unfold, rather than through the lens of their outcome.

Finally, it will require greater modesty in the claims that researchers make. Any claim of best should be clearly placed in its relevant context. The possibility that factors beyond those stated, such as luck, could have played a significant role should be acknowledged, with conclusions given appropriate caveats.

Back in the real world this is unlikely to happen, at least not in the short term. The challenge then is to make sure that maximum benefit is gained by those who invest their valuable time in reading research that has been generated using current flawed approaches. Despite reservations about the veracity of the findings, I do believe they have some value, not least for the Hawthorne effect mentioned in the Deloitte research. The challenge then is how to build on this while keeping readers from falling into the easy trap of imitation. This requires the research to stimulate divergent rather than convergent thinking, so that each person who reads it can build on it in a different way – the creation of a rhizome of ideas rather than a single trunk-like truth.

To stimulate original thinking, readers of management research also need to treat any conclusions posited as ideas for testing and provocations for creativity, rather than as a prescription for success. It also requires the adoption of a more contrarian mindset to mitigate the natural tendency to follow the herd. This should particularly be the case with competitors – studying what they do but seeking out opposite courses of action. When 'stealing with pride' the practices of other companies, an obligation should be felt to change and improve one aspect before implementing the idea, both to encourage the habit of enhancement and to stay ahead of others with access to the same information.

One way to make people think more about what they are reading would be for them to be aware that all research should come with a health warning, perhaps something along the following lines:

Implementing the conclusions presented in this article is no guarantee of replicating the superior performance of the sample companies in the period under review. The *post hoc* nature of the review both introduces selection bias and means that the value contribution of different factors can never be accurately determined. System complexity (combined with the functional selectivity of the researcher) is likely to have excluded factors that may have contributed more to superior performance than those posited in the conclusions, including luck brought about by natural systematic variation. It is not sufficient for an outcome simply to follow an action or even to be correlated for them to be causally linked. Any description of a practice as best should be treated with scepticism unless contextualized by who has made this assessment and their qualification for doing so, the comparator set reviewed, the strategic objective it supports (e.g. cost reduction, value addition, customer acquisition etc.), the volume of activity and the investment level for which it is deemed best. Without this context, any such classification is strategically misleading at best and legally questionable at worst. Finally, any assumption that imitating other companies can replace the need for original thinking and experimentation will only damage long-term corporate health.

I have no hopes that such a warning would ever be mandated, but like management research, the value resides in the thoughts and questions it provokes.

One such question is: if the findings of management research are questionable, what are the implications for providers of management education and their flagship offering, the MBA programme? It is to business schools that the next chapter turns.

Six
Too Smart to Go to Business School

I n one of the first lectures on our MBA course, the professor admonished the slightly shocked class with the following: 'You're all failures. If you were successes you wouldn't need to be here.' Being a European business school, prior work experience was almost a prerequisite for admission (there were a couple out of 160 who had no business experience, but everyone else had a minimum of two years' experience, with some having over ten). And our provocative professor's reasoning was simply that if we were rising up the career ladder at a swift pace, what need did we have to incur the costs of tuition and the opportunity costs of lost earnings to attend business school?

Judging by the figures, however, more and more people are equating going to business school with success rather than failure. Studying for an MBA has become increasingly popular, its career value remaining unquestioned. From fewer than 5000 graduates in the late 1950s – all from US business schools, the attendees almost exclusively North American[1] – the number graduating globally some 60 years on is estimated at 100 times that amount, around half a million per annum.

But in parallel with this growth in popularity, an increasing number of studies and commentators have questioned the value of the MBA qualification. Particularly in the aftermath of the credit crunch, when whizzkid business school graduates were cast as the greed-driven and immoral perpetrators of the design, development and trading of the financial instruments of wealth destruction.

The accuracy of this charge is questionable: you don't have to have an MBA to be greedy and immoral, or to work in the structured debt markets. However, some of the high priests of management education, including Joel Podolny, Dean of Yale Business School, have perceived it to be serious enough to argue that business schools need to regain society's trust by emphasizing values and ethics in their teaching programmes as much as analytics.[2]

Yet arguably there is another, perhaps more fundamental question that deans of business schools need to answer relating to the value of attending business school: whether the enhanced salary on graduation is more a function of factors other than the education provided, notably selection bias. This has been recognized by some of the more questioning members of business school academe, notably Henry Mintzberg.[3]

Despite this growing chorus of dissent, the popularity of the MBA continues unabated, in part because an absence of well-recognized alternatives means that potential candidates do not question the accepted wisdom that it provides a career launchpad for the ambitious. Normally a huge mismatch in value addition (the selection process) and cost generation (the tuition) is trumpeted as an opportunity for disruptive innovation, but so far little has been forthcoming. Mintzberg's International Masters in Practicing Management is a notable exception, but evolving current offerings rather than creating revolutionary alternatives has been the response of most institutions to the challenges voiced by their heretics. So in an attempt to remedy this deficiency, one is outlined at the end of this chapter.

Mastering the MBA

The business education market has grown steadily in its US heartland over the past 50 years, with the number of master's degrees in business (most of which are MBAs) growing from just over 4000 in 1958 to exceed 150,000 in 2007[4] (a compound annual growth rate of 7.7 per cent, in MBA-speak). Even more remarkable has been the growth of business education outside the US. In the UK, for example, the number of programmes has grown from 3^5 in the late 1960s to over 100 currently. Continental European universities have taken a similar approach, as increasingly are those in Asia, with the result that estimates place the number of graduating MBA students each year at approaching the half million mark. Such growth would not have been achieved unless there was a strong belief in the value conferred by the MBA qualification, on the part of both graduates and employers.

The MBA was first introduced in the US in the early part of the twentieth century. It underwent serious revision in the late 1950s on the basis of two studies into US business education commissioned by the Ford Foundation and the Carnegie Foundation respectively. Both reports derided the quality of scholarship and suggested that greater academic rigour was needed; and that to achieve this business schools needed to hire people trained in traditional academic disciplines that emphasized quantitative methods such as economics, statistics and operations research. Since the 1950s there has been little major change to either the ethos of the MBA or its curriculum, the irony of which Mintzberg highlights: 'Business schools pride themselves on teaching about new product development and strategic change, yet their flagship, the MBA, is a 1908 degree with a 1950s strategy.'

Its antiquated nature is reflected first in its curriculum. The MBA is a primarily a generalist qualification. Before specializing in subjects of their choice, students are required to pass exams in core courses such as accounting, economics, finance, marketing, operations management, organizational behaviour, politics, regulation and statistics; the vast majority of skills acquired in this process will never be used again. Ask the next ten MBA graduates you meet the percentage of what they learnt at business school that they have subsequently used. The overwhelming majority will probably state less than 10 per cent, maybe less than 5 per cent, possibly less than 1 per cent. What is really useful is learnt through experience on the job they go to after graduating; what they do use from business school could probably have been learnt on the job as well in far less time.

Outside of business schools, the ethos of generalism is in marked decline. Companies have sought to focus corporate resources on the elements that provide a source of distinction and the greatest return on investment, rather than the whole value chain as they might have done 20–30 years ago. Less profitable businesses have been divested. Suppliers now provide complete modules for final assembly rather than parts or raw materials for the in-house manufacturing process. Outsourcing has spread from peripheral activities such as facilities management, through functional activities such as IT and HR to complete process areas (such as accounts payable) that do not confer advantage. In addition, businesses have ceded end-customer segments to distributors, either because they could not be profitably served or to release working capital for limited margin loss.

The decline in generalism has also been marked by the decline in the criss-cross rise through different functions up the career ladder to senior executive positions that the MBA was designed to accelerate. Few companies can afford the lower productivity arising from staff having to learn the functional ropes from scratch in the first year of their initial few roles. At the other end of the scale, the top job often goes to the person whose experience is most critical to the biggest challenges the business is perceived to be facing.

Against a backdrop of increased corporate specialization, the educational generalism of the MBA is outdated. It is also the antithesis of clear strategic thinking, which is ironic, as many MBA graduates end up either in strategy consultancies or in strategic planning roles in large companies.

So why is there such a good return on investment from studying for an MBA? Ironically, the claimed returns may be more a case of confirmation bias (or self-justification bias) than rational analysis. In a paper called 'The end of business schools? Less success than meets the eye',[6] Jeffrey Pfeffer and Christina Fong of Stanford Business School wrote:

> *What data there are suggest that business schools are not very effective: Neither possessing an MBA degree nor grades earned in courses correlate with career success, results that question the effectiveness of schools in preparing their students.*

They concluded that there were almost no economic gains for an MBA degree except for graduates from a top-ranked programme.

Of course, one explanation for this could be that these programmes offer a superior education, but in fact the authors found 'that the course of study, and even the textbooks used, are remarkably similar across schools of different degrees of selectivity'. Selectivity rather than education drives the difference in return. Elite schools have the luxury of being highly selective in whom they admit, and they choose to admit only those they see as having exceptional capabilities and credentials. As the number of degrees granted continues to increase, this divergence is likely to widen. In the words of the authors of *Paths to Power*, a review of American business leadership in the twentieth century, 'the credential is threatened by a commodity status, which is likely to result in a focus on the "brand" value of MBAs earned at elite institutions'.[7]

The importance of selectivity has not escaped the notice of business school deans. Richard West, Dean of the Tuck School of Business between 1976 and 1983, commented in an interview with *Time* magazine, 'Business schools are like bottling plants... The product is about 90% done before we ever get it. We put it in a bottle and we label it.'[8] More recently, Podolny has highlighted how some business schools seek to increase their performance in the graduating salary rankings by focusing on seasoned students – those who have working experience prior to entering business school – as these will attract higher salaries than those who enter from university, an implicit recognition that input value is a greater determinant of output value than the process of value addition.

The top-ranked MBA programmes turn away five or more applicants for every one they accept; the percentage of applicants offered a place is 17 per cent at Wharton, 15 per cent at Harvard, 13 per cent at Kellogg and 8 per cent at Stanford.[9] This selectivity is compounded by self-selection bias on the part of those who have chosen to apply. As Nobel Prize-winning economist Michael Spence has pointed out, higher education is an economically valuable signalling device: enrolling at a business school signals drive, ambition and a commitment to a career in management. The top programmes can be highly selective from a pool of applicants who are highly motivated and would probably succeed whether they went to business school or not.

This double dose of selection bias also highlights a further much-cited benefit: the development of a robust network of peers and alumni. Again, we need to look at cause and effect. Those who are good at networking (connectors, as Malcolm Gladwell calls them in *The Tipping Point*) will develop a large network and wring financial value from it whether they go to business school or not. Those who are average to poor at networking will not.

As a final piece of evidence, consider the following. The increase in number of institutions in the UK that are granting MBAs – typically universities that have created business faculties – has also increased the number of business studies degrees on offer, either individually or as part of a joint honours degree (e.g. with economics). In so doing, the stigma attached to business studies has been reduced; previously it was seen as something only offered by polytechnics, the poor relations of higher learning, and as more vocational than academic. What is the point in incurring the additional costs to obtain a postgraduate business qualification when there is an undergraduate equivalent taught out of the same faculty as the master's? The answer would be very little – unless there is some benefit other than from the knowledge gained.

Adding value?

What value is there in a postgraduate business school education? Over the past few years this question has been addressed directly or in part by many leading lights of the business school world, including Pfeffer, Podolny, Warren Bennis and Nitin Nohria,[10] now Dean of Harvard Business School. And three Harvard Business School professors have written a book called *Rethinking the MBA: Business Education at a Crossroads*. However, the most comprehensive criticism comes again from Mintzberg, who lays out a number of charges regarding the value of MBA programmes. The key ones are as follows.

First, he criticizes the functional silos into which business education is split, highlighting that most were in place a century ago:

> *That the established functions are fonts of important knowledge cannot be disputed. But that they contain all the relevant knowledge certainly can. That these functions have a central role to play in M/B schools is likewise indisputable. But that they deserve a stranglehold over everything these schools do should be accepted nowhere. It is accepted almost everywhere.*

Podolny echoes this concern, even going so far as to describe himself as angry about the disciplinary silos in which business schools teach management. One impact of the reports commissioned by the Ford and Carnegie foundations was far greater emphasis on quantitative approaches. As a result, Podolny argues that the study of management challenges has become fragmented, with academics carving up problems to fit their areas of expertise. He also disputes the view that current teaching approaches compensate for this fragmentation:

> *Does the case method, with its emphasis on context, help overcome these problems? I have written and taught cases for years, but my answer is no. Cases can be a source of interdisciplinary integration, and a way to focus on the various dimensions of leadership, but they rarely are.*

Mintzberg's second major criticism is 'that old joke about the MBA standing for management by analysis is no joke at all' (in both senses). In contrast to effective management, which requires art, craft and science to meet, conventional MBA education is about the last of the three in the form of analysis. Citing research findings that about 80 per cent of the MBA curriculum in top-rated business schools is just concerned with analytical problem solving,[11] Mintzberg continues:

The practice of managing is not so much excluded from MBA pro-grams as reduced to one particularly narrow dimension of itself: deci-sion making as analysis... Reducing managing to decision making is bad enough; reducing decision making to analysis can be far worse.

He makes the point that many stages in the decision-making process are soft (e.g. identifying the issue in the first place, diagnos-ing its character, generating solution options, implementation) so are not amenable to systematic analysis. 'The one exception is the evaluation of possible choices, so this is where decision-making-treated-as-analysis is focused. It is a narrow view indeed.' Effective management requires synthesis. Synthesis is about putting things together, whereas analysis is about breaking things down into their constituent parts. Analysis is an input to this process, but synthesis is the hard part. Mintzberg comments:

Teaching analysis devoid of synthesis thus reduces management to a skeleton of itself. This is equivalent to considering the human body as a collection of bones: Nothing holds it together, no sinew or mus-cle, no flesh or blood, no spirit or soul.

This point is echoed by Bennis and O'Toole:

When applied to business – essentially a human activity in which judgments are made with missing, incomplete, and incoherent data

– statistical and methodological wizardry can blind rather than illuminate.[12]

In weighing what counts and what can be counted, hard analysis inevitably leads to overweighting the latter. Podolny also highlights that the faculty members who rely on quantitative methods and mathematical models vastly outnumber those who emphasize qualitative techniques and inductive approaches, the consequence being that 'many academics aren't curious about what really goes on inside companies'.

Mintzberg's damning verdict is:

MBA programs by their very nature attract many of the wrong people: too impatient, too analytical, too much need to control. These characteristics together with the MBA credential may get them into managerial positions. But with what consequences?

Answering his own question, he concludes that as an education for management, 'conventional MBA programs train the wrong people in the wrong ways with the wrong consequences', one of those consequences being that they 'turn out staff specialists who promote dysfunctional styles of managing'.

Nevertheless, his most devastating criticism is that what is taught in MBA programmes gets in the way of what businesses need to do to succeed.

Companies generally do only two things of ultimate consequence: They make things, and they sell things. Not market things, not analyze things, not plan things, not control things. These support the physical making of something, or the provision of some service, and then getting some final customer to buy or use it. It can thus be said without great overstatement that MBA programs take people who have hardly ever made anything or sold anything and then make damn sure they never will.

In evaluating the value added by an MBA, we also need to reiterate the point made in the previous chapter, namely that professors are selected on the basis of research rather than teaching capability. When representatives from our class complained about the teaching skills of some of our professors, the disingenuous response given was that if we were to be educated by people at the cutting edge of their subjects, their research record was more important than their teaching skills. Given that we were talking about core courses, this was quite evidently not the case. A solid grounding in the basics by someone who could explain them was what we were looking for; the cutting edge could wait until the more advanced, elective courses. The real reason is that business schools are run in the interests of the professoriat and not their other stakeholders.

In addition, the criticisms of management research summarized in the last chapter should be taken into account, notably the questionable validity of research that seeks to codify success, with the elevation of imitation over originality resulting in herd-like behavior. This tendency to follow the herd is clearly exemplified in the job selections of MBA students on graduating, to the degree that they have become recognized as good contra-indicators of fortune.

I first became aware of this when working as an investment analyst at Fidelity over 20 years ago, even before the recent surge in popularity. In the mid-1980s Leo Dworsky, a noted contrarian and former manager of Fidelity Investments' Contrafund, wrote a series of provocative thought-pieces for internal circulation. One of them highlighted how the graduating class of Harvard Business School had on several occasions proved to be a good signal of a likely change in fortune, notably that if a higher than usual proportion entered a particular sector, that sector would shortly turn down. Among others he mentioned Florida property companies in the early 1970s and computer game companies in the early 1980s.[13] More recent cycles of boom and bust have confirmed the same tendency. The rationale is simple. By the time a sector has grown big enough and profitable enough to offer sufficiently interesting remuneration to an above-average number of MBAs, its upswing will have been underway for long enough to attract the excess of capacity (a disproportionate number of business school graduates being one manifestation) that inevitably leads to a downturn. The consistency with which downturns are preceded by increased intakes of MBA graduates only serves to question the strategic foresight acquired during their studies.

Professionalizing management

In the face of this criticism, or self-criticism, the business school establishment is launching a counter-attack. This backlash is focused on making management a profession, akin to the legal or medical professions, a keystone of which would be – surprise, surprise – the MBA qualification. Professionalizing management, so the argument runs, would improve competency levels and ethical standards. The argument was most forcefully put by Rakesh Khurana and Nitin Nohria in a 2008 article titled 'It's time to make management a true profession'.[14] The core of their argument runs thus:

> To regain society's trust we believe that business leaders must embrace a way of looking at their role that goes beyond their responsibility to the shareholder to include civic and personal commitment to their duty as institutional custodians.
>
> On balance we believe that a profession, with well functioning institutions of discipline, will curb misconduct because moral behavior is an integral part of the identity of professionals – a self-image most are motivated to maintain.

They go on to describe the impact that professional status might have on management roles:

> One could imagine a much more open system in which management positions would be attainable by individuals with varying cre-

dentials, depending on the job responsibility: none, experience only; experience plus education; MBA only; MBA plus Certified Business Professional; CBP only (which might be granted to an experienced manager who passed the certification exam without having completed an MBA, as people without a law degree are allowed to pass the bar and practice in some states).

There are a number of assumptions that underlie this argument that are, at best, questionable. First, that the vast majority of managers lack any notion of civic responsibility or professionalism in how they perform their roles currently. That is obviously the case with the most egregious examples of corporate leadership, but tarring all managers with the same reputational brush requires a logical leap that inaccurately and unfairly portrays the vast majority.

Secondly, it assumes that membership of a professional body would provide a more compelling deterrent than the current combination of law and market forces, whereby law breakers are disqualified from office and the unethical or incompetent find the damage to their reputation restricts future employment opportunities. Most managers would choke on the idea that lawyers are their moral superiors, even if they have signed up to an ethical code. At the heart of this is the difference between ethics and morals, which Kurana and Nohria blur. Lawyers are obliged by their professional ethics to defend someone whom they believe to be guilty of a crime they feel is morally reprehensible. For lawyers ethics must trump morals for the justice system to work, while for most people morality would trump ethics.

But which would be more important in driving managers to behave in a more civic-minded way? Kurana and Nohria assume that a course on ethics would help achieve this. At the margin it may – in his article Podolny cites students who believe it is acceptable to do something if the majority believe it is OK – but that could be more a reflection on those who choose to attend business school. If we are more guided by morals, such a course would have little impact, as most psychological studies suggest that our perception of right and wrong is imprinted at a much earlier age. A manager who has attended a course on ethics may have a greater understanding of ethical behaviour than one who has not, but that may not result in more moral behaviour.

Thirdly, Khurana and Nohria's argument presumes that MBA graduates make more competent managers than those who don't have the qualification. However, more educated does not always equate to more able. When my father graduated from university in the late 1940s he was told by his tutor: 'Give it 20 years and it is usually the thirds employing the firsts.' This encapsulates the idea that those who had embraced the full breadth of university life at some expense to their academic studies were better equipped to succeed in business than those who had focused solely on their academic studies in the pursuit of first-class degrees. More recently it has been a case of give it ten years and the drop-outs will be employing the firsts, seconds and thirds. There are more than a few examples of billionaires in both the UK and the US who did not finish university, let alone business school.[15]

What this highlights is that managing is fundamentally different to practising law or medicine. In these two professions extensive study – of legislation and precedents; and of body mechanics, symptoms and treatments, respectively – is a prerequisite just to become a trainee. This is not the case with management, which can perfectly well be learnt on the job without previous training; indeed, without any training at all. Business success results from being different in attitude, capabilities, propositions to customers – something that does not typically result from being squeezed through a standard learning and training process. Being different requires a break with current practices, something that a professional body would understandably frown on. While that is appropriate for the medical profession, where the cost of a single mistake can result in someone's death, in business mistakes (health and safety apart) are less costly.

More fundamentally, as Richard Barker, former director of the Cambridge MBA programme at the Judge Business School, has pointed out, management is too esoteric to be made into a profession.[16] For a professional body to function, a discrete body of knowledge must be defined, boundaries established and a reasonable consensus achieved as to what that knowledge should consist of. Otherwise there will be too much variability for professional standards to be established. However, that is clearly not the case as far as management is concerned, and the need for innovation and diversity means that such constancy never will be achieved, nor would it be valuable.

In practical terms, the straitjacket that Khurana and Nohria envisage is unlikely to be applied.[17] They are also aware of the weaknesses in their own argument, first with regard to the value of study in general: 'In the absence of empirical evidence, the idea that people can improve the practice of management by mastering some body of knowledge rests on faith.' (Not a great argument from the point of view of logic. As the philosopher Jamie Whyte notes, 'from the point of view of truth and evidence, faith is exactly the same as prejudice'.[18])

Further, they acknowledge the detrimental effect of the MBA programme specifically, in that it creates a negative attitude towards continued learning:

> *Data on enrolment in executive education programs offered by business schools suggest that people who possess an MBA are less likely than those who don't to invest in lifelong learning in the form of continuing education.*

To me, one explanation is that graduates assume that their period of intense study removes any future need; an alternative would be that their experience has led them to question the value of what can be learnt from business school professors.

This raises the following question: if the incremental financial returns of an MBA are more a function of how it signals ambition and intellectual capability than the education received, but the educational element accounts for the vast majority of costs both in fees and lost earnings, does such a disconnection offer a major opportunity for disruptive new entrants to the management education market? Is there an opportunity for a provider that combines the highly selective entry criteria of top business schools with more targeted tuition that would deliver a better return on investment?

TooSmartToGoTo Business School

Welcome to TooSmartToGoTo Business School (henceforward known as TSTGTBS), an educational establishment based around the principle of not consuming valuable time and money to educate people with stuff they will never use again, but instead giving attendees exactly what they need, when they need it, over the course of their career. In practice this would involve individual assessments to ascertain what is required for each person to achieve their potential. The assessment process would involve interviews, psychometric and attitudinal testing and a review of annual career progress evaluations. The result would be a tailored programme of education, training and coaching.

The flagship course of TSTGTBS would be its unique 'I'm No duMBA' programme. Given that the greatest value business schools offer is in their screening of candidates, the simplest way to manage the entry process would be a requirement for the applicant to have a place at a leading business school that they have no intention of accepting. However, this runs a little counter to the ethos of avoiding the waste of valuable time. As a result, the two key entry criteria would be that all successful applicants must have a professional qualification in their functional area of expertise – marketing, accounting, production and so on; and that they are progressing well on their chosen career path and have no need for an extensive period of remedial study.

The objective of the 'No DuMBA' course would be to help those who have achieved a management position within a function to start broadening their understanding as the first step towards a general management position. It would be based around seven core components that cross traditional functional silos and together deliver the conceptual, personal and executional competencies necessary for business leadership. These seven elements would be:

- how to acquire and retain profitable customers;
- how to create value for customers and extract value from those relationships;
- how to manage the innovation and change necessary to keep progressing;
- how to achieve the organizational alignment to deliver the first three components;
- how to attract good people and retain them;
- how to lead these people effectively;
- how to communicate, as much as with oneself as with others.

These would be taught in a seven-day boot camp, with each day focused on one particular component.

The first three are the conceptual skills required for successful business leadership. Businesses always need customers and understanding those customers – who they are, what they value, how they can best be served – is a critical component of continuing business success, but one that often gets forgotten. The more people in a business are removed from direct customer contact, the more customers tend to be taken for granted, with internal matters receiving more focus. With increasing size, the job of the marketing department becomes more overweighted towards persuading customers to buy what the company would like to sell and away from developing the deep understanding of customers' real, often unstated, needs and then designing products to meet them. Deciding which customers or segments to prioritize is a key strategic decision, as is how to create value for these customers and how best to deliver it in such a way as to meet the business's strategic and financial objectives regarding customer relationships. Ultimately, this is a decision about how to allocate scarce corporate resources to generate the greatest long-term return – the keystone of strategy.

Improving the value delivered to customers requires innovation. Successful innovation drives distinction and growth in revenue and profits. Both increasing the value delivered to customers to grow the revenue line and serving customers more efficiently to reduce costs require innovation. Given the struggle that companies have generating organic growth, the creation of value for customers is a particular challenge.

Achieving organizational alignment and attracting and retaining good people are the executional skills of business leadership; execution being as, if not more, important than conception. The first focuses on top-down prioritization while the second is more bottom up, covering the skills necessary to motivate and develop staff. Effective execution requires an organization that is aligned behind its key objectives and has clearly stated targets and priorities. These will help drive the desired behaviour. But in the end, decisions are made and implemented by people, and success is a function of the quality of the individuals concerned. Developing high-quality lieutenants is a critical component of business leadership.

The final two components cover personal skills. Leading in such a way that others will follow requires strong conviction, which in turn requires critical self-evaluation, deep self-knowledge and a strong desire for self-improvement. It also requires an ability to convince oneself. However, conviction is not enough on its own. Convincing people to join you on a journey requires you to communicate compellingly where you are going, why you wish to go there and how you intend to reach your destination. That in turn requires the ability to set yourself targets.

To keep the programme simple, each of the seven components outlined above would comprise a further seven legs, each involving a seven-step 'how to' approach. Such a 7×7×7 approach to developing the skills of business leadership would be scoffed at by the professoriat in business schools. But then as one of their number, Clayton Christensen, has pointed out, most disruptive innovations gain a foothold at the low-price end of the market because incumbents have overengineered their products to be more functionally rich and costly than customers really need. And they catch on because the new service helps customers reevaluate exactly what is worth paying for.

It would require an enormous leap of faith to argue that TSTGTBS – something that is as much a provocation as a serious business concept – could be such a disruptive innovation. Nevertheless, that the management education market presents such an opportunity is clear. All it probably needs is for a few bright sparks who (unlike me) didn't go to business school to put their heads together and come up with a compelling proposition for people like themselves. If there were ever a case, or opportunity, for crowd-sourcing, then the co-creation of an open-source alternative to the MBA delivered by an alternative organization to traditional business schools is it. I hope that will prove to be the case; and if so, I look forward to seeing what emerges.

Seven

The Value Trinity

Strategy is not what it used to be – or what it could be. In the past 25 years it has been presented, and we have come to think of it, as an analytical problem to be solved, a left-brain exercise of sorts. This perception, combined with strategy's high stakes, has led to an era of specialists – legions of MBAs and strategy consultants – armed with frameworks and techniques, eager to help managers analyze their industries or position their firms for strategic advantage.

Cynthia Montgomery, Putting Leadership Back into Strategy[1]

When executives develop corporate strategy, they nearly always begin by analyzing the industry or environmental conditions in which they operate. They then assess the strengths and weaknesses of the players they are up against. With these industry and competitive analyses in mind, they set out to carve a distinctive strategic position where they can outperform their rivals by building a competitive advantage...

This 'structuralist' approach, which has its roots in the structure–conduct-paradigm of industrial organization economics, has dominated the practice of strategy for the past 30 years.

W Chan Kim and Renée Mauborgne,
How Strategy Shapes Structure[2]

As the above two quotes highlight, the assumption that strategy development is predominantly an analytical exercise has hardened into accepted practice over the past quarter

century or so. Kim and Mauborgne attribute this thinking to FM
Scherer's work on how industrial market structure determines economic performance. However, its roots are far deeper than that,
analysis having long been a pillar of western philosophy. Its exalted
status has shaped how our intelligence is measured and our minds
schooled. For the smart and well-educated – for which read
Montgomery's legions of MBAs and strategy consultants – analysis
is the default approach to problem solving.

Much of western intellectual tradition is founded on the thinking
of the Greek philosophers of antiquity: Socrates, Plato and Aristotle.
Plato's search for truth, Aristotle's classification system and Socratic
questioning and challenge have shaped our approach to education
and, through that, prevailing mental models and approaches to
problem solving.

The focus on why things were so, justified by argument, logic and
reason, has played a significant part in the scientific advances made
in Western cultures. But those advances have also required creativity
– what de Bono calls the possibility system – to generate visions for
the future and drive the development of new hypotheses about the
potential opportunities that new technologies unleash. Yet as de
Bono points out, this receives far less attention:

> *Even today in schools and universities very little attention is given
> to the 'possibility' system... This is because there is the belief that
> thinking is all about the 'truth' and 'possibility' is not truth.*[3]

Such thinking is clearly displayed in the world of management science: the preoccupation with codifying success and case studies
being a search for truth about profitability or growth or both. The
landmark breakthroughs in the historical development of strategy
– those that have prove long-lived such as SWOT analysis, the
growth–share matrix or Michael Porter's five forces – are those that
have provided tools for analysing the attractiveness of a business
environment and the strength of a company's position within it,

typically to identify where investment should be funnelled. Such frameworks all reflect Aristotelian categorization and judgement. There are some exceptions to this where there is more of a design focus: the work on value-mapping undertaken by Kim and Mauborgne, Gary Hamel's work on business concept design. But these remain the exception in terms of number, recognition and application.

The bias towards analysis is also reflected in business education. As highlighted in the previous chapter, roughly 80 per cent of the traditional MBA curriculum in top schools is focused on analytical problem solving. Some schools have recognized the limitations of the traditional approach to business education and the need to inject creative thinking into their curricula, particularly to support innovation, and have paired with design schools to address this gap – Stanford with the Hasso Plattner Institute of Design, INSEAD with the Art Center College of Design. Equally, a number of educational establishments, such as the Illinois Institute of Technology, are offering a dual Master's in both Business Administration and Design. However, as *BusinessWeek* reported in its review of all such courses, 'At this stage, the true impact of design thinking has yet to be seen in industry, as classes are small and graduates are a mere drop in the ocean of global business.'[4]

The first job for many graduating MBAs is with a strategy consultancy, who directly via consulting assignments or indirectly through their alumni in corporate planning roles influence the strategy development of many companies. And the left-brain predisposition is accentuated by the business model of these firms, which is completely geared to producing detailed analysis. Typically such organizations employ a pyramid organizational structure: a wide base of new associates, narrowing significantly with promotion to a small group of partners at the apex. The profitability of this model requires the effective deployment of large numbers of bright but inexperienced graduates and postgraduates. And analysis is what these people do best.

How are these new associates selected? By asking questions to test whether they are logical, quantitative, systematic and structured – particularly whether they can break down problems or issues into their component parts. Analytical aptitude is the number one must-have competency. As Robin Buchanan, former senior partner of Bain in London, put it in an interview: 'The people here are awesome... amazing analysts, brilliant communicators'.

LEK is arguably even more passionate in its enthusiasm for analysis, co-founder Iain Evans having exhorted his troops to be 'the fundamentalists of analysis'.[5] This theme continues on the firm's website:

> Our understanding of market trends and drivers, along with deep technical skills and analytical firepower, enables us to develop actionable strategies that create measurable long-term value for your organization. We tap our depth of industry knowledge and expertise to uncover hidden opportunities and provide the evidence-based analysis for executives to make informed decisions.[6]

This emphasis on analysis is mirrored at other strategy consulting firms. 'Our customized approach combines deep insight into the dynamics of companies and markets',[7] states Boston Consulting Group in the 'mission' section of its website, while under 'values' it adds: 'Objectivity is crucial. Valid data, rigorous analyses, external perspectives, root causes, and explicit logic serve as our foundations for objective decision-making.'[8] Marakon avers that one of its key differences from competitors is that it helps its clients to 'discover their own highest-value opportunities through rigorous, fact-based analysis of their markets, customers, costs and competitors, and through the application of new standards'.[9]

Only McKinsey doffs its cap to a more creative side to strategy: 'We have the courage to invent and champion unconventional solutions to problems.'[10] Nevertheless, for the most part it echoes its competitors, the creativity counterbalanced by its 'structured problem–solving approach, where all opinions and options are considered, researched, and analyzed carefully before recommendations are made'; elsewhere stating:

> We take an overall, independent, and fact-based view of a client's performance. We rely on facts because they provide clarity and align people. Facts are the global management language. We work with facts to provide credible recommendations.[11]

While these consultancies would all be keen to stress the differences in their value propositions, they are all built around the same core: a Platonic (even Gradgrindian[12]) search for truth based on fact collection and analysis (rigorous, of course). Effective strategy requires a compelling value proposition to be complemented by a profitable business model. The focus on analysis has enabled strategy consultancies to set new associates to work collecting large quantities of data and applying their analytical capabilities to transforming it into the insights that clients find valuable. (As a test, in the next strategy presentation prepared by a consultancy you attend, calculate the percentage of slides that are analytical in content; that is, involving the manipulation of quantitative data or the categorization of qualitative data into charts, graphs or tables. My guess is it will be not less than 90 per cent.)

Analysis can have value...
In business, strategy has become the preserve of the smart and analysis is what smart people excel at (and enjoy doing, for that matter). The emphasis it receives presupposes a causal correlation between how we define intelligence and value creation. And the presumption of value in the analysis produced by the bright young things at the base of the consultancy pyramid allows them to be hired out at a significant multiple of their salaries. It is a model that has proved very profitable to consultancies and sustained the growth of the industry, particularly since personal computers

became commonplace, enabling increased computational power to be applied to an increasing number of clients' problems.

This presumption has been validated by the contribution that analysis has made to improving corporate profitability over the past 25 years, the role it has played in identifying opportunities for productivity gains bequeathed by the supply-side revolution. And it has been given wings by Moore's Law: ever-increasing data-processing speeds enable both the replacement of people by computers and the mining of the ever-expanding bytes of data generated by enterprise systems for the purpose of identifying further potential cost savings.

With cost reduction, the greatest value is added by analytical processes: benchmarking against comparators and defining where gaps exist; comparing bids from different suppliers; determining profitability by manufacturing facility, product, segment, country; identifying which costs are fixed and which variable and so on. Once the analysis is complete, the solution as to where and how to cut costs – which factories to close, which services to drop, which customers to stop serving, which suppliers to terminate – makes itself obvious. The answer simply drops out.

Analysis is powerful when there is real data to work with and so a high degree of certainty exists. For example, most businesses will have real data and therefore an accurate understanding of their current costs – raw materials, salaries, rent. As a result, there will be a high degree of certainty around what benefits will be delivered if a production facility is closed, raw materials are only purchased from the lowest-cost supplier, or customer service is relocated to an area where rents and salaries are lower. The confidence in the benefits being delivered should certainly be far greater than if a similar amount were invested in a campaign to win more customers. This greater degree of certainty with cost-saving initiatives stems from the fact that the focus is inward. The impact on the benefits case of external factors such as the reactions of customers and competitors, which by their very nature are far less accurately quantified, is limited (though not completely negligible, as competitors will tempt customers to defect if service levels drop due to cost savings).

The productivity gains that analysis brings are not just limited to the cost side of the income statement. It can also help generate revenue growth through identifying opportunities to reduce customer churn, increase share of wallet and improve acquisition rates. These outcomes require a detailed understanding of customer profitability and lifetime value to ensure that the right customers are being prioritized; the implementation of root-cause analysis to identify reasons for defection; the benchmarking of salesforce effectiveness and identifying gaps between best and worst performers. Research techniques such as conjoint analysis can also determine which elements of the proposition deliver most value to different types of customers, thereby enabling propositions and pricing to be optimized. Pricing analysis also highlights where excessive discount levels are being granted. Ensuring that discounts are strictly managed and correlate with the value of the customer to the business frequently offers significant, quick wins. Again, the solution becomes self-evident once the analysis is complete.

...but analysis ≠ strategy

The scenario promulgated by some around the turn of the millennium that productivity gains would start to dry up, all the low-hanging fruit having been picked, has proved to be far from the case. And for as long as Moore's Law continues – even maybe for 10–20 years after it ceases as practices catch up with the technological capacity – and globalization continues, businesses will continue to be able to improve cost and capital efficiency through automation, optimization and labour cost arbitrage. The wealth of insights that sit in the database silos of disparate corporate enterprise resource planning systems, accumulated through acquisition but never consolidated due to the excessive implementation costs, has hardly been tapped. And the integration of all this disconnected data will uncover numerous further opportunities for improving operational performance by transforming management information into genuine business intelligence.

This rich seam of productivity opportunities that companies have sought to mine has had far-reaching consequences, however, creating a view that improving operational effectiveness is sufficient, blurring its distinction with strategy and subverting the art of differentiation in the process. Such thinking has inevitably elevated the value attached to analysis in strategy development, enabling consultancies in particular to promote the idea that strategy equals analysis.

Michael Porter has defined the distinction between strategy and operational effectiveness as follows:

> *Strategy is about making choices, trade-offs; it's about deliberately choosing to be different. Operational effectiveness is about things that you really shouldn't have to make choices on; it's about what's good for everybody and about what every business should be doing.*[13]

Smudging the boundaries has damaging consequences. As Porter goes on:

> *What's worse, a focus on operational effectiveness alone tends to create a mutually destructive form of competition. If everyone's trying to get to the same place, then, almost inevitably, that causes customers to choose on price. This is a bit of a metaphor for the past five years, when we've seen widespread cratering of prices.*

Porter's comments were made in 2001, in the middle of the post-dot-com boom fall-out, so no doubt the 'cratering' of prices was exacerbated by that particular downturn. Downward pressure on prices will obviously be far less in buoyant times, but strategy weaknesses will always be more clearly revealed in downturns, so his comment is likely to be even more appropriate in the even harsher economic conditions brought on by the credit crunch. More dangerous than the assumption that 'strategy equals analysis' is the belief that 'analysis equals strategy'.

In part the misconception arises because analysis adds more value in improving operational effectiveness than it does in strategy development. The former involves looking backwards to identify opportunities for improvement in the near-term future. The fundamental but usually unstated assumption that all business analysis rests on, that all other things will remain equal, is valid given the abbreviated timeframe. On the other hand, strategy development requires projecting forwards into the medium- and long-term future, not just the very short term. Such an assumption is far less valid, and even dangerous. Furthermore, when focusing on improving operational effectiveness, there is a wealth of hard data to work with, so analysis is extremely powerful. But with strategy development there is no hard data about the future, just projections about which there is far less certainty, not least because they are susceptible to the biases of whoever develops them. Any analysis is only as good as the assumptions on which it has been predicated.

This limitation is generally ignored, in part due to the confusion of uncertainty with risk. Risk is defined by a distribution of outcomes that can be accurately defined – the broader the spread, the greater the risk – and the assumption that the past provides an accurate estimate of the future can be made with a high degree of confidence; that is, that all other things will be equal to a fairly high degree. Such an assumption can reasonably be made regarding changes in the prices of traded securities, for example. The high volume of past data and the ability to limit the spread of possibilities enable quantification and the application of analytical techniques to the data set.[14]

However, when the distribution of outcomes cannot be projected with any degree of confidence, the assumptions become all important. In such circumstances, the value of analysis is a function of the accuracy of the conjecture on which it is built. Disregarding this fundamental limitation will generate greater confidence in the conclusions than the accuracy merits; the spreadsheet models, graphs and presentations developed to justify major strategic decisions become twenty-first-century equivalents of the emperor's new clothes.

This is not to say that analysis is valueless in strategy development – not being able to project perfectly does not obviate the need to try, and then to assess options based on those best-effort predictions – merely that it is necessary but not sufficient, and that it receives a focus that is disproportionate to the value that it adds.

One example would be the role analysis plays in supporting corporate strategy decisions, where the focus is mostly on where to play: which industries, markets, geographies or customer segments offer the greatest opportunity. Effective allocation of scarce corporate resources requires investment to be funnelled to those businesses where it will generate the best returns; ideally those with advantaged positions in attractive markets. As Warren Buffett has emphasized on many occasions, 'A good managerial record (measured by economic returns) is far more a function of what business boat you get into than it is of how effectively you row.'[15] Put another way:

> When it comes to growth, it also helps to have a following wind at your back. A study of 100 of the largest companies in the US across 17 sectors over the two most recent business cycles identified that companies achieving a superior revenue rate of growth to that of GDP while delivering shareholder returns above those of the S&P500 were highly concentrated in four sectors – financial services, health care, high tech and retailing.[16]

No one would dispute the good sense in this, but it does highlight an implicit assumption: that growth (a key determinant in defining the attractiveness of a market) is endogenous. It also raises a couple of questions: how much does analysis really contribute in this process; and what about businesses that do not find themselves in advantageous environments, what can they do?

The first question will probably have traditional consulting types spluttering with indignation. Nevertheless, one of the most critical insights we have from behavioural science is the susceptibility of analysis to bias and distortion when uncertainty prevails, as it must in all strategic decisions. At the risk of repetition, analysis is only as good as the assumptions on which it is built. Relying on sophisticated strategic analysis and financial modelling that are presaged on flawed assumptions is akin to constructing a cathedral on foundations of clay.

Analysis is at its most powerful when it is built on truth, when the review period can be reasonably assumed to approximate the future and it is being applied to large quantities of hard data. Truth and fact are one and the same: something either happened or it did not. If we seek to apply judgement to that fact – why it happened, what it means in a broader context – there is more than one possible interpretation and the corridor of possible truths starts to widen. Attempting to understand the relationship between multiple facts, specifically any correlations or causal links, widens the corridor still further. If we then build the analysis on projections built up from analysis of past events rather than fact, the range of possible truths resembles more a canyon than a corridor.

Given the greater levels of uncertainty inherent in strategic decisions, relative to more data-rich operational ones, the accuracy of any conclusions is much reduced. Confidence in the findings should be lower than often it is. As highlighted in Chapter 4, we tend towards overoptimism in our forecasts and overconfidence in the quality of our assessment. Not surprising then that, despite being underpinned by huge tracts of analysis from investment bankers, strategy consultants or both, the track record of companies making acquisitions shows a tendency to overpay in the majority of cases.

In part this arises from a failure to appreciate and adjust for probability. Take as an example an acquisition valuation where there are three key variables: the growth rate of the market in which the business operates, the target company's share of that market going forward, and its profitability. If the assumption for each variable (or a better outcome) has a probability of 75 per cent – superficially very reasonable – the probability of all three occurring together is 0.75 × 0.75 × 0.75, which is just over 42 per cent, somewhere between possible and unlikely. Change the probability to 70 per cent and the compounded likelihood is just over 34 per cent, definitely in the unlikely territory.

Spreadsheet tools that allow probability distributions to be assigned to each key assumption for the purpose of running Monte Carlo simulations have been available since the late 1980s. These tools automatically run the financial model 1000 times using probability-adjusted random sampling for each variable. Each individual simulation will produce a single result, but the 1000 results together will generate a probability distribution for the different results – the probability for each possible result. The advantage and disadvantage of such an approach is that it blurs the findings, softening the conclusions that can be drawn. On the one hand this represents a truer picture of the confidence: if you pay $5 for each share there is a 64 per cent likelihood that you will be paying more than the company is worth. On the other hand, such a nuanced view provides a less clear-cut case for action, uncertainty leading to procrastination. Such an answer reduces the risk of a Type 1 error – a false positive, or paying too high a price – at the risk of increasing the chance of a Type 2 error – a false negative, not proceeding with a bid that would have been successful and created value. Given the track record on acquisitions, an increase in Type 2 error risk is probably an acceptable price to play. By the same token, it may explain why such an approach is not believed mandatory for all acquisition valuations.

The other problem with using such a technique is the erroneous tendency of subsuming uncertainty into risk. If the probability distribution of possible outcomes is known with a high degree of confidence, for example due to the presence of thousands of historical data points, the distribution can accurately be mapped (albeit with a caveat that the future may not be like the past). But with variables such as market growth rate, market share trends or profit margin, there may only be a few years from which to derive a proxy distribution. There should be a high degree of uncertainty around the distribution posited. While the resulting distribution of outcomes overtly recognizes the presence of uncertainty, the median, mode or mean value that the distribution generates may be no more accurate than a point estimate.

As has been said, critical to any strategic evaluation are the projections on which it is based, but often these receive a fraction of the time and attention that is focused on the process of analysis and its implications. These projections are usually derived from an extrapolation of the past, any differences being in degree more than kind. There needs to be sufficient historical data for the projection to be built from. As a consequence, there is a distinction in the validity of operational versus strategic assessments.

A number of companies have successfully applied predictive analytics and used analysis of historical customer purchase patterns to predict how customers will behave in different situations in order to persuade customers to spend more or reduce defection rates.[17] Though as Dan Goldstein, an assistant marketing professor at London Business School, has warned: 'While such models can perform admirably when conditions are right and data is abundant, they provide no particular advantage under the all too common conditions of having limited knowledge.'[18]

This is typically the case with the variables that influence strategic decision making. The forecast growth rate of a market may be modelled bottom up on the basis of estimated saturation, penetration rates and replacement spend; but all of these will require assumptions derived from the historical experience of a proxy product or the experience with that product in a different geographical market. It may also be modelled top down using an extrapolation of the past, perhaps adjusted for the experience of similar markets at the same stage. This, again, is highly assumptive. As Roger Martin, Dean of Rotman Business School, has argued, businesses often confuse reliability with validity. A reliable prediction is one generated by a process that has worked reliably a number of times in the past. A valid prediction is one that turns out to be true. Validity cannot be known in advance; inferring validity from reliability is a fallacy of induction, but one that is all too common.

Another requirement for such an approach to be valid is that the industry or market being modelled is stable; that is, that past experiences are a reasonable guide to the future. Relative to what has historically been the case, stability, if anything, is declining. Certainly change is perceived to be increasing, due to globalization and corporate hyperactivity arising from the perceived shortening of timeframes for achieving success.

That said, there will always be industries that are more stable than others, particularly when looked at in terms of market maturity. This can distort the corporate resource-allocation process. As Joseph Bower and Clayton Christensen have put it:

Using rational analytical investment processes, it is nearly impossible to build a rational, cogent case for diverting resources from known customer needs in established markets to markets and customers that seem insignificant or do not yet exist.[19]

As they further point out, market research can seldom help, as no market currently exists. This information can only be created by experimenting rapidly, iteratively and inexpensively – by getting something into the hands of customers and observing the results. Experimentation provides the real data on which analysis thrives. David Garvin has also argued the need for a more iterative approach:

It follows that perfectionist cultures (and planning-oriented managers) are in for a rude awakening, since it's seldom possible to figure out product designs or business models fully in advance. Repeated investments in rigorous, fact-based planning or quantitative research inevitably produce diminishing returns.[20]

Yet despite this, companies proceed as if their assumptions are facts. The limitations of analysis with regard to uncertainty tend to be ignored and the appearance of rigour only serves to increase the risk of incorrect decisions being made.

It's a mystery

At the heart of the problem is the way the challenge or issue is framed. In this respect, the military intelligence expert Gregory Treverton has drawn a distinction between puzzles and mysteries. Puzzles are questions that can, in principle, be solved definitively if the right information were to be available; for example the number of weapons of mass destruction that Iraq possessed or the whereabouts of Osama bin Laden. Conversely, a mystery is a question that cannot be answered with certainty, even in principle: what would happen in Iraq in the aftermath of the defeat of Saddam Hussein was a mystery, as is what will happen in Afghanistan once NATO troops withdraw. In *Reshaping National Intelligence for an Age of Information*,[21] Treverton argues that intelligence agencies have been mistaken in focusing on puzzle solving when the most critical questions facing foreign policy makers are more typically mysteries.

Exactly the same charge can be levelled at corporate strategy departments and their advisers. Strategy is treated as a puzzle to be solved when it should be treated as a mystery. A puzzle requires a closed and controlled environment. Such an assumption is reasonable for inward-facing initiatives that improve operational effectiveness, but for strategic decision making the opposite is true. To borrow another famous expression from the Iraq war, strategy developers face a plethora of known unknowns and a few, but intractable, unknown unknowns. A puzzle-based approach will generate strategies that are assumptive, simplistic and opaque. Assumptions are necessary to bound the environment so that analysis is possible, but these assumptions are likely to oversimplify the inherent complexity that businesses face. Equally, many assumptions are implicit; not making them explicit reduces the transparency of the strategy-development process.

An alternative distinction to puzzles and mysteries is thinking of the challenges business face as either hard or wicked problems. The expression 'wicked problem' was first used by C West Churchman as the title to a guest editorial in *Management Science* in 1967.[22] This piece referred to the work of Professor Horst Rittel; and in 1973, Rittel with Melvin Webber formally described wicked problems,[23] specifying ten characteristics, the first of which was 'There is no definitive formulation of a wicked problem'.

Rittel and Webber were focusing on wicked problems in a social planning context, but they are equally present in business. In a note in Roger Martin's book *The Design of Business*[24] describing the difference between hard and wicked problems, Jennifer Riel confirms the orientation of business education to solving the former:

Hard problems are complex and take many steps from beginning to end, making it difficult to see your way clear to the solution from the outset. Hard problems face us at every turn, but fortunately business schools specialise in giving us the analytical tools that allow us to tackle and solve these problems.

Wicked problems, in contrast, are 'ill-defined and unique in their causes, character, and solution' and, as a result, 'Analytical thinking alone, no matter how skilfully applied, isn't going to generate an answer to a wicked problem.' Analytical thinking fails because it requires the problem to be defined, but the very nature of wicked problems means that the primary focus has to be on understanding the problem; finding the solution is secondary.

The wide range of uncertainties that a business faces – potential new entrants, competitor consolidation, the impact of environmental disasters, regulatory changes, technological developments, raw material shortages, changes in buying behaviour – mean that strategy development is more akin to solving a wicked problem than a hard one. The challenges, threats and opportunities that will present themselves cannot be accurately defined. As a result, the decisions that will need to be made cannot be framed and the questions that will need to be answered cannot be articulated. Indeed, treating strategy as a hard problem to be solved by analysis will provide misleadingly confident answers. Instead, the focus needs to be on uncertainty management, seeking to bound and reduce uncertainty in a systematic way (described in more detail in the next chapter). In turn, this needs strategy to be seen as a challenge requiring design thinking more than analytical thinking, for as Roger Martin highlights, it is the art of problem definition at which great design thinkers excel.

Keeping score

Two consequences of framing strategy as a puzzle or 'hard' problem and the consequent emphasis given to analytical thinking are a bias towards hard data and an overemphasis on keeping score. An example of the former is 'qualiquantification', the translation of qualitative information into quantitative data, a process that enables aggregation and manipulation for graphical display but removes all valuable insights and therefore the opportunity to improve. Typical examples are Likert or 5-point satisfaction scoring scales in customer research.

Both quantitative and qualitative data are important and ideally should be collected in parallel. But this increases the time required of interviewees and risks a lower hit rate or higher drop-out rate mid-interview. It is much easier and quicker to ask a time-pressed interviewee for a score rather than an explanation. The innate bias to collect something that can be more easily averaged and displayed will always lead to greater focus on the quantitative unless accentuating the qualitative is specified.

Quantitative data provides valuable information on how well the business is performing, but not *why* that is the case and therefore how improvements can be made. Alan Mitchell, writing in

MarketingWeek, put this a bit more bluntly: 'Knowing a "willingness to recommend" score is like knowing how profitable you are: it's a good indicator as to how well you've done but tells you little about how to do better.' And he concludes: 'As systems thinker Peter Senge pointed out years ago, coaches who manage their teams by looking at the scoreboard never get very far.'[25]

Keeping score is obviously important to improving operational performance, but it is not everything. The popular saying that 'you can't manage what you don't measure' is flawed on two counts. First, it equates measurement with management – all you need to do is to set up a balanced scorecard and you are implementing strategy – when it is significantly more than that. Secondly, it presumes that only what can be measured is valid. The measure-to-manage quote is often incorrectly attributed to Dr W Edwards Deming, father of total quality management, but Deming was firmly of the same view as Einstein. Managing by visible figures alone was one of Deming's seven deadly diseases of management, and as he said, 'the most important figures that one needs for management are unknown or unknowable'.[26]

A well-run business should have clearly defined key performance indicators (KPIs) that it tracks via a series of scorecards to monitor performance. However, that is not enough: qualitative input is required, first to articulate why that particular performance indicator is key to strategic objectives (nothing blinds decision makers more than excessive or misaligned performance reporting) and secondly to explain trends in results, to close the feedback loop. Quantitative data needs a qualitative explanation to make it mean something. This is especially the case when loads of data is available, for example with websites. As web analytics guru Avinash Kaushik describes it:

> *no matter what tool you use, the best that all this data will help you understand is 'what' happened. It cannot, no matter how much you torture the data, tell you 'why' something happened. This is the rea-*

son qualitative data is so hyper important. It is the difference between 99% of the website analysis that happens that yields very little insights and the 1% that provides a window into the mind of a customer.[27]

Or as a sales manager once put it to me: 'We spend most of our time in sales meetings trying to understand why performance on our KPIs is worsening.'

Hard data – even that which has genuinely hardened into facts – is often not as valuable as it may seem to strategy development. Mintzberg has highlighted a number of limitations, what he calls the soft underbelly of hard data. First, it is limited in scope and lacking richness: some important information, such as the look on a customer's face or the tone of her voice, never becomes hard fact. In addition, it can often be too aggregated (the obvious solution to a manager burdened by too much data being to aggregate it). Thirdly, it takes time for information to harden into facts and more time for it to be collected and included in reports. As a result, it can often arrive too late. Finally, he points out that a surprising amount of hard information is unreliable, having been subjected to some of the distortions described in Chapter 4.[28]

One example of the last point is the 'full potential' concept (though as Chapter 5 described, fallacy is a better descriptor). The idea is to benchmark a business's competitors and identify best-in-class performance on each key activity. These best-in-class performance levels are then applied to a financial model of the business to create a mythical view of its 'full potential', what it would generate if it was the 'best of the best'. Such an exercise requires research, quantifying and applying uplifts to revenue and profitability to create a target profit level; all good left-brain fun for the analytically inclined. Its intention is to invigorate aspirations by setting audacious goals that shake the business out of its lethargy. The problem with such studies, however, is that the stretch targets are unlikely ever to be achieved. The idea that a business would be able to match the best-in-class performance delivered by multiple competitors and sustain that parity is arrogant in its assumption that competitors will not respond and dangerous because of it. It is the antithesis of strategy, encouraging breadth of effort rather than prioritization and specialization.

A further limitation with such highly quantitative analyses as full potential studies is the weakness of the link to execution. By definition they focus on the size of the prize, the uplift in profit, more than how it can be achieved; a case for action more than an action plan. But therein lies the fallacy: any determination of viability that floats over feasibility (that is, it only takes a high-level view) is inherently flawed. The devil (the financial costs, management time, front-line resources required to support initiatives) is in the detail. Such analyses may state 'what' is required to achieve such gains, but only in generic terms (e.g. the forecast returns may be predicated on becoming the lowest-cost producer, perhaps even going so far as to state what the target cost level per unit of production should be). And in failing to specify how that is achieved (the specific assets and capabilities that are required, the initiatives that need to be undertaken), the constraining impact of limited corporate resources is underestimated. Managers may leave presentations on a high, the potential prize being at the forefront of their mind. only to come down within a short space of time as the lack of 'how' sinks in.

Full-potential studies are the Chinese takeaway of consulting offerings – you feel bloated after consumption but starving half an hour later. They are certainly not the strategy equivalent of the low-fat, energy-sustaining meal that athletes favour, much as those who provide such services would like to describe them in those terms.[29]

The preoccupation with quantification is the twenty-first-century expression of the command-and-control philosophy: top-down strategy dissemination via metrics with no guidance provided on how the metrics should be achieved. As such, there is no risk to the strategist should these targets not be met; it is for others to take the fall. But to reiterate the point made by Senge, you don't score many points by looking at the scoreboard. The game is won or lost on the field; the scoreboard only records the results.

For strategists to help the team to score goals, they need to appreciate the limitations of the analytical approach in strategy development. It is necessary, but not sufficient for a business to deem its strategy complete. Where to play and what to be may be answered, but the most crucial question of how to achieve this is ignored, or thrown over the wall to operations. In many situations analysis helps improve the quality of decision making. But in many others, particularly where uncertainty is high, analysis adds limited value and can serve to deceive. It is a starting point, nothing more.

Creative strategy

Strategy needs to be more than analysis, both to be genuinely strategic and to avoid the risk of focusing excessively on operational effectiveness. It is not lack of productivity opportunities that makes a blinkered focus on operational effectiveness dangerous. But underweighting the importance of other factors that contribute to strategic differentiation does encourage the commoditization, price-based competition and profit margin collapse of which Porter warns. Differentiation requires creativity, the generation of different options. However, the left-brain hegemony tends to downplay it or relegate it to part of the execution process. Design, in particular, has become lost as a business competency. The problem is, as de Bono has highlighted, that analysis cannot solve all problems, specifically those where the cause is unfindable. 'There is a need for design. We need to design a way forward.'[30]

The essential difference between left-brained thinking and right-brained thinking is one of convergence versus divergence. Analysis seeks to use logic and the process of elimination to reduce possibilities, while the objective of creative thinking is to generate new ones. For analysts rationality is critical, whereas designers prize imagination and structured creativity, which together enable them to peer into uncertainty to define the challenge, then look at it from multiple perspectives, using multiple lenses to stimulate multiple – even opposing – ideas.

Both are important, but left-brain dominance in business is particularly damaging. If it is not built on foundations provided by divergent thinking, convergent thinking is susceptible to bias. Generating possible alternatives illuminates the uncertainty and the assumptions nested in each one. It highlights different possible causes for observed effects. Only thinking convergently risks missing what is implicitly assumed.

The errors that result from convergent thinking are, arguably, unconsciously intended. This is especially the case with decision support analysis, undertaken to help senior management make a decision regarding significant funds (for example an acquisition) or significant strategic consequences (whether to back a new technology or not). As Ariely has pointed out, businesses seek clear-cut answers so that they can move from deliberation to action. The purpose of analysis is to give confidence that action can be taken. This creates a pressure to report substantive conclusions, certainly not nuanced findings requiring further investigation. The desire to take action also leads to a focus on confirmation rather than refutation – in-built bias to what the analyst is seeking to find (even if unconsciously).

It is not hard, then, to see how this results in overoptimism and overconfidence. In the context of the uncertainties that surround strategic decision making, analysis is a confidence trick – a trick to generate confidence that action can be taken – perpetrated on themselves by those who perform it. It is for this reason that applying probabilistic weighting to the outcomes of key variables, an approach that would generate a more balanced picture, is not seen as mandatory. A distribution of possible values with probabilities attached does not generate the confidence to proceed in the same way that a point estimate does. Given the desire to take action, less accurate but more clear-cut evaluations are preferable to more accurate and nuanced ones.

Knowledge is advanced by the process of generating multiple hypotheses and refuting those that do not fit the facts. Absence of hard facts and figures may mean that not all hypotheses can be eliminated, but the possibility of multiple causes is critical to business decision making. Even if there is not time to disprove all possibilities and one course of action has to be selected, at the very least the appreciation of the risks involved is clearer.

As well as improving the quality of analyses, creative thinking is valuable in its own right. In *New Thinking for the New Millennium*,[31] de Bono differentiated between design and analysis, somewhat cryptically, as follows: 'What "truth" is to analysis, "value" is to design.' The distinction he draws is in terms of their ultimate purpose. In so doing he introduces a temporal distinction. Truth, by definition, can only refer to what has happened, the past, whereas the creation of value has to reside in the present or the future. The implication is also that they are, if not mutually exclusive, at least distinctly different.

Analysis, design and execution

While the temporal distinction is true, the implication that truth plays no role in value creation is not. There is what might be called a value trinity – analysis, design and execution – which combine to generate value for both customers and the business. Analysis locates value, design unlocks value and execution delivers value. An opportunity for value creation needs to be uncovered through research and analysis[32] (e.g. an activity that is costing more than it should, an unmet customer need or underserved customer segment). Next a solution that releases the value in the opportunity has to be designed. Finally, that solution has to be implemented, either fully or as part of an experiment. The results of implementation are then analysed and the process begins again.

All three stages are present in any value-generation initiative, but the contribution to the total that each stage makes will vary with different initiatives. For simple productivity-improvement initiatives, analysis creates most value through illuminating what has happened and why, for instance where the bulk of costs have been incurred or where costs or working capital exceed industry benchmarks. Analysis will typically reveal the answer and thus the need for design is limited.

More complex cost-saving initiatives will possibly involve redesign of the business operating model (though not the value proposition). When it comes to generating profitable organic growth the importance of design increases still further, as the challenge is creating increased value for an increasing number of customers in a way that is increasingly profitable for the business. As de Bono puts it, there is a need to design the way forward.

While the degree of design or redesign necessary in the different instances will vary, some element will always exist. More critically, design is the link stage between analysis and implementation. Analysis highlights 'what' should be done and design articulates 'how' it should be implemented.

However, while the role of execution is fully appreciated, that of design is not. To meet the growth challenge, strategy needs to incorporate more right-hemisphere thinking (to be whole-brained not just half-brained). That starts with more recognition of the importance of design skills.

As strategy gurus from Peter Drucker to Michael Porter have emphasized, business strategy has to start with defining the value proposition that will be delivered to customers, underneath which are nested the specific product and service offerings that customers will buy. Design skills are required at both levels, not only to make them attractive to customers, but to manage the trade-off between making them attractive to customers and profitable for the business to deliver. Such decisions are as much about what you leave out as what you include. One test of a thought-through strategy is the ability to articulate what will *not* be done and why as clearly as what will.

Designers, whatever their field, have a fixed set of elements or dimensions that they need to manage according to the constraints presented by budget and objective. Product designers need to consider shape, colour, texture, material, pattern and ornament. The emphasis on each will differ according to whether they are seeking to design a product that is practical or beautiful, disposable or long-lived, basic or functionally rich. Similarly, interior designers must work with space, light, colour, pattern, texture and focal point when creating new kitchens or remodelling living areas. Again, achieving what their client desires will require them to make choices in each dimension based on the constraints presented by the physical space, choosing which to emphasize, where to spend more money to create the desired effect.

In the same vein, value proposition designers also have a number of core elements that they can use to deliver benefits to customers – performance, choice, convenience, feel-goodness, speed, security and price. All these dimensions need to be included when the product or service offering is being created and the customer experience designed. Critically, the business must be able to sell its offerings in sufficient volume at a price that covers all variable costs and delivers sufficient gross margin to absorb its share of overheads and deliver an attractive operating profit margin. It is worth emphasizing that the key skill is finding what to exclude, what delivers least value to target customers in the context of all the other elements (that is, each element not taken in isolation, but as part of an integrated whole). There are a number of research techniques that can help with this, conjoint analysis being one, but all the elements need to be brought together holistically.

The same approach and mindset are required when creating the operating model that the business will use to deliver the value proposition and achieve the desired financial returns in terms of both growth and profitability. This requires clear prioritization of the capability that the business must have. As mentioned above, the natural human response is to want a capability of four out of five on every element and subelement in the value chain, but that would never be sufficiently profitable to deliver a return on the capital invested. Hence trade-offs need to be made and an appropriate capability model designed. This requires deciding which of the component activities that make up supply chain, manufacturing and customer management are most critical and should be executed to the highest level possible, then identifying those that only require a basic level (so could possibly be outsourced) and those that do not even need to be performed at all.

Once the capability level being aspired to is defined, the way it is to be built needs to be designed. Capability is a function of how a business is organized, the competencies of the people, the culture that the business embraces, the processes that it follows, the degree of automation and technology enablement of those processes and the metrics that it will measure performance against. Each of these will vary depending on the value proposition and profit model: some may require a high investment in process design and automation, whereas others may be more dependent on having highly skilled staff.

If being intimate with customers is important – typically the case if the proposition to customers incorporates a high degree of added value – the organization may be designed to have integrated teams serving different segments. If the focus is on efficiency, then a functional orientation is probably better. Or there may be a hybrid, with customer-facing activities organized in one way and back-office activities in another.

A similar debate needs to be had about process design. What is the main objective: reducing cost or creating value for customers? In the case of the former, the process orientation may be towards reducing defects and rework, maximizing speed, minimizing working capital. In terms of creating customer value, there may be greater emphasis on collecting information about customers enabling greater proactivity, even greater customization. Again, the priority may differ with different processes.

With competencies there is the decision on how well-trained employees need to be, and whether some activities can be performed by well-trained offshore or near-shore staff. It also involves deciding which competencies should be accentuated. Typically there is a trade-off to be made between people and process automation. The higher the investment in systems – for example those that automate steps, deliver online support through answers to frequently asked questions and provide a full history of the account and all relevant customer information – the lower the need for experienced and highly trained people.

However, high levels of automation are only feasible once there is sufficient volume of activity. So this is affected by whether the profit model is predicated on high volume and low margins or vice versa. Equally, it may depend on the number of customers being served. If you are serving only five or six customers, you don't need a customer relationship management or CRM system to retain all the information necessary to be proactive and customize offerings. But if you have several hundred or even thousands, then a sophisticated CRM system that captures all the information and provides customer-relevant prompts is critical if customer intimacy is a critical capability.

The above highlights just some of the trade-offs that exist and the need for design when developing value propositions and operating models. Some purists may argue that this is part of operations, not strategy. But strategic planning, if it is to be in any way meaningful, needs to identify the initiatives that the business will carry out. This requires identification of the capability gaps that need to be bridged, which can only happen if strategists include operating model design within their remit.

Focusing on the importance of design is the starting point for more whole-brained strategy, but it needs to be supplemented with increased imagination. That may strike some people as strange, but as the trendspotter Magnus Lindkvist has put it:

in these unpredictable times, imagination is the one skill we need to master. Imagining what could be. Imagining what could be done with tomorrow's technology.[33]

He highlights the recognition of this by the 9/11 Commission, which stated that if we want to avoid further atrocities, 'It is of crucial importance that we routinize, even bureaucratize the exercise of imagination.'

The problem is that most strategists do not have the training in design or the right-brain thinking to do this. While some business schools have started to recognize the importance of design, as yet the number of courses is small, as we saw at the beginning of this chapter, with the design component often minor and typically geared to meeting the recognized need for innovation rather than the less recognized gap in creative strategy development.

The history of business leadership in the twentieth century showed three distinct phases, with leaders typically drawn from the profession most critical for business success. In the first instance many business leaders had legal training; the law was seen as the best preparation for a business career, especially given 'the thicket of legal issues, from anti-trust suits to increasing levels of industry-specific regulation, being faced by firms in the early 20th century'.[34] Next, in the era of industrialization and mass production, engineers tended to rise to the top posts. Most recently, as capital markets became ever more important, acquisitions more frequent and cost cutting the source of profit growth, many of the top jobs went to those with MBAs and a background in finance and analysis.

The twenty-first century has seen increased focus on the importance of innovation to generate organic growth. Even in the period preceding the credit crunch, this was proving elusive to large businesses, despite much senior management attention. Given the lack of emphasis on design and the 'how' in strategy development, perhaps this is no surprise, since the analytical orientation of larger companies was leading them to focus on improving operational effectiveness where the 'how' is subsidiary to the 'what'.

Design skills and creativity are central to product and service innovation; and they are also critical to innovative strategy development. So if this aspiration for accelerated growth is to be achieved, the next generation of leaders will need to have well-developed right-brain capabilities. Lindkvist concludes that the ultimate challenge for any leader today is 'To create and maintain an environment where imagination – beyond creativity – thrives and is rewarded.'

It may take time for management education to provide enough people with formal training in right-brain thinking. But the starting point is greater appreciation of the importance of design, creativity and imagination. A willing mind is a prerequisite for learning and demand for knowledge will create its own supply. As the *BusinessWeek* article on design thinking in business concluded:

educators, executives, and public officials around the world are investing in the potential of the technique [design thinking] to provide new insight and enhance innovation in a time that desperately needs both.

Just not enough, at least not yet.

Eight

Customer Advantage

S trategy is preoccupied with competition. Think of a business analogy or expression and there is a very good chance it will be adversarial in theme and drawn from the battle or sports fields.

Award yourself one point for any of the following that you have heard or used in a business context (if used in a self-aware, semi-ironic sense, only award yourself half a point[1]). We need to:

play hardball;
have big hitters;
step up to the plate;
knock the cover off the ball;
have bench strength;
have team players;
block and tackle well;
pick up the ball and run with it;
make the most of open-field running;
have a level playing field;
kick a bad idea into touch;
make a ball park estimate;
keep score;
parachute in a SWAT team;
hit the ground running;
fly under the radar;
have senior brass provide air cover;

employ judo strategy;
get a black belt on this;
gain first-mover advantage.

As a bonus, give yourself two points for any analogous use of military or sporting endeavour that I have missed. The higher the score, the more time you have obviously spent in alpha-male environments.

There is a long tradition of management scholarship focusing on military strategy, going back to the writings of Sun Zhu and the battles fought by Alexander the Great. Blend this with economics' pre-occupation with different forms of competition; add in studies that show the competitive environment to be the key determinant of profitability; mix in some ambitious business school graduates and bake in a culture where testosterone outranks the emotional intelligence required to regulate it; and you have a recipe for business strategy that is overly focused on beating the competition.

So what's wrong with that? On the surface very little, but once a behavioural lens is applied, the costs of an adversarial mindset become more obvious. Relativity – making judgements in relative rather than absolute terms – is a characteristic of highly driven people. And as mentioned in Chapter 4, such a perspective can induce self-harming behaviour, for example rejecting offers that would have made us better off because the other party benefits too much (a tendency that increases with testosterone levels), or a preference for a lower standard of living but one that is better than everyone else we know. When we introduce this bias, the risks of strategy focusing on beating the competition become more apparent.

This has major implications for competitive strategy and its central theme of competitive advantage. A behavioural perspective raises a number of questions, similar in theme to those raised in previous chapters. Does the popularity of competitive strategy stem more from psychological than economic factors? Does this in turn increase the likelihood of irrational implementation? How damaging is irrational implementation? For every one success story that is written up, how many businesses have been damaged through applying the same principles and approaches?

The idea that competition is the main dimension of strategy stems, in part, from the links between business strategy and microeconomics. As Cynthia Montgomery, a Harvard Business School professor, summarizes it:

> *When the head of the strategy group at one major business school was asked recently to describe the common denominator among faculty members in his department, he replied, 'We are a group of economists with a lively interest in business.' An honest man and a telling comment.*[2]

From the perspective of economic theory, the purpose of a firm is to compete. Those that use the resources they have most efficiently will grow at the expense of their less efficient competitors. As a result, resources will be drawn to those who use them best and so be optimally allocated across the whole economy. (At least that is what happens if you have what microeconomics calls perfect competition, lots of small firms competing against each other. It breaks down somewhat when there is the sort of imperfect competition – monopoly and oligopoly – that typically exists.)

Montgomery highlights how the infusion of economic thinking into strategy has brought a number of benefits, but also costs:

> *That merger added much-needed theory and empirical evidence to strategy's underpinnings, providing considerable rigor and substance. But the benefits have not come without costs. A host of unintended consequences have developed from what in its own right could be a very good thing. Most notably, strategy has been narrowed to a competitive game plan, divorcing it from a firm's larger sense of purpose; the CEO's unique role as arbiter and steward of strategy has been eclipsed; and the exaggerated emphasis on sustainable competitive advantage has drawn attention away from the fact that*

strategy must be a dynamic tool for guiding the development of a company over time.

Competitive advantage

The term 'competitive advantage' was, of course, coined by Michael Porter, who was an economist before shifting his attention to strategy. He begins the preface to his seminal book[3] on the subject with the comment: 'Competitive advantage is at the heart of a firm's performance in competitive markets.' He then goes on to define it in the following terms:

> *Competitive advantage grows fundamentally out of the value a firm is able to create for its buyers. It may take the form of prices lower than competitors' for equivalent benefits or the provision of unique benefits that more than offset a premium price.*

The starting point is creating differential value for customers; he could just as well have called it *customer* advantage.

While the idea that strategy must start with a customer value proposition is one that Porter has reiterated in interviews,[4] this critical foundation has never been that widely acknowledged. The concept of customer advantage doesn't resonate as clearly with driven strategy professionals as competitive advantage. The question this raises is whether in minting the expression with which he is synonymous, Porter has unintentionally legitimized the focus on relativity that typically characterizes alpha male-dominated management environments. Equally, in these environments the cycle of adoption, adaption and corruption has led to a more monolithic interpretation of competitive advantage, one that loses much of the original subtlety and multiple dimensions of competition as Porter described it. When taken at face value, competitive advantage becomes a justification for macho inclinations, giving credence to the idea that the objective of strategy is beating the competition.

Such thinking confuses an objective – what should be focused on directly – and an outcome. Developing a sustainable competitive advantage is the outcome of serving customers more effectively via a profitable business model, with competitive positioning one contributory factor to the latter. It is an example of what the economist John Kay calls obliquity, achieving goals through oblique means. However, the disproportionate focus on competitors that the relative mindset brings means that the subtlety of the distinction between outcome and objective can be lost. Competitive measures become the standard currency of strategy.

One example of this is the enduring appeal of relative market share as a measure of strategic positioning, no matter that the relationship with profitability has long been dismissed. Through a behavioural lens this resembles the stereotypical male belief that size is important, no matter how much shareholders may say it's what you do with it that counts. The preponderance of sports and military analogies also provides a clear picture that, for all the talk of wanting win–wins, the prevailing mindset is more often win–lose: for me to be a winner, everyone else has to be a loser; and if I can have a direct hand in making them lose, so much the better.

Market share

One irony of the concept of competitive advantage sustaining the credibility of market share as a measure is that Porter's five forces model, with its much broader definition of competition, sought to challenge its preeminence as a definition of competitive positioning that had prevailed for a decade or so. BCG's growth–share matrix, which had its origins in the early 1970s, identified relative market share – a business's market share divided by that of the largest competitor (the market leader in most cases, but if the business is the market leader, the next biggest) – as the key determinant of how well a business was positioned in its market, with growth being the key determinant of market attractiveness. The rationale for this was the experience curve, which mapped how unit costs of production reduced as cumulative volume increased. The implication of this phenomenon, first observed in aircraft manufacture but then tested in other industries, was that the business with the highest relative market share had accumulated the most experience and would therefore enjoy the lowest costs.

The relationship between profitability and relative market share was further confirmed by the research of Robert Buzzell into the profit impact of market strategies, or PIMS. The second phase of his research was published in 1975, when Buzzell and his fellow authors concluded:

> *It is now widely recognized that one of the main determinants of business profitability is market share. Under most circumstances, enterprises that have achieved a high share of the markets they serve are considerably more profitable than their smaller-share rivals. This connection between market share and profitability has been recognized by corporate executives and consultants, and it is clearly demonstrated in the results of a project undertaken by the Marketing Science Institute on the Profit Impact of Market Strategies.*[5]

The authors explained the positive correlation between market share and return on investment as resulting from economies of scale, market power and quality of management.

The strategic imperative of both the experience curve and PIMS research was that a business should maximize its relative market share: the higher the relative market share, the stronger and the more profitable the competitive position. Companies with a relative market share of 1.5 times the next biggest player have a strong market position. At the other end of the spectrum, a relative market share of less than 0.5 implies a struggle to be profitable.

In his much-praised book *The Myth of Market Share*,[6] Richard Miniter highlights a number of problems with the underlying thinking, not least of which are a number of subsequent studies that found the largest company in an industry to be seldom the most profitable. None of these received the attention of Buzzell's original study. Despite this, the idea that a company with a dominant market position will enjoy the highest profitability has become entrenched: 'That sentiment appeared over and over again in dozens of major business journal articles in the past few decades and it was often the unstated assumption in hundreds more'; the result of which is that 'companies do an astonishing array of self-destructive, counterintuitive, and downright strange things to maximise market share'.

Miniter highlights the dot-com boom as an example of how willingly people believed that size was a panacea. 'Get Big Fast' was one of the more forgettable consulting catchphrases of the era, the idea being that if you could get scale, profitability would look after itself. More pervasive is the enduring appeal of acquisitions despite repeated evidence that most of them do not deliver the gains expected and fail to create value for the acquiring company.

The original objective of the growth share matrix was to help the corporate planning departments of conglomerates allocate financial resources to different component businesses on the attractiveness of each one's market and its relative position in that market. Industry growth was a reasonable proxy for market attractiveness and relative market share a reasonable proxy for a business's competitive position. As a tool for corporate resource allocation, the concept is valid and useful; GE's mantra of 'be number one or number two in an industry, or get out' is an example of a similar approach to deciding where to invest.

Nevertheless, problems arise when such thinking influences the strategy development within a business and high relative market share is seen as a pot of gold at the end of the rainbow; if achieved, superior margins should follow automatically. This takes a static relationship between profitability and market share, where there was no observation of the processes that led to that relationship being reached, and attempts to use it for dynamic policy making. As soon as relative market share (the end) becomes a focus for strategic action without consideration of how it is achieved (the means), Goodhart's Law – once a measure is made a target for the execution of policy, it loses its value as a measure – takes effect and any causal relationship with profitability breaks down.

What might have existed if it had been achieved through superior business practices (that is, without any forced targeting) doesn't when the natural state is disturbed. And in a rush to achieve a superior market position, the risk is that it is achieved at excessive costs, either in the form of discounts, promotions and price cutting or by overpaying for acquisitions – often paying a premium to prevent others from buying them – then finding the costs of integration higher than expected, or not properly integrating them at all in the hurry to move on to the next consolidation opportunity. Not surprisingly, a pot of gold is seldom found: competitors match price cuts and everyone's profitability suffers; customers resist attempts to raise prices or reduce discounts; and the aggregate of assorted acquisitions never achieves the predicated profitability.

Overfocusing on achieving a dominant market share can also be growth limiting by implicitly supporting the view that the size of the pie is fixed and the battle is for as large a slice as possible. The more management focus there is on competitors, the less there is on customers and understanding their needs in order to grow the pie. Such thinking becomes self-fulfilling. Attempting to maximize market share has proved particularly tempting for companies with proprietary innovations (such as Polaroid with its instant photography, Apple with its Mac operating system). However, success in locking competitors out and maintaining a dominant position only results in the market potential never being realized, as alternatives or substitutes prevail. High margins are achieved but on low volumes.

Such aversion to competition is misguided, though not surprising given the relativist mindset. It ignores the benefits of competitive clustering and accelerated learning that all can benefit from – the commons of the knowledge economy. It also misses the role of competition in market growth stimulation, helping to boost customer awareness and encouraging customers who otherwise would not to opt to buy through providing a choice and justifying why prices are reasonable.

One reason the customer dimension is typically overlooked is that, at its core, the focus on relative market share reflects the belief that at the heart of a firm's competitive positioning is its cost position. The greater its experience, the lower the unit costs of production. As such, it presumes that competitive position is derived from the supply side of the equation; relative cost position studies have long been a service provided by strategy consultancies. A business may choose to invest some of its superior margin in marketing and branding, but ultimately this is enabled by lower costs of supply. And in the process, the dimensions of competitive advantage have been collapsed to one side of the income statement.

The risk with a relative cost-derived view of competitive position is that businesses lose a clear picture of their uniqueness in terms of how they create value. It is far easier to quantify the cost of a capability than to quantify the customer value that it delivers; and in a world where benchmarking and analysis have disproportionate weight, the tendency will be for the more certain outcome of cutting cost to trump the less certain one of creating value for customers.

Behavioural economics also highlights that we have a natural tendency towards herding. In business this plays out in the form of competitive convergence that a focus on the cost side accentuates: if one player cuts costs in an area, others feel pressured to follow, even if difference is threatened. As companies become more similar in their capabilities, so do their offerings, until there is little but price to compete on, creating a downward spiral in margins and return on capital. Focusing on cost as the key dimension of strategic advantage increases the risk of price-based competition, with value transferred via lower prices from corporate margins to customer pockets. Beyond cutting the price they pay, the ability to create value for customers becomes lost and with it the ability to generate sales-led or organic growth.

The dangers of targeting market share are now much better understood. But, as Miniter comments:

> *Even if relative market share is not so closely monitored as before, the two beliefs that underlie it – namely that the objective of strategy is to obtain an advantage over the competition and the way to achieve this is through having a better cost position – remain very present.*

Playing hardball

The macho, win–lose mentality was aptly demonstrated by a couple of BCG consultants, George Stalk and Rob Lachenauer, in an article in the *Harvard Business Review* titled 'Hardball'[7] and a book of the same name. The article includes insights such as:

> *winners in business play rough and don't apologize for it. Hardball players pursue with a single-minded focus competitive advantage and the benefits it offers: leading market share, great margins, rapid growth.*

Prescriptions include suggesting that it is better to weaken a competitor to the point of near-death and keep it there rather than kill outright and risk a phoenix-like rise from the ashes thanks to Chapter 11 bankruptcy protection. According to *The Economist's* review:

> *In their original draft of the book, they had urged businessmen to focus not just on creating 'competitive advantage' but also 'unfair advantage'. That phrase was replaced with the decidedly softer 'decisive advantage'.*[8]

Hardball demonstrates that competitive strategy is about making the market as anti-competitive as possible: creating an uneven playing field. It is not about seeking to do good for society and generating profits from serving customers, just seeking to do good for shareholders through legal acts of competitor destruction. In the authors' words:

> *Hardball involves playing the edges, probing that narrow strip of territory – so rich in possibilities – between the places where society clearly says you can play the game of business and those where society says you can't. The hardball player ventures closer to the boundary, whether it be established by law or social conventions, than competitors would ever dare.*

Stalk and Lachenauer try to draw a distinction between the companies they admire, such as Microsoft and Wal-Mart, with those that have broken the law, such as Enron and WorldCom. They refer to the latter two as using a classic softball tactic: manipulating results to make themselves look better. 'Hardball players don't cheat', they opine. Maybe not, according to the way they conveniently define hardball companies, but the underlying philosophy is the same, the distinction between 'win at all costs' and 'win at all legal costs' being minor for most people. In the authors' words again:

> *to play the edges, you have to know where the edges are. This is perhaps the most complex and daunting aspect of hardball. So hardball players do their homework. They know their industries cold. They have the legal and accounting counsel to help them determine what they can and can't do.*

So there you are, in the world of hardball, the personnel who contribute most competitive advantage are legal and accounting counsel, not designers and engineers working with marketers and salespeople to create something unique and valuable to customers.

In a 2006 follow-up HBR article, analogously titled 'Curveball', Stalk bemoaned the fact that his view of competitive strategy had been seen as 'primitive' – a good choice. The approach he and

Lachenauer advocated is exactly the right one for a primitive society. The problem is that we live in an advanced one and the challenges we face are the ones advanced societies face; they will not be solved by primal solutions.

It is perhaps no surprise that such thinking has emanated from a leading strategy consultancy given the preponderance of driven overachievers that are drawn to and typically thrive in those organizations. As Robin Buchanan, for a long time Bain's senior partner in London, has put it: 'We never get rid of people's competitiveness. That's a disaster. We're massively competitive on behalf of our clients.' This can get a little extreme. One partner in a leading consulting firm had a reputation for beginning meetings with new clients with: 'Beating the competition is like drowning puppies or clubbing baby seals... are you prepared to drown puppies?' He sold very successfully, probably because his audience were equally alpha oriented.

Are such competitive instincts a bad thing? Not at all; I would argue the opposite to be the case. But the risk is that they lead to damaging behaviour. Anyone with strong competitive instincts will be able to recall a time they have got them into trouble, in either their personal or professional lives: rage at being cheekily overtaken leading to driving too fast and causing an accident; a fun game of football becoming feisty, with increasingly aggressive tackling resulting in a trip to hospital; a desire to avenge a put-down resulting in a soon-regretted outburst; denigrating colleagues to win a prized promotion and it backfiring, ambition recast as politicking. Now imagine something similar exaggerated by the compounded confidence that group think brings: 'We can't possibly let our biggest rival win that account, acquire that company, license that technology and so on.' Such behaviour is to be expected. As Warren Buffett has noted, driven people are driven to get one over on each other. The danger arises if the corporate mindset and strategic frameworks accentuate that tendency – and its inherent risks – rather than counterbalance it.

In this regard, the sporting analogies used are not helpful, not least because they tend to overemphasize the adversarial element. Such metaphors are usually applied bluntly, categorizing winners and losers, and inaccurately. If you have had the opportunity to attend a motivational talk given by a successful sportsperson, you will most likely have heard a different story, with the day-to-day focus being applied to performance goals: target time, height or distance that they aspire to achieve at the Olympics and the intermediate targets they need to achieve on the way to ensure that they peak at the right time. These performance goals are set with an outcome goal in mind, whether it be making the final, standing on the podium or winning gold, but in terms of focus these are secondary. Performance goals are within an athlete's power to achieve, so merit single-minded attention. Outcome goals provide the motivation, of course, but they depend on factors beyond an individual's control – how others perform on the day – and they can only be influenced indirectly. Only one person can gain first place, but the mentality is: if I achieve my performance goal I am a success even if I have come second or third or lower.

It is similar in golf. In his book *Golf Is not a Game of Perfect*, sports psychologist Bob Rotella tells a story about Tom Kite recommending him to other tour pros. One pro asked Kite why, if Rotella was so good, he was recommending him to his competition. Tom replied:

The way I see it, there's more than enough money out here for all of us. You guys are going to help me get better. And I am going to help you get better. We are all going to help each other have fun seeing how good we can get.

Rotella goes on to say:

Tom had the ideal attitude towards competition and fellow competitors. He recognized that the other people on the golf course are not the real opposition that a golfer faces. The first opponent is the game itself. The course, the club and the ball are all idiosyncratic and unpredictable foes, and they will humble the best golfers more than occasionally. [All of which sounds remarkably similar to the challenge of keeping customers happy.] The second opponent is the player himself. Can he discipline his mind to produce the best score his body is capable of? [Again, analogous to the organizational challenges a business faces.] Only after these two foes have been confronted do the other people on the course come into the picture.

To Rotella's way of thinking, competitors set a benchmark, providing the inspiration and motivation to improve. The real competition is with yourself – being the best you can be.

The problem is that the winner-take-all interpretation of sporting success does not acknowledge this. It encourages an exaggerated focus on the competition, which, to use a sporting analogy, is equivalent to running the 100 metres with your head turned sideways towards the other sprinters rather than focusing on the finishing line – not a recipe for a great outcome.

Customer advantage

None of this seeks to say that competition shouldn't be used for motivation; the goal of overthrowing an 'evil empire' can be a particularly powerful way of engaging employees. Nor that competitor analysis is irrelevant in the strategy development process; it provides both a valuable external challenge to internal thinking and a source of insight into new trends and what customers really value. Nor that a business should disregard opportunities to shape the competitive landscape so that greater profitability can be achieved; a compelling profit model is the counterpart to a compelling customer value proposition. But competitors need to be monitored, not obsessed over. They are an input to strategy rather than the starting point; the more energy is directed towards competitors, the less there is for customers. A desire to outperform them is healthy, but intending to destroy them is sociopathic. Relative success should be viewed as an outcome and not an objective. It is about proportion and focus.

Competitor analysis, for example, is a crucial input both at a corporate and a business strategy level. Allocating resources to business units that face strong and aggressive competitors will yield lower returns than if those resources were allocated to businesses where the competitive environment is more attractive. While customers determine the size and growth of any market, competition – in all its forms – determines profitability. For that alone, understanding likely future trends in the competitive environment, what opportunities exist to make it more attractive, remains a critical part of corporate strategy.

At business strategy level, competitor performance provides insights into the attractiveness of different offerings in the market. Without a clear view of the relative value of its offerings (that is, versus those provided by competitors), a business will not be able to optimize its price levels. Profits will be left on the table or disappear into the pockets of customers, or opportunities to do profitable business will simply be lost.

In the same vein, competitor analysis is critical for understanding which customers to go after, which competitors have an inferior value proposition and have customers that will be most easily tempted away. Or alternatively, which competitors are most likely to steal existing customers.

Equally, competitors provide an important performance benchmark for both customer value creation and corporate value extraction. Competitors that are winning in the marketplace provide clues to what customers need and value. Competitors that are achieving superior profitability should also cause a company to reevaluate what it is doing: what capabilities do they have that allow them to achieve that superior profitability, how can we leapfrog those capabilities?

It is also important to reiterate that the focus on reducing the cost side of the income statement (which competitive positioning emphasizes) has enhanced corporate profitability: profits as a share of US GDP reached a 50-year high in 2006, before credit shortages took their toll on business activity. In some industries, no doubt, further opportunities exist to consolidate and cut costs. But the question remains: for how much longer can cost reductions drive profits growth? If growth requires greater attention to the demand side of the equation, a different emphasis is required. Unlike in a wrestling or chess match, the interaction with the competitor is indirect. There are some opportunities to influence competitors directly, most notably by acquisition, but most of the struggle is enacted in the customer arena. You only beat a competitor by attracting away its customers (or leaving it the least profitable). Beating the competition is an outcome of serving customers in a superior manner. This is the very essence of Porter's definition of competitive advantage that seems to have been lost. To change this we need to reframe the strategic mindset; recast the focus from competitors to customers; retain Porter's definition of advantage but rename it customer advantage.

Such reframing is even more important given increases in relative customer power. Manufacturers are finding that their distributors and retailers are consolidating. Globalization has increased the choice available to customers, international companies having entered markets previously the domain of national players. The internet has provided the means for these companies to serve customers in multiple markets when they might otherwise be locked out by traditional suppliers dominating retail shelf space. For customers, the internet has also increased transparency and facilitated the consolidation of disparate buying groups to increase bargaining power. As a result, customers are in a far better position to command what they want at the price they want. Sam Walton's adage that we can all be sacked by the customer has never been more true. In Porter's five forces definition of competition, customers are increasingly powerful in the competition for profitability.

However, even if the term competitive advantage is susceptible to relativist subversion, Porter's definition remains as appropriate as ever and contains the seeds for dealing with this challenge of increased customer power. To reiterate: 'competitive advantage grows fundamentally out of the value a firm is able to create for its buyers'. Renaming this customer advantage would support the necessary switch in focus, emphasizing that creation of value for customers needs to be the foundation of strategy. This can be achieved in a number of ways: being able to supply (when others cannot), supplying at a lower price, reducing a customer's operating costs, delivering a better customer experience, enabling the customer to do things that otherwise would not be possible, or reducing customers' risk.

Customer advantage gets to the heart of what business is about – a customer buying from a seller. A seller will only win a customer's business if it has something superior to offer and it will only keep that customer's business if it continues to do so. The seller will only grow its business by increasing the range of services where it can offer something superior to its customers, or by increasing the number of customers it can offer something superior to. Growth requires existing customers to be retained and either for those relationships to grow or new customers to be acquired. And rapid growth only occurs when the value created increases for an increasing number of customers – a combination of increasing relevance for new customers and increasing value for existing ones. It requires a mindset of seeking to increase the size of the pie *and* gaining a high share of the increment.

Obtaining a position of customer advantage requires constant innovation, but creation of value for customers should be the focus, not innovation. Innovation is the means, not the end, and focusing on the means increases the risk of behavioural distortion – its becoming the end – by those involved in the process. Jeff Bezos, Amazon CEO, has captured this distinction neatly:

we work hard at being very customer-obsessed and expressing that through innovation. We see our customers as invited guests to a party, and we are the hosts. It's our job every day to make every important aspect of the customer experience a little bit better. We have a big team of people who from the very beginning have thrived on that. They're attracted to the idea of inventing on behalf of customers.[9]

Customer advantage is not about being nice to customers. It is about understanding them extremely well, discovering what really delivers value to them in terms of products, services and interactions and, as importantly, what doesn't. It also requires an understanding of what else is available to customers and the relative value provided so that value extraction – the share of the value created that the business retains as its gross margin – can be optimized.

Customer advantage is as compelling a motivation for employees as defeating a rival. More importantly, whereas hardball competitive strategy promotes an attitude of maximizing shareholder value whatever the cost to society, customer advantage seeks to create shareholder value through serving society. It aligns with HP co-founder David Packard's description of a company's *raison d'être*:

I think that many people assume, wrongly, that a company exists simply to make money. While this is an important result of a company's existence, we have to go deeper and find the real reasons for our being. As we investigate this, we inevitably come to the conclusion that a group of people get together and exist as an institution that we call a company so that they are able accomplish something collectively that they could not accomplish separately – they make a contribution to society, a phrase which sounds trite but is fundamental.[10]

Business is not analogous to boxing or judo, which involves head-to-head combat. It is far more complex and subtle than that, as the battle with competitors is indirect, fought out through relationships with customers. Competitors are important, but the focus on them should only be secondary to that on customers. Beating competitors is an outcome of doing something else well. As soon as it becomes an objective in itself, innate relativity will distort behaviour in potentially damaging ways, especially the more competitive, driven and alpha-male the environment.

While prevailing strategic approaches have contributed significantly to increased profitability, arguably the challenge of achieving profitable organic growth would be less daunting if Porter had suggested that businesses seek a customer advantage. Such a term, however, would not have had the same psychological appeal to driven people. Possibly little would have changed had he done so, while he might be less revered in business circles. However, given our increased understanding of behavioural economics – that cognitive biases can distort decision making and that we need to incorporate the costs of irrational implementation into our evaluation of different approaches – perhaps the time is now right for such a reframing. The logical conclusion of a behavioural perspective is that we should seek to counterbalance irrational inclinations rather than accentuate them.

Businesses need competitive people in order to succeed, but an emphasis on customer advantage will temper their damaging instincts and direct their energies towards the critical arena, towards customer objectives which, if met, will deliver to them the outcome they desire.

Nine

Big Decisions, Little Decisions

A CEO's most important decisions fall into two categories: big bets on people and a big bets on strategy.
David Nadler, Confessions of a Trusted Counsellor[1]

The business-as-gambling metaphor is popular with both commentators and business leaders (particularly 'heroic' leaders). It stems from the preoccupation with the big bets a business places: the acquisitions, divestments and joint ventures it makes; the technologies it backs; the investment projects it sanctions. The primacy given to such matters reflects a belief that strategy is first and foremost about making big decisions. Given the sums involved, this is understandable.

The willingness – enthusiasm, even – to make big bets also shows great confidence in the tools and techniques used to support the decisions being made. But, as touched on in Chapter 6, prevailing analytical approaches have a number of limitations when dealing with uncertainty. Analysis is a powerful tool for facts, but when it is forward facing it encourages the treatment of assumptions as if they were facts, especially when a probabilistic view of variables achieving their assumed levels is not taken.

This results in an increased risk of a behavioural double bind, a compounding of overoptimism with overconfidence. And the costs of this can be seen in the track record on acquisitions, in most instances value being destroyed because the price paid is too high.

For strategists, uncertainty is the final frontier. We can never know what the future will bring, so uncertainty permeates all strategic decisions; assumptions must be made, providing fertile ground for bias to flourish. However, the models used for strategy development often obscure the foundational role that assumptions play. Assumption accuracy is presumed and attention focused on constructing elegant analytical edifices rather than solidifying the base on which they are built. As a consequence, confidence in the results increases at a faster rate than does their accuracy.

Behavioural factors are at play here. We are highly averse to uncertainty; it discomforts us hugely. We prize feeling that we have, if not control, at least a firm grasp on the world around us. Subconsciously we are seeking confidence, confirmation that we can take action, as much if not more than we are seeking accuracy. Our psyche conspires in the delusion. Unfortunately, fallacious confidence results in resource misallocation – the bigger the decision, the greater the cost. And better decision making (the manifestation of accuracy) requires us to suffer the anxieties that fully recognizing the existence of uncertainty provokes.

This idea was captured by John Keats in a letter to his brother describing the quality that defined what he called a Man of Achievement (equally applicable to someone we might call a genuine strategic thinker): 'I mean Negative Capability, that is, when a man is capable of being in uncertainties, mysteries, doubts, without any irritable reaching after fact and reason.'

A nineteenth-century romantic poet would seem an unlikely source of wisdom for a twenty-first-century business manager, but Keats' insight into human nature – particularly how individually we are discomforted by uncertainty (and collectively we are panicked by it, as stock market reaction often shows) – is timeless. 'Irritable reaching after fact and reason' in the face of uncertainty is counterproductive. Results appear reassuringly concrete, but confidence is increased by more than their validity, the divergence between confidence and validity being psychologically appealing but economically damaging. Keats' negative capability celebrates the search for beauty and those antithetical skills to analysis: creativity and imagination. Both are important in discovering – uncovering, if you prefer – the world of possibilities inherent in coping with uncertainty.

Discovery

Despite its criticality, uncertainty receives relatively little attention; far less than the strategy frameworks that take accuracy for granted in what must be assumed. To improve the quality of big decisions, uncertainty management needs to become central to the process. Rather than analyse based on a set of assumptions, the process needs to be set on its side: the assumptions become the predominant focus, the task of increasing their accuracy absorbing most of the time and energy. The emphasis on analysis is replaced by an emphasis on discovery, an approach encompassing a series of stages designed to reduce the band of possible outcomes for each variable in order to reduce the opportunity for error in the final decision.

An orientation towards discovery further requires strategy to be cast in a different way, providing managers with some flexibility to experiment within prescribed guidelines – giving them freedom within a frame. First, this means that decisions can be delegated to the manager who is best informed to make them, improving the likelihood of success. Secondly, the results of the experimentation help to reduce uncertainty by adding to the business's overall stock of knowledge. Thirdly, by clearly communicating the business strategy and priorities throughout the business, greater alignment across the organization is achieved. Fourthly, it helps break down the barriers between strategy and operations.

Rather than only focusing on big decisions, strategy becomes as much about shaping the little decisions. To do this, it needs to be cast in a form that will guide and improve the choices made every day by middle managers – sometimes even those made by front-line employees – that collectively determine success with customers, suppliers, employees and thereby levels of profitability.

Strategy as big decisions

Given the perceived pressure to deliver results within a short time-frame, CEOs' preoccupation with big bets should come as no surprise. A few big, bold moves are a much quicker way to change the fortunes of a company (so long as they are successful) than changing the way it works on a day-to-day basis. (Easier, too, as only a small dedicated internal team is required, supported by third-party advisers.) Michael Hammer neatly captured this allure when he wrote:

> deals are easily explained to and understood by boards, shareholders, and the media. They offer the prospect of nearly immediate gratification, and the bold stroke of a deal is consistent with the modern image of the executive as someone who focuses on grand strategy and leaves operational details to others.[2]

As Hammer highlights, deals are a way to make a mark with City and Wall Street analysts, some of the most influential stakeholders CEOs need to keep happy. This, however, is a double-edged sword. If they do not agree with the decision made – if they feel it is flawed strategically or the price being paid is too much – such events provide an opportunity for these analysts to downgrade their stock recommendation. If they believe it to be a good move, they can advise their mutual fund and pension fund clients to buy. Either way, big decisions are popular with analysts, as they provide an opportunity to generate brokerage commissions.

They are also popular with consultants and investment bankers. Bain's website explains: 'We help management make the big decisions: on strategy, operations, mergers & acquisitions, technology and organization.'[3] Big decisions create a distinct event with an inbuilt requirement for third-party advice and a scale of investment

that makes the fees appear negligible in comparison. When consultants or investment bankers leave to join the strategic planning
departments of large corporations, their ingrained belief in strategy
as big decisions accompanies them into their new roles, further perpetuating it.

Of all the types of big decision, the sheer scale of investment
makes acquisitions the most significant in terms of absorption of
corporate funds. Given the dismal performance record, the primacy
of acquisitions as a use of corporate funds would appear to be perhaps more of a gamble than shareholders would like (and almost
a certain loser). Despite all the analytical firepower deployed to support such decisions, only a small minority can be classed as creating
value for acquirers. Such a track record cannot help but raise questions about the validity of prevailing approaches.

The problem with acquisitions, or any large decision outside the
day-to-day operations of the business, is that no matter how much
research and analysis you do, there remains an intractable element
of uncertainty. On one assignment I worked on, supporting the
acquisition of a competitor by a private equity-backed auto parts
company, a director of the private equity firm explained to the management of the acquiring company that through due diligence, 'you
only discover less than 20 per cent of what you would really like to
know', an appreciation born of the experience of multiple acquisitions, and no doubt shared by many such firms (perhaps one of the
reasons their track record is superior to that of their corporate
counterparts).

Insufficient recognition of uncertainty typically results in overestimation of benefits and overconfidence in findings (for the reasons described in Chapter 4). This is accentuated by the risk of the
deal acquiring its own momentum: a mindset that the deal must
be done, almost whatever the cost, to avoid the time spent and costs
incurred thus far being wasted. This is a form of loss aversion that
replaces the certainty of a small loss with a significant risk of a much
larger one. But, as Chapter 4 also describes, when faced with a loss

our risk profile increases. On top of the time spent and advisers' fees incurred, there is the emotional investment, the expectation or hope of completion, that must also be written off. When emotional ties exist, economic irrationality usually follows.

This risk is further compounded by groupthink, whereby independence of thought is subjugated to conflict minimization, no one wanting to play the potentially career-limiting role of devil's advocate. The unstated primacy of group cohesion allows the critical assumptions to be flexed so that the valuation rises to the price needed to win the bid. Or the preconceived answer becomes an anchor to which the outputs of the analysis are drawn. Paying more for a company than it is worth is not such a surprise in these circumstances.

A further drawback of 'strategy as big decisions' is the divide it cements between strategy and operations. Strategy is the preserve of an elite group at the centre, those clever business school graduates and ex-consultants in head office. Everyone else is in operations; and it is the role of people in operations to execute on what the strategists have decided, to manage to the scorecard they have been set. What becomes lost in such thinking is the idea that strategy should support operations through providing criteria, both qualitative and quantitative, that inform and guide the hundreds of decisions that need to be made every day. And with it goes the ability for strategy to shape the creation of value for customers that sustains margins and drives growth.

That businesses often need to make big decisions requiring the investment and risking of large sums of company funds is indisputable and making big bets will continue to be an important part of the role of the chief executive and the board for the foreseeable future. Changes in industry environment, new technologies, one-off opportunities that arise will all require bold action. However, as the acquisition track record shows, there is a need to improve the quality of big bet decision making. In addition, there is a need for strategy to cascade through an organization in such a way that it can shape day-to-day management decisions and encourage the creation of new insights.

As mentioned above, the problem with big strategic decisions is the uncertainty involved – assumptions need to be made. Research can help improve the accuracy, but lack of time, particularly where acquisitions are concerned, and lack of hard data militate against the careful accumulation of the relevant fact base necessary to validate such assumptions. The quality of insight increases as the fact base matures, time allowing data to emerge and harden. Collecting information over a six-month period will produce more accurate assumptions than attempting to do the same exercise in one month, even assuming the same amount of time spent, the additional time allowing for the review of key hypotheses, the generation of alternatives, further targeted data collection and actual testing where possible.

Externally driven timetables may not allow this luxury of extra time, but that does not excuse accepting lower-quality assumptions. What is needed is a more proactive approach to managing uncertainty, most importantly starting the process earlier – in advance of when it will be needed.

Uncertainty management

Such an approach has further advantages. At first blush, uncertainty would appear to be the enemy of good decision making in business. But uncertainty exists for everyone. Rather than downplaying its presence, why not revel in it, see it as an opportunity for advantage? The corollary is seeing strategy development as it should be seen – as a mystery or a wicked problem. Those who do so are immediately at an advantage over those who have cast it as a puzzle or hard problem to be solved, both an oversimplification of the extent of the challenge and one that produces strategies that are highly assumptive. Puzzles and hard problems yield to analysis (with assumptions). Wicked problems require a different approach, uncertainty management being the starting point. Better management of uncertainty, shrinking its dimensions and its scale, will inevitably result in better strategies. Embracing it is the first step towards profiting from it.

Uncertainty management, as a discipline, has yet to be defined. Nevertheless, there are a number of long-standing tools that could be used in an integrated fashion to manage uncertainty on a systematic basis.

The objective of uncertainty management is to identify the key dimensions of uncertainty that have a critical impact on business strategy, specifically the big decisions that a business is likely to have to make, defining the range of possibilities and systematically seeking to shrink this range, reducing the degree of uncertainty and band around any assumptions in each case. As such, it needs to starts well in advance of when the assumptions become critical, not as the result of an event-driven requirement. It is the careful and deliberate accumulation of strategy-critical insights as part of an ongoing process rather than a quick binge of fact collection to enable a specific decision to be made.

The process would start with defining the areas where greater insight will improve the quality of strategy development. For internal variables – those that are under the business's control, such as product and service offerings, capability levels and how those capabilities are developed – the focus would be on revealing implicit assumptions:

- How do we want each to evolve?
- What are we implicitly assuming about external variables?
- Which parts of our value chain do we believe are becoming more or less important?
- Why do we think that?
- What evidence is there to support or refute our assumptions?
- What assumptions do we have in common with competitors?
- What would cause us to change our assumptions?
- Which assumptions would we most like to change and why?
- Can we use what we fear most to our advantage?

The aim of these questions is to uncover the tacit beliefs that people hold about the company and its business environment so that they can be tested and potentially altered to create plausible (and profitable) new scenarios.

With external factors (such as technology trends, market opportunities, competitor activity), the process would involve creating scenarios for how each one could evolve, then attributing likelihood and impact scores to each scenario. Defining the range of possible scenarios for these factors – the best and worst cases along with some estimate of the most likely – also requires a number of questions to be asked:

- What are the trends?
- What would happen if these trends accelerated or reversed?
- How likely is that?
- What would be the worst and best changes to the business environment?
- How will customers and customer behaviour change?
- What is the most disruptive move a competitor could make?
- What is the most beneficial?
- Who is the most dangerous new entrant?
- What makes them dangerous?
- Who would be the least dangerous?
- What will drive pricing?
- What are the best- and worst-case economic and political outlooks?
- What circumstances will create the greatest and least pressure on prices?
- How are critical technologies likely to evolve?

Once all the possibilities for each external variable have been defined, the most unlikely would then be excluded. Prioritizing those that remain requires first estimating which, if they came to pass, would have the greatest impact on the business, present the greatest opportunity or greatest threat. This should be followed by a further round of likelihood assessment, the idea being to identify the potential trends that have a high impact and high likelihood, then those with a high impact and medium likelihood or medium impact and high likelihood. In this way the value of information – the benefits from reducing uncertainty – can be defined.

Once this prioritization is in place, two things would happen: the development of contingency plans for each high–high or high–medium scenario; and the definition of an approach to systematically reduce uncertainty with each one. The first focuses on ensuring that the business is prepared so that it can maximize the impact should the identified opportunities arise, or minimize damage should the threats manifest themselves. The second is concerned with refining the likelihood side of the assessment and establishing an early warning system, with identified trigger points at which point the contingency plans would come into play.

Contingency planning involves the creation of considered responses to different potential scenarios – identification both of trigger points and the specific actions that would be taken as a result. These actions would need to encompass everything from making a bid or putting up a business for sale to launching or withdrawing products, altering prices and issuing public statements and staff announcements, depending on the scenario.

Better understanding the likelihood of different possibilities and creating a best view of what will transpire necessitate identification of what insights are required, with processes put in place for their acquisition. One source would be enterprise resource planning and customer relationship management systems, but not all valuable data would be process driven and systematically collected. Some external information would have to come from *ad hoc* research. Other data would come from the interactions that staff have that are not systematically collected.

The involvement of everyone – staff, suppliers, partners – in the quest for insight increases the chances of data being collected.

Simply defining the key areas of uncertainty and what data would help improve the quality of decision making (and who such data should be passed to) increases the chances of valuable insights reaching those who need them. Communicating the key questions that need answering is a start, but the wisdom of employees could also be tapped in more fun ways using prediction markets.

Prediction or decision markets provide estimates of what will happen through the aggregation of opinions using a mechanism similar to the stock market. Participants in the market buy or sell shares of 'claims' about a particular prediction. Popular examples predict the outcome of presidential elections, the box office takings of new films or Oscar results. However, the same mechanisms can be used for better predicting business-critical events. The claims usually state that if proved true, owners of one share will receive a given amount, often $1. Participants can buy either Yes or No shares, depending on whether they believe that the claim will transpire or not. They can make money by either holding on to the shares until the claim has proved to be true so that they receive the payout or by selling the share in the market if they feel that the claim has become overpriced.

For such markets to work, the uncertainty needs to be distilled to a simple choice – for example which of two or three technologies will prevail – and the results need to be measurable, for instance the technology becoming declared the industry standard by a qualified body. Where such definition or measurability is less clear, it can be manufactured through the incorporation of timescales and the creation of a threshold. Companies seeking input from staff on whether a new product will be successful can offer them the opportunity to buy Yes or No claims on whether it will achieve the threshold sales or gross profits for it to be deemed a success, for example sales of $50m in its first year following launch.

From a business's point of view, aggregating opinions produces a better forecast than that of almost any participant in the market. As James Surowiecki described it in *The Wisdom of Crowds*, crowds are almost always smarter than the smartest people in them (so long as the behaviour of one participant does not influence that of another). The profit mechanism also means that people with good insight are rewarded, while those with only poor predictive abilities are discouraged from trading. Participants are incentivized to seek out information as they profit from doing so. Perhaps most important of all, there is no hierarchy: the voice of a senior manager does not receive disproportionate weight or discourage others from sharing their opinions.

All the different feeds – system-generated information, research findings, *ad hoc* interactions, predictions of decision markets – would then be used to populate a dashboard covering the key strategic questions that senior management would like answered, with a best estimate of the likely outcome and some attachment of probability along with the range of possibilities. The dashboard should be updated on a regular basis. The objective of the process would be to reduce the range and thereby increase the estimated probability of the most likely outcome in each case, thereby elevating the focus on uncertainty to the management level that most needs to consider it.

This would then link to the next stage of uncertainty management: discovery-driven planning. The purpose of discovery-driven planning, as outlined by Rita Gunther McGrath and Ian MacMillan,[4] is to increase the ratio of knowledge to assumption. They identified this as being primarily relevant to new ventures. However, the planning dangers that they highlight also exist in more mature environments; as the banking crisis has shown, even supposedly stable markets are more unstable than previously believed.

McGrath and MacMillan highlight a number of planning risks. The first is a false sense of security: companies lack hard data but proceed as if the assumptions about customer needs and size of the opportunity were facts. The second arises from failing to test these assumptions. The third risk comes from overestimating (either implicitly because it was not considered or explicitly) the business's capability to execute on the plan. The fourth arises from starting with the right data but failing to notice that a key variable has changed.

Two key elements in the process are the maintenance of an assumption checklist (under the aegis of a Keeper of the Assumptions) and milestone planning. The former is to ensure that each assumption is flagged, discussed and checked as the initiative unfolds, then looped back into the business case to check whether it remains viable. The assumptions and business case are reviewed at milestones in the plan, the objective being to postpone further financial commitment until the stage gate has been passed and there is sufficient evidence to justify taking the next step. Stages for launching a new product might include the production of a proto- type for customers to test; then subcontracting production of the new product to test market demand, pricing and competitor reac- tion; and only then scaling up production, either in an existing facil- ity or building a new one or buying an existing producer.

The value of this 'crawl, walk, run' approach (as Jim Collins described it in *Good to Great*) would be a significant reduction in the risk of resources being allocated to initiatives where they will not generate the required return. It is commonly used in R&D: at each different stage of its development a pharmaceutical compound will have to meet certain criteria and pass various tests for more funds to be made available for further research. However, the same approach could be applied to strategic initiatives such as whether to enter a new country or not. The starting point could be as simple as creating a trading relationship with an agent in a new country. One stage on from this would be a more formal partnership or joint venture – again with limited investment. In certain markets, partic- ularly those still in a high-growth phase with fragmented competi- tion, the best entry route may be via buying a small, existing player. Since the objective is learning – the immediate revenue or profit impact of any move is secondary – the best form of entry is the one that yields the most knowledge. What is learnt determines whether the company scales up its investment and makes it a core business area or exits.

The stage-gate approach would go hand in hand with Monte Carlo simulation, the running of multiple scenarios using levels for each variable that have been randomly selected according to the defined probability distribution. Each stage should see a narrowing in the band around each assumption that should be reflected in a more concentrated distribution of financial outcomes, in both profit and net present value terms. The distribution illustrates the compound probabilities across multiple assumptions that are obscured in a static, single-point model, even when sensitivities are included.

The tools underpinning uncertainty management are not new – scenario planning has been around for nearly half a century, as has its counterpart contingency planning. Assessing likelihood and impact is a straight lift from risk management. McGrath and MacMillan wrote about discovery-driven planning in the mid-1990s. Collins was singing the merits of the 'crawl, walk, run' approach in the early years of the new millennium. Monte Carlo simulations were first used in the development of the atomic bomb and software to run them on spreadsheet-based financial models has been around for over 20 years. However, if used at all, these tools tend to be employed in isolation. Proactive uncertainty management uses them in an integrated way to systematically improve assumption quality and the quality of big strategic decisions.

Don't forget the little decisions

Improved uncertainty management is one aspect of improving strategy formulation; another is expanding our definition so that it helps shape the little decisions as well as encompassing the big. As well as providing some freedom for uncertainty-reducing experimentation, casting strategy in this way strengthens the linkage between strategy and operations, improving the communication flow backwards and forwards between the two. Additionally, it encourages greater alignment in the initiatives pursued by different teams or functions – they are all guided by the same criteria. Effectively, strategy becomes the organizational middleware that guides the everyday choices made across an organization, allying decisions made at different levels and in different departments to the same goals and objectives.

The idea that strategy, if codified into simple rules, would help businesses deal with uncertainty by enabling managers to follow opportunities within given guidelines was first described by Kathleen Eisenhardt and Donald Sull.[5] Their thesis was that such an approach would help businesses in fast-growing markets. And while the value of such an approach is most obvious when the environment is fluid, it is still valid in more stable industries, not least because the degree of uncertainty is often underappreciated.

Managers and employees have to make decisions every day and the basis for such decisions tends to be precedent, the way such things have been dealt with before. Precedent reflects accumulated experience, so it may indeed support the best decision. But equally it may not – change having rendered it now suboptimal – and without testing no one will know for sure. Such a backward-looking approach also does not encourage continuous improvement, increasingly important for maintaining profitability. That requires experimentation, but within stated boundaries. If the experiment passes the rules, permission to proceed is automatic.

One of the rules would need to constrain time or money, limiting financial discretion. But they could also be cast in quite a general form, for example providing discretion to try something that will improve customer satisfaction. As well as encouraging limited risk taking, such an approach would also help front-line staff make more informed decisions, for example which customers should be prioritized, guaranteed product if there is a shortage or given special treatment if there is a complaint.

Part of the benefit accrues from improved communication, so simply outlining how the business seeks to differentiate itself provides helpful strategic context – the dimensions on which it aspires to be ahead of the competition (and why), where it seeks competitive parity, where it will offer nothing (again outlining why). However, this needs to be balanced by articulating how the business plans to make money: where it will spend to develop capabilities, where it will not. A clear statement of capability priorities – highlighting those that are most critical to achieving differentiation and meeting strategic objectives, explaining why that is the case, detailing where improvement is being sought and publishing the strategic criteria against which initiatives will be prioritized – helps ensure that decisions made below board level are the decisions that the board itself would have taken.

In addition, when the strategic direction is made clear, the quality of feedback improves. People in front-line roles are repositories of insight, which provides a robust testing ground for strategic hypotheses developed by people some way removed from operational realities. Once the strategic intent and the assumptions on which the strategy is predicated are published, the opportunity to challenge will highlight potential weaknesses, critical dependencies that need further verification or monitoring. The process also identifies those in the front line with the ambition and potential to progress, as for those people the opportunity to challenge will prove irresistible.

More importantly, such a process shapes and prioritizes the feedback provided and stimulates suggestions for operational improvements. By including operational staff in the process and encouraging their contribution, the context is set for an ongoing dialogue that provides an early-warning feed about competitors catching up, changes in customers' priorities, rumours of a new entrant; all of which might otherwise not be escalated as quickly as required.

However, the principal benefit of casting strategy as organizational middleware is in aligning business initiatives – the programmes and projects that a business is executing – with the high-level strategy they should be supporting. This happens in three ways, first through the clearer communication outlined above. Secondly, the steps from design to implementation are clearly laid out as part of the strategy – the 'how' is included alongside the 'what'. Thirdly, through holistic implementation all change levers are pulled at the same time in the same direction.

One way to test existing alignment between strategy and implementation is to run this process in reverse, starting with the current initiatives that are receiving most funding. How do the initiatives currently being undertaken support the business's priority objectives? How are they aligned with the business profit model? How cross-functional are they? How are different initiatives aligned? Such an exercise may be revealing. As the marketing director of a chemicals company once honestly admitted, 'We are good at high-level business strategy. We are also good at executing on projects. What we are not good at is linking the one with the other.'

The balanced scorecard

Ensuring that the right projects – large and small – are enacted requires strategy to be cascaded through the organization to make priorities clear and the trade-offs explicit. One popular way of enforcing strategy execution is using strategy maps and the balanced scorecard, devised by Robert Kaplan and David Norton. The philosophy behind this approach is cause and effect between the underlying components. Learning, growth and innovation support internal business processes and together they increase customer intimacy, satisfaction and loyalty, the result of which is the achievement of the financial objectives.

The benefits of this approach have been eloquently described by Gary Cokins, a performance management expert at the business intelligence software firm SAS:

With these cause-and-effect relationships linked in sequence, one could argue that maximizing shareholder wealth creation winds up not as a goal, but rather the result of accomplishing all the strategic objectives in the strategy map. One could also argue that executives do not really have a strategy, but rather a vision of where they want their organization to go. The linked strategic objectives, like the musical instruments in a Beethoven symphony, then become the strategy. This is not about every instrument playing loudly, but rather playing together in harmony.

The problem with the balanced scorecard is that the causality outlined is, at best, simplistic; at worst, fundamentally flawed. First, the customer and shareholder perspectives are as much in conflict as linked by cause and effect. The best way to delight customers would be to sell stuff very cheap or give it away free, but obviously this would not be in shareholders' best interests. On some points the interests of shareholders and customers conflict, on some they are aligned; it is a problem of constrained optimization rather than simple cause and effect.

Secondly, it oversimplifies the picture with regard to capabilities. Capabilities are made up of a number of different elements: organizational design (for example around customer segments or functionally), the culture of the business (for example values and attitudes oriented towards efficiency, innovation or customer centricity), staff competencies (design of roles and responsibilities, skills required, how role performance is measured), process design and enablement of those processes via IT systems. To some degree these should be complementary, aligned to achieving the same goal. But in terms of overall capability level they are also substitutes. Heavy investment in process design and documentation with a high degree of technology enablement means that you need staff with less experience and less initiative. You can achieve customer intimacy in how you organize teams (for instance around customers or customer segments) or through significant investment in a CRM capability. The different elements of the operating or capability model need to be developed holistically so that the trade-offs are explicit; and not sequentially, starting with staff competencies and assuming that these must be developed to ensure that operational processes are executed effectively.

However, the lure of its purported causality is strong. In a recent online debate about the merits of the balanced scorecard, one participant cited that one third of the world's largest companies used the balanced scorecard or balanced scorecard-based approaches. The question this raises is: how much of its appeal is derived from its flaws? We want to believe in the simplistic cause and effect outlined – it gives a sense of controlling our destiny. Any approach that raises conflict and forces trade-offs makes us far less comfortable.

The stakeholder scorecard[6]

Critical to strategy is how conflicts or trade-offs are resolved. These are the hard choices a business must make. Complementary demands are easily dealt with; how scarce resources are allocated in the face of competing demands is the true test of strategy. Rather than seeing the flow as causal and complementary, this requires strategy to be crafted from multiple, often opposing perspectives so that the inherent tensions are surfaced and choices made in the face of conflicting forces.

These opposing perspectives can be derived from thinking in terms of the different stakeholders a business has: customers, shareholders, debt holders and staff being the most important, but also suppliers, partners and society. Recent research[7] suggests that focusing exclusively on profit (and therefore the interests of shareholders) is not the best way to improve profitability, with more balanced consideration of the requirements of all stakeholders serving shareholders better than when they are anointed paramount.

Why might this seemingly counterintuitive finding hold true? Put simply, viewing a business from the multiple angles afforded by different stakeholders' standpoints increases the perspective on the challenges faced. Conflicts and inconsistencies reveal themselves more distinctly, assisting in the allocation of scarce staff time, funding and management attention across competing requirements. And focusing on the critical trade-offs – raising them to ensure that they are fully discussed and explicitly decided on rather than suppressed and fudged – improves the quality of the choices made, the strategy that is developed; as a result of which, growth and profitability are more sustainable.

What the research is less clear on is how businesses can start developing strategies using multiple stakeholder perspectives. One way is to think in terms of the value exchange they are targeting with each stakeholder group. While such an approach has been tried and tested in the development of customer strategies, it can equally be applied to all stakeholder groups.

This starts with identifying the subset of each stakeholder group that the business is targeting: the customers or customer segments, the kind of people it wants to attract as employees, which types of suppliers provide the best fit, which interest groups it feels best represent the interests of society the business wishes to serve, even the sort of shareholders it is seeking.

Next comes the design of a stakeholder proposition, the benefits offered and how they will be delivered, and what the business expects to gain in return. For customers, at a high level the potential benefits include enabling improved productivity, superior choice, greater convenience, higher responsiveness, more feel-good factors, greater security or lower cost. The business must choose on which of these dimensions of utility it chooses to excel, trade them off against one another to decide which will offer the greatest value to its target customers, and define its customer value proposition. This describes how it will create value for its customers better than its competitors and the attributes that deliver those benefits.

A business that creates lots of value for customers but not for itself will soon be out of business, so value creation for customers needs to be matched by value extraction by the business – the specific benefits the business is seeking in return for delivering the value proposition. With customers, a business's strategic objectives can be summarized as acquisition of new customers, retention of existing ones, growing existing customer relationships and improving customer profitability.

The same process can be applied with suppliers, partners and employees. The primary levers a business has to create value for its suppliers (both in absolute terms and relative to other potential customers that its suppliers have) relate to the terms of business: the volume it provides, security of contract, relative price paid, payment terms. But there are additional ways in which it can create value for suppliers: sharing knowledge such as research findings, co-developing new offers or collaborating on processes and integrating the businesses more tightly with cost savings for both parties. All of these provide value to suppliers while forging a closer relationship. In return, the business needs to specify the value it expects to gain from delivering this superior supplier value proposition: lower prices or security of supply if there are shortages, the knowledge it will receive in return, introductions to potential customers and partners.

For partners, the proposition would specify how it would augment the partners' offer to its clients: what information it will share, the introductions it will provide. In short, how it would be a better partner than its competitors. Again, value extraction is likely to take the form of information sharing, discounts on training, introductions to potential customers and shared marketing initiatives.

As with all stakeholder groups, the starting point with employees is articulating the type of people the business is seeking to employ, but with employees this is particularly important – an organization's culture is a function of the beliefs, attitudes, values and aspirations of the people who comprise it. The business should also specify the critical competencies sought – as defined for delivering the propositions to the different stakeholder groups outlined above – both in absolute and relative terms (for example top-ranked graduates from particular programmes, or those seen as leaders in their fields of expertise).

The staff or employee proposition outlines why people should work for the business: what it will offer in salaries and benefits relative to alternative employers and what it will offer in non-financial benefits such as organizational culture. From the business point of view, the value it should seek to extract will take the form of staff loyalty (reduced churn) and higher productivity. This again defines the metrics that would be tracked.

For society as a whole, the proposition needs to outline how the business plans to be a good corporate citizen. This would cover health, safety, environmental and regulatory issues, where the business plans merely to meet threshold requirements and where it intends to exceed, along with the rationale for incurring this additional cost. Here the benefits sought will include enhanced reputation (and its impact on all forms of loyalty), lower risk of regulatory investigation or savings on supporting mandatory investigations and preferential government support.

For all stakeholder groups (excluding shareholders), the benefits the business intends to deliver need to be translated into key performance indicators and targets for each one. These KPIs would typically be a combination of internal performance measures and stakeholder satisfaction scores. Taken together, these measures provide a pan-stakeholder view of how successfully the business is creating value. Equally, it needs to translate into KPIs the benefits it is seeking in return from each stakeholder group so that it can measure its effectiveness at value extraction. The combination of value creation and value extraction metrics across these stakeholder groups creates a stakeholder scorecard – a genuinely balanced view of business performance.

Optimizing capabilities and assets

The priorities expressed provide clear guidance for the next stage in the strategy-development process: defining the capabilities and assets required. Effective value creation and extraction will require certain activities to be performed to the highest level and some only to a basic level (or not at all). Clearly defining the value-creation and extraction priorities enables the desired capability level to be selected within each group of stakeholder-facing activities and activity metrics defined so that resources can be allocated accordingly.

With both capabilities and assets, optimization is a two-stage process: clarifying the levels required for creating (and capturing) value and meeting strategic objectives; and building to those levels and no more. Once these levels have been agreed, they need to be compared with current levels (both in terms of performance on metrics and more subjective assessment of capability) and the gaps defined. The high-priority gaps then need to be addressed in a holistic manner. This means that both assets and capabilities are addressed together; and that all capability dimensions – culture, competencies, organization, process and information technology – are addressed in an integrated way.

The importance of the different components will vary according to the specific capability required. Some will be more culture and competency related, others may be more process and technology oriented. However, any capability-building initiative needs to consider all the different dimensions; an attempt to pull on one lever alone is likely to be unsuccessful and it is even more important to pull the levers in the same direction. This is probably the biggest challenge, as the levers are typically owned by different parts of the organization – human resources being responsible for culture and competencies, the strategy team for organization and scorecards, operations for processes and IT for technology.

Each part of the organization will understand the components they control and have ideas about what could be done better. But integrated improvement requires functional walls to be demolished, with all areas aligned both in terms of where effort should be focused and how the capability should be improved.

The above process covers the non-shareholder stakeholders, but the business also needs to articulate a shareholder proposition: the returns that it is targeting for shareholders in terms of return on investment, earnings growth and so on. In most cases businesses have little choice about who their shareholders are, for instance if they have a parent company or are quoted on a stock market. However, if the opportunity is available, for instance with private companies seeking funding, it can also define the characteristics of the shareholders sought. The profit proposition shapes the targets in the profit model. In turn, the profit model caps the total cost, and therefore capabilities, that the business can afford.

This model also provides the link between the different stake-holder components of the strategy, as each one will have revenue, cost and asset implications. The profit model will highlight that the business cannot afford all that is desired, forcing choices to be made about which capabilities should be prioritized, both within the sep-arate stakeholder-facing activity sets and across stakeholder groups.

Through constraining what would otherwise be an unbounded appetite for capabilities, the profit model forces discussion about priorities. The resulting trade-offs, so long as they are made explicit and the rationale is given, clearly communicate organizational pri-orities and help to increase organizational alignment. Capability prioritization is critical to the cost control that maximizes the trans-formation of value captured into operating profit; and operating efficiency needs to be complemented by asset efficiency to ensure that the return on investment is maximized.

The capability levels that a business can fund are determined by the gross margin that the business is targeting. The higher the value added, as reflected in the gross margin percentage, the higher the level of overhead the business can absorb. Lower gross margin busi-nesses require a significantly leaner organization and sharper pri-oritization. Finally, the profit model should also provide the financial justification for the capability-building or cost-reducing initiatives that the business is targeting.

The objective is to construct all the stakeholder propositions so that they are as complementary as possible. Some are obviously so, while others will be conflicting. There is a long-established link between employee satisfaction and customer satisfaction, so an attractive employee proposition will support the delivery of an enhanced customer proposition. However, the profit proposition will require the additional associated costs to be justified in terms of additional revenue or other savings (such as reduced staff turnover) and this will not always be possible. By placing a cap on what can be spent, the profit model will force compromises to be made in some capabilities.

Complementariness and conflict in partnership deliver the alignment and prioritization required for effective strategy development. Ensuring that the different stakeholder value contracts are mutually reinforcing and selecting between the demands of the different stakeholder-facing activities when they are competing encapsulates the critical decisions that senior leaders need to make – the real essence of strategy.

In addition, through the clear articulation of the business's priorities and the trade-offs it is willing to make, the leadership's strategy is unambiguously communicated to managers and staff. And by providing guidance and boundaries, it enhances the quality of decision making. It enables delegation to those with the most information while increasing knowledge and reducing uncertainty, through providing managers with a frame within which they can experiment, confident that what they are seeking to achieve is aligned with what the business would like them to achieve.

Perhaps counterintuitively, taking a multistakeholder approach to strategy development does not conflict with the pursuit of shareholder value. The systematic stakeholder-by-stakeholder process simply ensures that there are no blind spots in strategy development. And while more balanced prioritization may result in lower short-term profits, over the longer term profitability and growth are more sustainable.

The stakeholder scorecard approach embraces complexity and conflicting demands rather than pretending that they don't exist. The environment in which businesses operate is messy, with multiple factors having an impact on success, some of which are under the business's control but most of which are not. There is also a lack of clarity on cause-and-effect relationships, even between the factors where some control exists due to the presence of confounding variables; the result of which is a high degree of uncertainty. Yet rather than acknowledge this, we pretend that it doesn't exist, simplifying the environment and bounding it so that we can make assumptions and analyse.

Psychologist Dorothy Rowe, author of *Why We Lie,*[8] has argued that to ensure we aren't overwhelmed by the uncertainties that are inherent to the world in which we live, we shut them out by lying to ourselves. In strategy development, the lie we tell ourselves is that our assumptions are facts. And by treating strategy as a hard rather than a wicked problem – irritably reaching after fact and reason – strategists fail to display Keats' negative capability. Until strategy genuinely becomes the province of men of achievement, success will continue to be as much due to luck – or lucky guesses – as to judgement.

Ten
Rise of Marketing Form, Decline of Marketing Function

The view that an industry is a customer-satisfying process, not a goods-producing process, is vital for all businesspeople to understand. An industry begins with the customer and his or her needs, not with a patent, a raw material, or a selling skill. Given the customer's needs, the industry develops backwards, first concerning itself with the physical delivery of customer satisfactions. Then it moves back further to creating the things by which these satisfactions are in part achieved...

...the entire corporation must be viewed as a customer-creating and customer-satisfying organism. Management must think of itself not as producing products but as providing customer-creating value satisfactions.

Theodore Levitt, 'Marketing myopia'[1]

As for generations of MBA students, the required reading for my first marketing class was 'Marketing myopia', Theodore Levitt's seminal article from which the above two quotes are taken. It made a big impression then and, if anything, an even larger one when I reread it after it was reprinted in the *Harvard Business Review* in 2004. The HBR website describes it as 'the quintessential big hit HBR piece',[2] the type of article that is routed round organizations with its vocabulary becoming familiar to managers everywhere and fundamentally changing behaviour. The website goes on that the article 'introduced the most influential marketing idea of the past half-century: that businesses will do better in the end if they concentrate on meeting customers' needs rather than on selling products.'

Levitt was challenging the inside-out orientation of businesses at that time, which started with what the company wanted to produce then sought to persuade customers to buy it. He cited a number of examples of industries that had once qualified for the 'magic appellation of "growth industry"', but had since disappeared into terminal decline.

Levitt's argument was that this decline arose from management failure, specifically defining their companies by the products they sold rather than the customer satisfaction they delivered. Confident in the seemingly unchallenged superiority of their product, managements in these industries disregarded the threat of substitution. Put another way, managers fell victim to the distortions of perspective that result from innate human egocentricity – the belief that the economic world revolved around what they were selling, only to find their products eventually shunned, in much the same way that overly egocentric people eventually are.

The solution that Levitt proposed was elevating marketing from its status as 'stepchild'. He also advocated making a clear distinction between selling – which was internally oriented, concerning itself with 'the tricks and techniques of getting people to exchange their cash for your product' – and marketing, which should be externally oriented and focusing on the needs of the customer.

Selling has evolved a great deal since those days; sales training courses emphasize the need to listen to customers, understand their needs and frame the product or service they are selling in terms of satisfying those needs. However, the question arises as to whether marketing has also changed, though not for the better, falling victim to the complacent egocentricity Levitt was criticizing.

Brand worship

In Levitt's article, the word brand is not mentioned once. Even 20 years or so ago when I was at business school, it was still just one of many topics covered in marketing and certainly not a prominent one. But since the early 1990s the importance attributed to branding has inflated massively, with building a brand seen as the only way 'to cut through the clutter in today's marketplace' (to use one of the many eulogies you can find on the internet). Indeed, branding has arguably transcended being just a component of marketing – even the defining one – to become its ultimate purpose. Al and Laura Ries, authors of several books on marketing, have argued that marketing and branding 'are so inextricably linked that it is impossible to separate them'.[3] They emphasize this by stating both 'branding is marketing' and 'marketing is branding'.

The question that such brand worship raises is whether it has returned marketing to the inside-out thinking that Levitt railed against, albeit with product-centricity replaced by brand-centricity, with only lip service being paid to the importance of customers. Or as one of the few marketing academics to challenge the brand orthodoxy, Roland Rust, has highlighted, managements have a blind spot when it comes to brands:

> *Listen to them talk, and you may hear customer, customer, customer. But watch them act, and you'll see the truth: It's all about the brand. Brand management trumps customer management in most large companies.[4]*

Rust goes on to argue that such a focus is incompatible with growth – in a business environment where customers have more choice and power than ever, the companies that grow will be those that are customer rather than brand oriented.

Another academic, Ranjay Gulati, came to a similar conclusion:

> *When I began this research [for his book* Reorganize for Resilience: Putting Customers at the Center of Your Business[5]*], I naively assumed that all firms must indeed have an outside-in orientation whereby they put their customers first in all their decisions*

and actions. After all, that is what business is about. Much to my surprise, I found that this was the exception rather than the rule for most businesses… Most companies with an inside-out perspective become attached to what they produce and sell and to their own organizations.[6]

Of course, brand is a higher-level marketing construct than product, encompassing a set of promises, a core idea, a distinct personality, a set of values, rather than performing a specific job. Champions of branding would also emphasize how branding, when done well, is informed by customer research and other tools of outside-in thinking. However, product development, if done well, would be similarly informed by an understanding of customers' needs. And even if it encompasses more sophisticated thinking, brand is still an internal construct, so when given preeminence, the perspective is drawn toward being inside-out, not the outside-in or customer-centric one that Levitt was recommending marketing should provide. It also accentuates innate egocentricity. And as when any behavioural biases go untempered, the risk of poor decision making increases. By definition, branding anchors mindsets to an internally generated set of values or promises, thereby blinkering perspectives. As a result it can both shape customer research, even down to the specific questions asked, and interferes with how customers are listened to – an interpretive filter for *ad hoc* comments that increases the likelihood of confirmation bias.

The word brand originally meant burn, as when ranchers used a branding iron to mark their cattle and identify ownership. With the advent of industrialization, this practice was transferred to the large, centralized factories that replaced smaller-scale localized production. Manufacturers of household items would identify their products through branding their logo, or trademark, onto the barrels in which they were shipped to local communities. The physical separation between producer and buyer caused by mass production created a corresponding gap in trust, one that trademarks helped bridge.

The next development was the advent of trademark advertising, introduced by J Walter Thompson, with companies adopting slogans or mascots to increase the chances of consumers registering and recognizing their logo. With the appreciation that consumers were relating to what they bought in more than simple utilitarian terms, manufacturers increasingly added social and psychological dimensions to their brands, giving them identities and personalities, seeking to equate them with words such as luxury, whiteness, freshness and so on.

By the 1980s, the value of the relationship forged between a brand and its customers was starting to be quantified financially and the concept of brand equity was born. By the end of the decade this had resulted in 'brand equity mania',[7] with acquirers paying huge premiums for companies with strong brand portfolios. In 1988 Philip Morris purchased Kraft for six times the value attributed to shareholders' equity in the financial accounts, the difference reflecting a valuation of brand equity not included in the accounts.

Both Philip Morris and Kraft inhabited the traditional heartland of brands and branding, the fast-moving consumer goods or FMCG sector (alternatively known as consumer packaged goods or CPG), comprising food stuffs and basic items regularly used and replaced by households. But the attractive valuations attributed to strong brands in these high-profile acquisitions came to the notice of managements outside the consumer goods sector. Seeking the fairy dust that some brand equity would add to their share price valuations, they sought to inject some branding expertise into their marketing functions, with seemingly every marketing job advertised in the 1990s demanding FMCG experience.[8]

As contrarians enjoy pointing out, such events often mark a turning point in the fortunes of the lauded, widespread recognition only occurring when fortunes have peaked. And the reputation of the FMCG sector for marketing expertise has since acquired a little tarnish. First there was Marlboro Friday (2 April 1993), the day Philip Morris announced that it would cut the price of its heavily advertised Marlboro cigarettes by 20 per cent as it could no longer sustain the price premium against cheap rivals. The realization that brands offered less price protection than had previously been thought led to a significant downgrading in estimates of the profit streams of branded companies, their share prices plummeting as a result.

The shudders caused by Marlboro Friday led some commentators to describe it as marking the death of branding. Such hyperbole has proved misplaced and brand blindness (as Naomi Klein, writing later, hoped would happen) has not transpired. Nevertheless, it did provide notice that the value derived from the power of branded products to withstand the pressures piled on them by increasingly powerful supermarket chains – either directly or through promoting own-brand or bargain-priced alternatives – was lower than previously believed. Less recognized was the implicit warning about the power of marketing – or marketing as it was being practised – to create an image or idea that would sustain a premium over functionally equivalent alternatives.

Further questions have been raised by approaches that have proliferated in recent years, notably the cross-category brand extensions that have become commonplace, a strong brand in washing up liquid seen as providing a platform for moving into adjacent categories, for example. For brand managers, who like proud parents look at their offspring through rose-tinted spectacles, such an extension appears credible, desirable (for customers), feasible and viable. But with everyone thinking the same way – or retaliating against incursions into their territory – even more power has been ceded to large retailers, manifesting itself in increased demand for trade promotions, slotting fees and return privileges.

The consequences have been extremely damaging, especially in markets such as the UK where retailer concentration is high. As Jacqui Hill, a former Unilever marketing director, put it back in 2005:

Between us, marketers and retailers have trained an entire generation of shoppers to buy only on promotion. It's not that they need

*to, but why shouldn't they when price deals are available on key
brands so often? Future generations may well look back on this time
as a time of anti-marketing unless we take action now.*[9]

In addition, the traditional FMCG marketing model – the expertise
that migrants from consumer goods companies were bringing to
their new employers – was increasingly being undermined by the
rise of new media. FMCG companies had traditionally relied heavily
on television advertising (the term soap opera being derived from
the product advertising that bookended each episode). When the
primetime audience for television networks touched 90 per cent of
households, it was a powerful way to reach the target market in a
concentrated way. But with the rise of alternative media – satellite
and cable shows, the internet – and entertainment, primetime audi-
ences could be as low as one third of households.[10] The fragmentation in reach required a more sophisticated model than these
companies had previously used. Once recognized, this was easily
remedied. More damaging, though, was that this fragmentation
provided a range of lower-cost advertising opportunities to those
previously priced out of promoting their wares in traditional media,
reducing barriers to entry.

Extensive advertising has always been an important element in
marketing household consumer goods, given its power to create differentiation in the way products are perceived; the benefits are primarily created in the minds of those who make the purchase
decision. In marked contrast to sectors where features and benefits
are more tangible (especially in industrial markets), there is little
discernible difference to consumers in the performance of products
such as toothpaste or soap powder. Differentiation is founded in
intangibles – the feelings inspired – more than superior function-
ality. The implicit assumption in importing of consumer goods marketers into other sectors was that the FMCG approach to brand
building could transfer from low-involvement, inexpensive and frequently purchased goods to more expensive, functionally richer and

infrequently purchased offerings such as cars, computers, mobile telephones, telephony services and financial services among others, even extending to B2B sectors such as professional services.

This ignores two key differences between these types of offering and those in the FMCG sector. First, measurable, functional factors play a much more significant role than in FMCG products, greater weight in the customer's buying decision being based on tangible factors, in good part because high-quality comparison data typically exist. This is not to say that intangible or emotional benefits do not exist with higher-value-added products and services; they do. But the second difference is that they accrue in a very different way, driven far more by the customer experience than an image created by clever marketing. The intangible benefits accrue from all the interactions that a customer has with a company and its products, the experience being primarily a function of measurable factors such as service levels, not solely a function of perception. Furthermore, this experience is far more complicated than the selection of a product from a shelf by the purchaser and its being opened at home by the user. It involves a more complicated buying and usage cycle – a function of greater product or service complexity, frequently involving interactions with multiple departments. To whatever degree intangible benefits play a part in driving preference, marketers play a far less important role in their delivery.

Does brand-led marketing destroy value?

This would not be an issue if the marketing function had the respect and influence to shape those factors that it does not control directly. However, an even bigger difference with companies outside the consumer goods sector than the mix of functional and emotional or tangible and intangible benefits is the influence that the marketing function has within the organization. In FMCG companies, marketing is critical to shaping customers' perceptions of the brand and therefore to the brand's success. It sits atop the organizational tree, containing the most prestigious roles and seen as a fast track to success. As a consequence, the marketing function holds sway over what other areas do – brand managers are, *de facto*, general managers.

Every industry has a functional area that enjoys favoured child status, typically the one seen as most critical for success – exploration in oil companies, R&D in pharmaceuticals, engineering in automotive, design in high-tech companies, risk management in financial services, sales in fast-growing sectors and finance in many declining sectors. Rarely outside FMCG is it marketing. Nevertheless, such differences have not stopped companies in other sectors from attempting to follow the advertising-led approach to building a brand. This reached its apotheosis in the height of the dot-com boom, with start-ups blowing funds raised from venture capitalists on expensive advertising campaigns. During Super Bowl XXXIV in 2000, more than a dozen dot-com companies paid an average of $2.2m each for a 30-second spot.

None of this seeks to dismiss the influence of brands on buying decisions. With the inexorable increase in self-service over the past fifty years – supermarkets replacing local grocery stores being the most significant, though not the only, example – products or services have become more bought than sold. Against such a backdrop brands definitely influence purchasing behaviour, offering a quality guarantee to engender the trust that used to reside in the shop owner's recommendation.

The challenge is not to the power of brands, but to the power of marketing to build them, particularly outside sectors where intangibles dominate the buying decision. Perhaps the challenge should be stated even more critically. Namely, does brand-led marketing actually destroy value, through a combination of creating a preoccupation with self, confusing an outcome with an objective and misunderstanding cause and effect? Moreover, the tools in the brand marketing kitbag tend to lead to the subjugation of function to form, substance to image and reality to perception.

In part there may be broader, societal factors in play. It is surely no coincidence that the rise of branding has corresponded with the increased prevalence of postmodern thinking. But there are definitely organizational drivers involved as well – form, image and perception being what marketing departments typically can control.

Form obviously outweighs function in a number of industries – FMCG, fashion, some luxury items (those that confer prestige rather than offer exceptional performance) – but employees with the word 'brand' in their titles have proliferated outside those sectors. Most would be able to cite case studies where brands have been successfully built by businesses that have deployed brand-oriented marketing. But as Chapter 5 highlighted, such examples suffer from the fallacy of sampling, even the fallacy of the lonely fact. Establishing a clear line of cause and effect in success stories is always difficult; and brand believers will understandably focus on the role that brand marketing has played and fall into the trap of confirmation bias, only collecting data that supports their beliefs.

That said, there are obviously companies that have successfully deployed brand marketing to build value, as a former colleague of mine used to argue strongly during our discussions on the subject. A stint at Procter & Gamble had made her an avowed fan of brand management and my scepticism irritated her deeply. In her eyes, my having never worked for a company like P&G or Unilever meant that I could never appreciate the effectiveness of brand strategy when done well.

In truth, I never tried to argue the point that FMCG companies had used brand strategy to profitable effect, my point was more that it didn't travel well.[11] The conditions and culture that led to effective deployment in FMCG companies are seldom replicated elsewhere. A truly scientific approach to the evaluation of any approach requires consideration of failures as well as successes (even though these are far less well documented), of those businesses that tried to market their way to brand success to moderate, even negative effect. Once you factor in behavioural science and the susceptibility of human bias to distort implementation, value destruction when done badly is as relevant in determining an approach's effectiveness as value creation when done well. The problem is that such instances are brushed under the carpet by the companies responsible and generally not sought out by marketing academics.

The challenge to marketing's preoccupation with branding is also as much philosophical as practical (in which case experience in a brand managing company is irrelevant): that by rooting marketing in an internal construct rather than an external constituency, brand-led approaches compound egocentricity, the innate pre-Copernican tendency to default to an epicentral perspective, albeit with individual identity subsumed into the corporate one. Thumbing through holiday snaps to find pictures of ourselves (or sharing personal experiences and opinions via blogs and social networks) is replaced by admiring company advertisements. The brand becomes a conduit for vicarious vanity, an opportunity to bask in its values, its personality adding to ours, associated prestige delivering the emotional bonus that forms part of our total remuneration. The problem is that those with a tendency towards self-admiration seldom make good listeners, especially when the message doesn't correspond with what they want to hear.

Perhaps the best evidence for the biases that branding induces comes from some leading proponents of branding. *The 22 Immutable Laws of Branding* promises to help readers build a product or service into a world-class brand. But the first question the book raises is: if branding requires 22 laws to be obeyed for success, is brand the right starting point for marketing strategy? 22 is over three times the 'magical number seven',[12] the number of information chunks that on average humans can receive, process and remember. And jokes about the mental capacity of those working in marketing apart, the number does beg the question of whether their basic presupposition that marketing equals branding and branding equals marketing is flawed; and whether treating brand as the primary currency of marketing, specifically making the starting point an internal construct, overcomplicates the process to a degree that makes it difficult to implement in the way believers argue it should.

Further support for this idea comes from the laws themselves, which describe the branding pitfalls into which businesses fall. To give the book its due, its focus on learning from failure as well as from success makes its insights all the more valuable; and while the automotive industry provides many of the examples of what not to do, a fair few are also drawn from the brand heartlands of consumer goods; even P&G is criticized for overextending its Crest toothpaste line.

Many of these pitfalls arise as a result of the tendency to be egocentric. Perhaps the biggest trap businesses fall into is the belief that an all-powerful brand can be successfully extended into adjacent categories and its brand equity milked. This tendency is covered in the laws of Expansion, Contraction and Extension. The Law of Publicity argues that brands are built by publicity rather than advertising; in contrast to what the Super Bowl dot-com advertisers tried. The Law of the Category states that a leader should advertise the whole category; similarly, the Law of Fellowship states that brands should welcome other brands, both of which go against the grain of self-interest. The Law of Mortality states that euthanasia is often the best policy, in contrast to the natural desire of the brand manager of a dying brand to attempt resuscitation, usually to limited effect.

Much of this egocentricity is baked into the organization through the role of the brand manager, not through the fault of any individual person, but just because it is derived from the job description – to be the brand champion requires seeing the world not as it is, but through brand-tinted spectacles.

Brand strategy

Authors such as Al and Laura Ries are one source of advice on branding for businesses. Of more significance are the brand agencies that have proliferated, a few of which have grown into multinationals. The leading brand agencies all offer a range of analytics or research services to help their clients better understand the markets in which they operate, the needs of customers, competitors' strengths and weaknesses and opportunities for the brand. And many are at the leading edge in terms of research techniques.

Brand strategy, another core offering, is typically founded on this research. Brand strategy as the agencies describe it is more than a communications strategy, but its implementation is typically communications led. Under brand strategy, Lippincott describes its offering thus:

> *What are your strengths? Your competitor's weaknesses? What drives preference? From analyzing your customers and competition to defining your brand's personality, we'll work with you to carve out a unique communications platform and build a comprehensive communications plan that differentiates your brand in the marketplace.*[13]

Meanwhile, FutureBrand asserts its 'commitment to ensuring that all strategy results not only in theory but in actionable, practical solutions that fuel design, environments, digital and activation'.[14] For Landor, 'once brand strategy is clearly in place, our team creates lasting brand experiences using events and environments, words and websites, pixels and packaging'.[15]

That branding requires the development of communications platforms, the expression of the underlying idea, the design of environments, wordsmithing and website creation should come as no surprise. Brand strategy engagements are commissioned by someone in the marketing team and these are the tools that marketing teams typically have under their control. Equally, the synergies between branding and communications such as advertising have long been recognized by the leading marketing services conglomerates – Landor is a WPP company, FutureBrand is part of McCann Worldgroup and Interbrand is owned by Omnicom.

One way in which this link is most clearly expressed is in the brand funnel. This idea is premised on the theory that people go through a standard set of stages on their way to purchasing a branded product. The first stage involves creating awareness of the brand, capturing the attention of buyers so that they can remember it. The second stage is interest, sometimes called familiarity, at which point the buyer's knowledge has increased to include some specifics about the brand. The third stage is action, a purchase or trial of the product. The final stage is preference, sometimes described as loyalty, at which point it has become the brand of choice.

As the word 'funnel' suggests, the model is typically displayed as a straight-line progression, either vertical or horizontal. Such displays collapse what are essentially two dimensions – knowledge and liking – into one that is amalgam of the two. It presumes, with the optimism that characterizes much behavioural bias, that knowledge begets preference: the more you know something the more you like it. The beauty of such a model for marketing services companies is that creating awareness and familiarity requires a communications campaign, with advertising often seen as the most effective means of achieving broad awareness.

The risk with such an approach is that advertising provides no check to self-delusion, with regard either to what customers value or to the brand's appeal relative to alternative choices. Ries and Ries argue that brands are built in the first instance by publicity, not advertising. Publicity only accrues if the offer is genuinely different and authentic. Consequently, it can be regarded as part of the market-testing process. Before funds are made available for mass media communications, a new brand should have garnered a certain level of publicity – it needs to have proved itself as having appeal.

This was how the internet companies that became household names approached marketing, not least because they had to, as Marc Andreessen, co-founder of Netscape Communications, highlighted:

The ongoing myth is that brands get built by advertising. Actually, the evidence is exactly the opposite. Brands get reinforced by advertising, but they get built by grassroots adoption and word of mouth: That was true of Amazon, AOL, Yahoo!, and eBay. It was true of Netscape. In the past 10 years, all the new Internet brands got built through grassroots adoption before the companies actually had enough money to mount a nationwide advertising campaign. [16]

Andreessen's words were intended as a rebuke to the later internet companies that had raised funds on the back of the success of the companies he mentioned, but in their rush to get big fast, frittered away capital on promotional spend before the value of what they were providing to customers had been validated.

The trouble is that publicity is often difficult to achieve (though that in itself should be instructive). It is much easier to spend money on advertisements that airbrush out flaws and paint over the mediocrity that proved an obstacle to generating PR coverage. The risk for companies that have funds available for such expenditure – typically large companies in this more austere age rather than venture capital-backed start-ups – is spending money to create a perception that is removed from reality, a point made frequently by Jeff Bezos, Chairman and CEO of Amazon:

What you absolutely cannot do – but you do see businesses try this – is they pretend to be something they're not. Even when people do advertise, the ones who advertise effectively are those who figure out what real value they genuinely bring, and then they shout about that. [17]

Under Bezos's leadership, Amazon has epitomized a different approach to building a brand. As with the other internet champions, Amazon's success relied on word of mouth (or keyboard):

We firmly believe that for us, the right way to build a brand is by delivering a great service. Customers learn about who we are as a result of interacting with us. A brand for a company is like a repu-

tation for a person. You earn reputation by trying to do hard things well. People notice that over time... We take those funds that might otherwise be used to shout about our service, and put those funds instead into improving the service. That's the philosophy we've taken from the beginning. If you do build a great experience, customers tell each other about that. Word of mouth is very powerful.[18]

Such conclusions are backed up by market research, a BIGresearch 2009 survey finding word of mouth to be the biggest influence in purchases of higher-value items such as electronics and apparel,[19] consistent with findings in previous years.

Word of mouth effectively inverts the brand funnel. Loyalists – those with preference for a service or product – stimulate those closest to them to purchase. The awareness and recognition phases are fleeting if they still exist at all. Either way, they are not worthy of significant expenditure.

More importantly, underlying word-of-mouth success is an obsession with customers rather than an obsession with brand, in the case of Amazon focusing on innovation to deliver the enhanced service:

We don't want to start with an idea and work toward the customer. We want to start with a customer problem and then invent a solution. That's how we approach everything we do.[20]

Outside the internet, the only brand that has grown to global proportions in the last 20 years or so is Starbucks, which also relied on word of mouth. Howard Schulz, CEO and Chairman, even called one chapter in his story of Starbucks' rise[21] 'The best way to build a brand is one person at a time'. One person at a time means that each new customer who enters a Starbucks store has a great experience so that they return (to keep having the same experience) and tell their friends.

As Schulz has pointed out, retail and restaurant businesses rely on their employees – their knowledge, attentiveness, passion and personality – more than anything else to deliver a great customer experience, yet they were typically low paid. He bucked the trend, providing staff with excellent benefits, even extending them to part-time staff. And expenditure on staff training as well as salaries and benefits meant that there was little money left over for promotion. Less than $10m was spent in the ten years to 1997, Starbucks' formative growth period.

If ever I cited such examples in discussions with my former colleague from P&G, her response would be along the lines of 'Well, of course, customer service and staff training should be part of brand strategy.' Ultimately, our differences of opinion arose primarily from strategic remit and organizational ownership. What was business strategy to me, and owned by the CEO, perhaps the chief strategy officer, was brand strategy to her, owned by the chief marketing officer or brand manager.

Such a distinction becomes moot if what is called brand strategy is the responsibility of the CEO, who has the authority to decide how scarce funds should be allocated, or marketing sits above all other areas (as is the case in FMCG companies) and has the influence to direct what other functions do. If not, then brand strategy risks only pulling on the levers that marketers own, typically the ones that relate to how the brand is perceived rather than how it is truly experienced. This may accelerate brand success, but it cannot create it.

The customer experience

At the heart of the challenge to marketing's preoccupation with branding is, once again, a belief that there is a confusion of objective and outcome. Brand value, like competitive advantage (see Chapter 8), is an outcome of serving customers in a consistently superior way. It is achieved by focusing not on brand strategy, brand personality, brand identity – not on anything brand related – but on *customers*. The objective – what the business should focus on, allocate resources towards – should be delivering a great customer experience, serving customers in the consistently superior way that ultimately delivers the desired outcome of increased brand value. Counterintuitively, the best way to build a brand may not be to focus on it much at all – it is another example of obliquity. And arguably, the problems Starbucks has encountered in the last 10 years have their roots in starting to think more in terms of brand as something to be built then leveraged via rapid expansion; a process that ultimately resulted in a 'watering down of the Starbucks experience', as Schulz put it in a leaked internal memo,[22] to the detriment of the business's performance.

Perhaps the biggest tragedy of the rise of branding has been its divorce from the more traditional idea of reputation: doing what you will say you do, each and every time. For Bezos, brand and reputation are one and the same, but that is not a view shared by the brand industry; the word 'reputation' did not feature once in over 9000 words drawn from the websites of five leading brand consultancies describing the services they offered.

Reputation is to experience what brand is to image. The increased preoccupation with the latter pairing has been to the detriment of a focus on the reputation–experience dimension. Relatively few companies buy into the idea, or manage their business, in such a way as to build their brand by delivering a great experience and earning a great reputation. As Rust has put it, a few shining examples aside, 'boards and C-suites still mostly pay lip service to customer relationships while focusing intently on selling goods and services'.[23]

One of the few shining examples would be P&G, as former CEO AG Lafley has described: 'We declared that the consumer – not the CEO – is boss, and made it our purpose to touch more consumers and improve more of each consumer's life.'[24] Equally, a number of brand agencies offer customer experience design services. Nevertheless, defining the brand customer experience – defining which interactions constitute moments of truth, what customers should feel at each interaction and so on – is the easy part. The hard part is making it happen, especially if links in the chain are glossed over. What is often missed in the design of the end-customer or consumer experience is its dependence on the experience delivered to the actual customer, typically a retailer or distributor.

Most branded consumer products businesses are not business to consumer (or B2C) but business to business to consumer (B2B2C). Some may even be B2B2B2C if there is both a distributor and a dealer between the producer and end-customer. The experience of the end-user is dependent on each link in the chain working effectively, most obviously to ensure product availability in the place where the consumer wants to buy. In turn, that requires thinking about the customer experience at each stage, though the intermediary customers are often forgotten about.

In the same article, Lafley outlined the importance of the customer experience in the following terms:

> When we look at the business from the perspective of the consumer, we can see that we need to win at two moments of truth: First when she buys a P&G brand or product in a store, and second, when she or another family member uses the product in the home.[25]

While this may appear simple on the surface and may seem to fall within marketing's remit to control, underlying the ability to deliver this is the far more complicated relationship between producer and retailer. That P&G also excels at managing its relationships with supermarket chains, notably Wal-Mart, receives no mention at all. But winning at the moment when 'she buys a P&G brand or product in a store' fundamentally depends on it.

In B2B sectors (including the B2B element of B2B2C sectors) the customer experience involves multiple functions as well as marketing: sales for purchase decisions, supply chain and logistics for inventory and delivery interactions, finance for invoicing, engineering for product reliability in use, customer service for queries and support, accounts receivable for late collections. And it involves nitty-gritty issues like process engineering and technology enablement; organization design and training; and the definition of metrics and service level agreements, all requiring broader skills than typically reside in marketing functions. Outside the consumer products industry, marketing usually also lacks the influence, interest and understanding necessary to shape the operations of these areas. A survey by Forrester found that 76 per cent of marketing groups do not even influence the customer service function.[26] In such instances, worthy statements of what customers should feel or perceive at brand interaction points are just slide-driven wishful thinking.

Marketing's direct role in the experience a customer has comprises creating offers and setting expectations. The latter is critical to a good customer experience, given the damage done to the relationship if expectations are set too high. In some situations what we expect shapes what we perceive. For example, if we are told that a wine is expensive, we are more likely to perceive it to be good. But relatively few offerings enjoy (or suffer) such inexactitude in evaluation. In most cases our expectations become the benchmark against which reality is measured. If we buy a luxury car but it proves unreliable, we are not going to be happy. If we receive four-star service but were expecting five-star, we are disappointed; but if we were expecting only two-star but received three-star service, we are happy. The ultimate level of service received is less important than how it compares to what we were expecting.

One counterintuitive result is that companies that dictate what customers will have – that is, they don't provide much choice or flexibility – are often perceived as providing a better experience than those seeking to be more customer-centric because the scope for disappointment is less. Expectations are low and as long as service is consistent, customers will know what they are getting and so be satisfied (but only if the service is consistent). In contrast, a business that tries hard to please its customers and markets itself accordingly sets high expectations, often ones that it cannot always meet, either because more has been promised than can be delivered, or because pressures to reduce the costs of serving customers result in service levels being scaled back.

The dilemma for marketers is where to set expectations. Setting them too low risks customer indifference, setting them too high risks customer disappointment. But in an effort to be distinctive in a cluttered market, marketers are more likely to err on setting brand expectations too high than too low, particularly if there is a disconnection between marketing and those functions responsible for delivering the customer experience.

The ownership of brand strategy

This risk is compounded if the flow is seen to be one way: an opportunity for marketing to dictate what other functions do, but not for other functions to have an input into what the brand strategy should be. Studies on persuasion show that to influence, you first have to show that you are open to being influenced. However, the brand is typically seen as marketing's toy and sharing is out of the question.

The first rule of branding should be that the value of any conversation on the subject is inversely proportional to the percentage of marketers involved.[27] Any discussion that only involves marketers is, by this definition, useless – just 'brandsturbation'. By contrast, when participants are drawn broadly from across the organization, including all the functions that interact directly with customers such as sales and service, make the products or deliver the services that customers buy, the value is significantly higher. The focus may be suboptimal – that is, on the brand rather than the customer – but at least it encompasses the reality of the experience rather than the creation of expectations based on wishful thinking dreamed up in a departmental vacuum.

All this will provoke howls of outrage from within the marketing industry, from the brand consultants and business school professors whose careers have prospered with the expansion of branding outside its consumer good heartlands. They would argue that all these criticisms are addressed when brand strategy is done properly, when marketing has the authority to shape it properly, and that it is certainly more than advertising.

I agree that when it is done well, brand strategy can be a powerful means of motivating employees and winning customers. However, done badly, it is a great way to waste resources. And done cynically, it is a great way to sell communication campaigns. The risk of done badly or done cynically reduces if the focus is on customer experience directly rather than on brand or customer experience as viewed through a brand lens. One reason for this is that organizational obstacles preclude brand strategy being done the way its proponents would like, simply because it is called brand strategy and owned by marketing. When it is called business strategy and owned by the CEO, these obstacles shrink and the different functions become more compliant. But if it is owned and executed by marketing, it is most likely to manifest itself in what marketing controls directly, promotional expenditure, look and feel – postmodern fripperies rather than substance.

More importantly, the whole idea of the brand panders to and so accentuates our innate egocentricity. We are programmed to see the world from our perspective, as if it revolves around us, continual underestimation of competitor moves or how they will respond to our actions being just one example. We can't be omniscient, but our response is frequently to believe what suits us best, collecting only confirming evidence; we are hugely overoptimistic as a result. Our default starting point is 'What's in it for me?' and only the truly altruistic or those with exceptional emotional intelligence are able to start with what is in it for someone else.

Brand-led marketing exacerbates these behavioural flaws, not least because shared belief across an organization increases belief in its rightness. As described in Chapter 4, groupthink generates overconfidence. Branding allows us to project what we would most like to be onto some organizational identity. It offers opportunities to do what we most enjoy – talking about ourselves, albeit vicariously, boasting even – while preserving some semblance of modesty by hiding behind the excuse of marketing necessity.

The implication of behavioural science is that we need management frameworks that counteract our natural tendencies, not ones that accentuate them, which are those that we typically find appealing. If marketing's focus is on customer experience and building a reputation, it starts to regain its external perspective. Most other functions in a business are introspective. Marketing needs to counterbalance that by thinking about the customer experience from the customer's perspective, not the company's and certainly not with brand blinkers on. Brand aficionados may argue that customer experience and brand are two sides of the same coin, the difference being merely semantic. Perhaps they are if done purely, but we need to recognize that behavioural bias distorts implementation and that they are done purely is a very unlikely outcome.

However, even if we accept that argument, for brand strategy to be substantive rather than image or perception driven it should be owned by someone with authority over the relevant parts of the organization. In consumer goods companies, the supremacy of marketing may confer this authority on the brand manager. But in most other industries, ideally it would be owned by the business's CEO (or nearest equivalent if the business offers multiple brands), with the next best alternative being the most senior executive in the part of the business that contributes most to the value customers receive.

That could, of course, be the marketing team in sectors where perception shapes the experience received, R&D or product development if the rate of innovation is high, design or engineering in luxury or high-performance sectors, perhaps even manufacturing if the brand promise is about low prices. Arguably, it could even be owned by HR. By far the most passionate conversations I have ever heard on the subject of brand have taken place among employees rather than customers.

In all these instances, marketing would have an important input: delivering the critical external orientation. It would provide customer research, evaluation of the marketplace and opportunities, and expertise on how the brand should be communicated. It would be consulted, make recommendations and execute some elements, but it would not decide. Removal of brand accountability would enable it to challenge on behalf of customers – be the customer champion, ensure that their voice is heard clearly in discussions – without having this perspective diluted by having to balance external with internal considerations. As Rust argues, 'the traditional marketing department must be reconfigured as a customer department that puts building customer relationships ahead of pushing specific products',[28] or brands for that matter.

Rust and his co-authors have made a number of recommendations for how this could be implemented. First, there is a need to make brand decisions subservient to decisions about customer relationships – the focus is on customer equity rather than brand equity, with customer metrics the primary means of assessing performance. One implication of this is building brands around customer segments and not the other way around: 'Brand managers, under the customer managers' direction, then supply the products that fulfill those needs.' This requires a shift of resources, principally people and budgets, and authority from product managers to customer managers. Rust echoes the point made by Ries and Ries that brands need to be cast as narrowly as possible, with brand extensions driven by customer needs. A critical capability that multibrand businesses need to develop is handing customers to other brands if they can serve them more appropriately. In parallel, a new mindset on the lifecycle of brands needs to be adopted, allowing them to die and be replaced by new alternatives if they become unattractive to the segment they are intended to serve.

However, most significant of all is the recommendation that achieving this requires the replacement of the marketing department with a customer department. Implicit in such an idea is the belief that marketing, like an ailing brand, is too broken to be fixed, so oriented to pushing products and brands that it is beyond resuscitation to customer orientation. Marketing has come to resemble Levitt's description of sales in 'Marketing myopia':

The difference between marketing and selling is more than seman-
tic. Selling focuses on the needs of the seller, marketing on the needs
of the buyer. Selling is preoccupied with the seller's need to convert
the product into cash, marketing with the idea of satisfying the
needs of the customer by means of the product and the whole cluster
of things associated with creating, delivering, and, finally, consum-
ing it.

Such a difference now appears far less clear. And if marketing has
become the new sales, where is the new marketing, focused on the
needs of customers, creating offers and experiences that deliver
value to both sides, resulting in long-term profitable relationships?

Marketing is too embedded for its elimination and replacement
to be possible in anywhere but a few genuinely innovative companies; there are too many professors of marketing, graduates with
marketing qualifications, executives on career paths through marketing, consultants with economic dependency on marketing
spend. In short, too many people have marketing as part of their
self-concept to allow marketing to be interred in the cemetery of
obsolescent brands. And of course, each would say that marketing,
when done properly, meets Levitt's description. But then we are
back to the whole 'done properly' argument, which returns us to
the central theme of how behavioural science makes such presuppositions questionable. The orientation to self that is innate to
branding may satisfy our psychological needs and wants, but such
a fit is not helpful, compounding as it does our inherent biases and
their associated distortions. We need to use frameworks that
through their construction force us to confront our biases, not those
that accentuate self-deceiving groupthink.

Anyone who is determined to look through a brand lens can find
successes and attribute them to brand strategy or brand management. Maybe this is so, though I would suspect that it is due to reputation and a great customer experience. This winning combination
may be the outcome of brand strategy. But wouldn't the chances of

success be increased if these factors were focused on directly and not viewed through a lens that encourages a communications-led approach and elevates style over substance and form over function? It is possible to design a great customer experience if the starting point is the brand, but wouldn't it be easier if the starting point was the customer?

It is almost 50 years since Levitt first articulated the need for customer-oriented marketing. Arguably, it is even more important now than it was then. And all we have really learnt in the meantime is that it is much easier to say than do.

Eleven

Marketing as Eyes and Ears as well as Mouth

'Today's marketing organizations are broken' was the headline of a 2006 Forrester report[1] emanating from a survey of over 100 senior-level marketing executives at large companies. One of the reasons given for this bleak assessment was that marketing departments no longer controlled the four Ps – product, price, place and promotion – that had traditionally been used to drive strategy and tactics. Most now only had power over one P: promotion.

Surprising as this might have seemed, the rise of 'one P' marketing had been presaged earlier in the decade by Philip Kotler. In a speech to the Marketing Forum in 2003 he laid out a number of criticisms of marketing practice. First, many marketing professionals were clueless about the effectiveness of their strategies. Secondly, marketing needed to become more rigorous, accountable and creative. And thirdly, in addition to marketing having become confined to promotional activity, television advertising didn't work, much of it being so average that 'it is a waste of money'.[2] (Predictably his comments caused 'uproar' among the UK marketing doyens attending, with the director-general of the Institute of Practitioners in Advertising, Hamish Pringle, responding with true British snobbery: 'Kotler is wrong, and seems to be heavily influenced by what he has seen in the US, where there is too much and too much poor-quality advertising. It is not the same in the UK.'[3])

This decline in the breadth and relevance of marketing has continued, in the process becoming a major source of angst for marketers. Prophet's 2009 'State of Marketing Study' describes marketing and its leadership as being 'firmly placed in a small box with a narrow set of responsibilities – even though the need for a more expansionary and visionary role has never been more needed'.[4] The report talks of a chasm between the CMO and CEO, echoing the findings of its predecessor study four years earlier.

The question this raises is how much marketers have contributed to their profession's demise. Have they prioritized promotion and willingly yielded the other Ps in the marketing mix? Or have they been forced to focus on promotion due the systematic stripping away of other responsibilities by functional competitors within the organization? The truth is probably a bit of both. Marketers have become enthralled with another P, positioning, specifically brand positioning. As a result, as described in the previous chapter, marketing has not lived up to the pioneering vision of what it could and should be, thereby contributing to its own demise. In parallel, creeping postmodernism, elevating perception above reality and style above substance, has resulted in promotion (the most fun part of the role) being prioritized. Marketing has defaulted to marketing communications. Worse, through a misunderstanding of the fundamental nature of communication, marketers are not even doing this part very well.

The talk–listen ratio

Lost in the marketing concept of communications is the idea that it should be a two-way process. Dictionary definitions include 'sending or receiving information' (*Oxford English Dictionary*); the exchange of information, ideas or feelings (*Collins English Dictionary*); and 'the imparting or interchange of thoughts, opinions or information by speech, writing or signs' (Dictionary.com). There is an old adage that we have two ears and one mouth and we should behave in proportion, listening twice as much as we speak. A more modern one, emanating from the world of NLP, is to listen, the idea being that if we truly want to understand someone with whom we are communicating, the talk–lisTEN ratio should be 1:*10*.

Asserting the importance of listening to effective communication would receive nods of agreement from all around; in the same way as would stating that a focus on customers is central to effective marketing. The challenge, once again, is behaving in accordance with pronounced beliefs. Anyone who has participated in an 'active listening' exercise – for example, being forced to check with the person who has just spoken that you have correctly understood what they have said before voicing your own response – will attest how difficult it is in practice. Innate egocentricity gets in the way. We tend to use the time while our conversant is speaking to rehearse in our mind what we are going to say. In the process, we just listen to the first part of their discourse, guess at the rest, then wait impatiently for them to finish, perhaps gesturing to say we have got the message so that the far more important process of our replying can begin. At our rudest, we may not even wait for them to finish.

The corporate equivalent of this is the imbalance between what is spent on advertising and other outbound communications (that is, corporate talking) against what is spent on market research, a measure of corporate listening. According to the Market Research Society, expenditures on market research in the UK were £2.2bn in 2008.[5] This compares with aggregate expenditure on advertising across media – press, television, outdoor and transport, radio, cinema and internet – and on direct mail of £17.3bn.[6] The talk–listen ratio implied by these two figures is 7.5:1 in favour of talking over listening, almost the inverse of the 1:10 advocated. Indeed, in 2007 the ratio was exactly the inverse of 1:10, but expenditure on advertising and direct mail fell significantly faster than expenditure on market research during the course of the recession and no doubt will recover faster.[7]

Obviously, calculating such a figure on an aggregated, countrywide basis is imperfect, as fundamentally the ratio should differ according to the number of customers a business potentially has, resulting in divergence according to sector and business size. A consumer products company or a bank with potentially millions of customers should have a different ratio to a supplier to the automotive industry, which will probably have less than 20. The more customers a business has, the more it can enjoy the benefits of sampling when it comes to listening; a benefit that does not play out when spreading the word. (As yet this concept has escaped the attentions of marketing researchers, so there are no studies providing indications of talk–listen ratios across industries of varyingly sized potential client bases, including the spread from highest to lowest, and across different sizes of company.)

Equally, funds spent on market research may not be a great proxy for listening. First, it may not capture everything; assignments performed by consulting firms frequently involve surveying customers and this will not have been included in the MRS estimates. Counterbalancing this, not all market research services really constitute listening to customers, being very much focused on the interests of the business. For example, market sizing and growth studies, which constitute a significant portion of research performed, seek to answer 'What's in it for me?' rather than 'What's in it for you, the customer?' The quality of listening certainly varies according to the purpose of the research being undertaken.

However, at an individual company level such a measure still has value, particularly for businesses pursuing a marketing strategy based on customer-centricity, though it is not a metric that businesses currently think to track. Try asking the next few CMOs you meet what their business's talk–listen ratio is and my guess is that they will struggle to come up with even an estimate.

In their defence, they may argue that such a measure is meaningless without anything to compare it against, that without any context provided by comparators – particularly those identified as delivering excellent customer service – evaluating whether too much or too little is being spent on listening is not possible. While such information would be useful, so long as the tendency for benchmarking studies to encourage imitation and convergence is eschewed, its absence does not render an individual company's measurement invalid. First, it can be put in context by a trend over time: is the ratio declining or falling? Secondly, the calculation itself is valuable, both to raise awareness of the importance of listening and to encourage managers to think about what the appropriate balance should be given their desired differentiation. If such a measure were monitored and published, it would also emphasize to customer-facing staff the importance of listening, specifically for continually improving the service delivered to customers.

Calculating the ratio also provides the starting point for some experimentation, reallocating funds from advertising to research and measuring the impact. Given the innate human preference for talking over listening (especially among those who have chosen a career in marketing), a reasonable starting hypothesis for any experiments would be that too much is being spent on outbound communications versus seeking out and interpreting what is being received. This is especially the case now that customers have become increasingly deluged by advertising, to the detriment of the messages' effectiveness:

> It has been calculated that the average American is subjected to some 3,000 advertising messages every day. If you add in everything from badges on cars to slogans on sweatshirts, the ads in newspapers, on taxis, in subways and even playing on TVs in lifts, then some people could be exposed to more than that number just getting into the office. No wonder many consumers seem to be developing the knack of tuning out adverts.[8]

A study by Yankelovich Partners found consumer resistance to the growing intrusiveness of marketing and advertising, with 65 per cent of those interviewed feeling 'constantly bombarded' by advertising messages and 59 per cent feeling that these advertisements had very little relevance to them. Unfortunately, saturation tends to compound itself, creating what Robert McChesney has called a commercial tidal wave:

One of the ironies of advertising in our times is that as commercial-
ism increases, it makes it that much more difficult for any particular
advertiser to succeed, hence pushing the advertiser to even greater
efforts. [9]

When drowned out by hubbub, the natural reaction is to shout
louder, or try to. And as one commentator has argued, CRM stands
more for Constantly Receive Mail than Customer Relationship
Management. [10]

The Yankelovich study also found that 70 per cent of those sur-
veyed would be interested in products that help them escape marketing pitches. It is not surprising, then, that advertising-avoidance
products and services have grown significantly over the past few
years. Spam filters are critical for anyone with an email address.
Door stickers requesting no leafleting are commonplace. And digital
video recorders, such as TiVo (or equivalent services provided by
broadcasters, such as Sky+ or V+ in the UK), have become increasingly popular, the time saving from being able to fast-forward
through advertisements as much a benefit as the ease with which
favourite television series can be recorded.

Dialogue marketing

By this point, any social media marketers reading this book will be
almost unable to contain themselves and will have spent the last
1700 words saying to themselves 'but, but, but, but...', trying to give
me a cue that they have something to say, rehearsing their arguments for how social media marketing replaces monologue with
dialogue, readying themselves to quote Marshall McLuhan's apho-
rism that 'the medium is the message'.

Maybe. That social media enables a conversation between business and customer is beyond doubt, but whether that is what will
happen is more doubtful, since marketers may just use social media
as another channel through which to broadcast. The fundamental
problem is more mindset than media. And for as long as the

mindset does not adjust for egocentricity, no amount of new media will change the preference for talking over listening. The mindset shapes the message (or 'mess age', as McLuhan might have punned) more than the medium. And the mindset remains egocentric or brand-centric rather than customer-centric.

For example, one of the buzzwords for Marketing 2.0, as 'dialogue marketing' is being dubbed, is customer engagement, which one of the UK's leading social media marketing agencies has defined as follows: 'Repeated interactions that strengthen the emotional, psychological and physical investment a customer has in a brand (product or company).'[11] Such a definition is disappointingly company-centric (or client-centric from the agency's point of view) – the benefit to the business is obvious, but there is no mention (or perhaps no thought) of what is the benefit to the customer from better customer engagement. Improved service? More relevant information? More tailored offerings? If you can only describe the benefit of a conversation for one side, it will rapidly turn into a monologue.

An article called 'Moving from monologue marketing to dialogue marketing'[12] states that evolved dialogue marketing 'needs to focus on making sure the customer can "pull" information and messages where they want, when they want, through the channels they want.' Better, but still not exactly customer-centric. Customers want 'information', perhaps 'suggestions', but not 'messages'. Messaging, like brand, is a company-centric concept, what the business wants you to hear.

I also recently received the following invitation to a webinar on social media marketing called 'Capitalizing on the Conversation', in which I would learn how to execute a well-planned social media marketing strategy that would generate exposure for my business, increase traffic to my website, build new business partnerships and bring in new qualified leads. Once again, no mention was made of how social media marketing brings benefits to my customers.

Finally, the 'Gartner Predicts 2010 for CRM' report forecasts that expenditure on social CRM will increase and that the focus of CRM expenditure will be on delivering qualified leads.[13] The report even predicts that by 2015 internet marketing, specifically the infiltration of social networks, will become regulated. It warns that given the degree of personalization possible, marketers will overstep boundaries, with social media marketing becoming more akin to stalking than enabling friends to make recommendations to each other.

It could be argued that agencies and software vendors need to focus on the 'What's in it for me?' angle with social media marketing to grab the attention of potential clients. But if that is the case, no amount of new channels enabling two-way conversations will result in dialogue if the same old broadcasting mindset rules company decisions. The tools may be Marketing 2.0, but if the mindset is Marketing 0.2 – pre-Levitt, pre-Kotler, pre-anyone else who has tried to make marketing focused on customers – the effect will be the same. Rather than being a case of the marketer's new clothes,[14] social media strategies risk being more like funky patches on old clothing – youthful, fashionable but not really different – unless there is a change in mentality, articulated in the replacement of company-centric language such as brand, engagement and messaging with customer-centric equivalents. And fundamentally this requires companies, and the agents that support them, to rebalance orientation and expenditure from talking to listening.

This raises the question of who and what should be listened to. In terms of 'who', the most important group is customers, the objective being to better understand their world: their stated and unstated needs, what their problems and pain points are, what triggers their purchases. But as part of walking in customers' shoes, businesses also need to listen to themselves, to hear what they actually say rather than what they *mean* to say. What we say about others reveals far more about us than it does about them. It shows our perspective, how we look at them more than it provides an accurate view of who they really are. And what we say about ourselves is equally revealing, though not always as we would like. Self-description veers more towards our hopes and aims than accurate self-evaluation, which to acute observers only highlights the gap between reality and aspiration.

The value proposition

One notable example of how language reveals true feelings is the seemingly innocuous term 'channel' when used to refer to distributors, wholesalers, retailers or any other intermediary with which a business transacts. The idea that these businesses are just a 'route to market', not sufficiently important to constitute a market in which each entity is a customer, unintentionally conveys disrespect. It implies that doing business with such companies is necessary for mass distribution, but is a necessary evil, and one that interferes with communications between the two most important parties: the company (for which read brand manager) and customer (for which read buyer or consumer or end-user).

Such assumptions stem from the pre-internet, pre-globalization, pre-productivity boom era of constrained supply, which gave producers superior bargaining power with respect to those businesses that helped distribute their products to end-users. But those three factors, particularly globalization, have reversed the supply situation and with it the power balance, a shift that distributors and retailers have used to their advantage, the existence of multiple possible suppliers allowing them to develop own-brand offerings. Disintermediation was one of the supposed benefits that the internet would bring: businesses would be able to showcase their wares via websites, enabling them to deal directly with end-customers. Yet if anything, intermediary customers have become even more important than before. Under the mantra of simplification, businesses have ceded to distributors tranches of end-user customers that they have been unable to serve profitably. Web purchases tend to be made through online stores rather than direct from the producer – one form of retailer replaced by another.

Not regarding these intermediaries as customers and treating them accordingly is an increasingly risky approach. While the economics of distribution are less sensitive to scale than the economics of production, they still exist, both in logistics and purchasing. One notable example is the rise of the supermarket chains such as Wal-Mart, Tesco and Carrefour, first nationally, then internationally. Consumer goods companies have learnt the hard way not to treat these businesses as mere channels. But type in 'distributor' or 'channel consolidation' into Google and legion other examples appear. There is a Tesco or a Wal-Mart coming to most industry value chains soon, if it has not already arrived.

With the distribution element of the value chain, whatever its organizational form, becoming more powerful and critical to success, treating the component companies as customers, not just a channel through which goods pass, will become ever more important. And a respectful attitude is crucial to delivering a good customer experience. The problem is that businesses have often seen their distribution chain as competition, at least competing for a share of gross profit: the margin over cost of supply paid by the end-buyer. But competing for a share of value exists with any customer relationship through the price being charged and paid. Problems only occur when such a focus comes to define the relationship. As with end-users, businesses need to refine their mentality to one of creating value. This requires the development of multilayered value propositions for each level of customer in their demand chain.

As highlighted in Chapter 7, the following benefits can be deployed to create value for customers:

- performance – typically the productivity enabled by speed, accuracy and so on;
- choice – the range of options, degree of customization, guidance provided;
- the feel-good factor – enjoyment, entertainment, ethical fulfilment;
- security – avoidance of feeling bad through guarantees and other risk mitigations;

- responsiveness and empathy – speed of service, delivery and issue resolution;
- convenience – ease of doing business;
- price – low, premium.

These benefits are just as valid for retail customers as they are for end-users, though the mix and what delivers the benefit are likely to differ in each case. In addition, for distributors and retailers there is an eighth value lever with which companies have to play, perhaps best described as 'margin uplift', enabling customers to sell more volume, turn stock over faster, and achieve a higher price and better gross margin.

A value proposition is typically formed of three components: the product/service offer, the customer experience and price. For end users most of the value is delivered via the product/service offer part of the proposition, typically a combination of performance, choice, feel-good and security benefits. Since much of the end-user experience is delivered by distributors or retailers, this can only be influenced through the support provided.

An attractive proposition to end-users is obviously attractive to intermediaries through the demand pull it creates. However, the value proposition to retailers can be augmented by designing a customer experience around their needs. Typically, the benefits delivered by a good customer experience relate to responsiveness and convenience in the first instance, but also to security and the feel-good factor. Designing a differentiated customer experience for distributor customers has two advantages. First, by broadening the dimensions on which benefits are delivered it removes a singular focus on price. Secondly, it provides the foundation for co-creating with customers the differentiated experience that together they will deliver to end-users.

While what delivers value for end-users (primarily the product/service offering) and distribution customers (primarily the experience delivered) are different, and the means of delivering those differentiated benefits are also different, both require a value proposition to be designed by a marketing team that focuses on value creation for customers as much as value creation for the business. At the core of creating value for customers is understanding what they need, better than they do themselves, something that requires questioning and listening. But it also means that marketers need to focus as much on retail or distributor customers as end-customers. This, however, cuts across organizational boundaries. 'Brand' and B2C relationships tend to be the responsibility of marketing and 'channel' or B2B relationships the responsibility of sales. Marketing creates demand pull and it is sales' responsibility to capture a rightful share of the value created.

This tension was described in a Harvard Business Review article called 'Ending the war between sales and marketing'.[15] This highlighted how, despite the close links in what they do, 'they're separate functions within an organization, and, when they do work together, they don't always get along'. The result of this is misunderstanding, mistrust and finger-pointing: 'In short, each group often undervalues the other's contributions.' All of this underlines another benefit of creating a customer department that covers traditional marketing, sales and service activities in one team, but organized around different customer groupings as well as business activities. In addition, having all customer-facing teams in one area would make the talk–listen ratio easier to measure and track.

An investment in listening

An accurate measurement of the talk–listen ratio would obviously include more than simply what is spent on promotional activities compared to what is spent on market research. First, it should take into account how sales and service employees balance their time between talking and listening, with the associated costs allocated to the respective buckets. For office-based staff, calculating such a split would be relatively simple, especially with modern CRM systems and integrated telephony. (Time spent updating the information held in the CRM system once the call had finished would need to be included as listening time.) For field-based staff the split would be harder to measure, requiring observation to generate an estimate.

Finally, the two different buckets should incorporate staff and system costs for marketing personnel. Collection and analysis of soft and hard customer data to understand needs and how the experience delivered can be improved would be included as a listening cost, with all activity associated with managing outbound campaigns constituting talking costs.

While understanding the total investment in listening is the starting point, not all listening is of equal quality. Broadly there are three types: selfish listening, service listening and scoring listening. All are important, but if listening efforts are biased to one category the complete message is not being heard.

The first answers the question 'What's in it for me?' This would include analysis to identify which markets, segments and customers are most attractive for the business to serve. At a macro scale this would include research seeking to define the size, growth, profitability and trends in a particular market or segment. On a more granular level it would include analysis that determines which customers are most profitable to serve or offer the greatest lifetime value.

Selfish listening ensures that a business allocates resources to where it will obtain the best return. This type of research provides little if any benefit to customers. It may result in some customers – the more financially attractive – receiving improved service. But to counterbalance this, others will find their importance downgraded and service moved to lower-cost delivery channels.

Calling it selfish listening is not intended to demean it, merely to describe it accurately. All business relationships involve a degree of conflict between what is in the business's best interests (for instance high prices) and what would deliver greatest value to customers (low prices or free); managing the trade-off is a key component of strategy. Overemphasis on the business's interests will result in a declining customer base. Insufficient emphasis will result in lots of customers but not much profit. The same is true of listening: it demands a balance. If all listening is selfish, profitability in the short term may improve, but the long-term ability to serve customers is diminished.

By contrast, service listening is the most important form for generating growth. Service listening answers the question 'What can I do for you?' It involves all efforts to understand customers' needs, both stated and tacit, so that the business can improve the service it provides. Insights should be mutually beneficial, identification of unrealized needs or improved service resulting in a better experience for customers and increased revenue for the business. Obviously research into what customers need in all its forms – surveys, focus groups, observation by user-centric design and human factors experts – falls into this category, the most effective being that which focuses on the outcomes customers want to achieve.

However, service listening is much broader than market research and would include the investment businesses have made in data analytics, for example mining customer purchase data to identify trigger points and predict future buying behaviour so that customers can be served most appropriately and presented with the right offers at the right time. It would also encompass analysis of other forms of customer data such as behaviour patterns, notably how customers navigate through the website in order to identify problems they encounter, the resolution of which would help future site visitors be served more effectively.

Into service listening would also fall the collection, collation and interpretation of softer information. This would include the review of feedback given to sales and service staff in interactions; analysis of the sentiment towards the business being displayed in blogs, industry forums, user groups and on social media sites; identification of the top ten reasons customers contact the company with a view to engineering out each need; root-cause analysis of service breakdowns, complaints and defections; monitoring telephone conversations to identify coaching opportunities for front-line staff; and analysis of customers' speech patterns, both the language and tone used, for triggers of stress or enjoyment (speech analytics). Finally, aspects of competitor research would also fall into this category: understanding why competitors are doing well or badly provides useful insights into what customers value or dislike.

The other aspect to competitor research, determining performance relative to competitors, is scoring listening. This seeks to answer the question 'How well are we doing?' The most obvious component is customer satisfaction research, whether that is focused on the net promoter method, customer effort score or some other. To be valuable – that is, to provide 'aha!' insights – such research needs to be more than just score keeping and close the feedback loop through the collection of qualitative information that explains performance. It also must be collected regularly from randomly selected customers at critical interaction points, so that insight into both how well the business is doing and what it needs to improve is timely.

Finally, the customer satisfaction score, however it is measured, needs to be linked to both key customer outcomes – acquisition, growth, retention and profitability – and key performance indicators. Linking the score to outcomes helps define the value of improvements (or costs of declines) on the measures that drive business revenue and costs to serve. Equally, the key performance indicators describe the experience being delivered to customers in functional terms, for instance timeliness of deliveries, completeness of deliveries, invoice accuracy, the frequency of first-time query resolution, average resolution time, the number of complaints. Relating these to the overall satisfaction score helps the business understand the impact of service levels for different interactions on customers' feelings about the business and, if possible, the impact that has on customer outcomes.

On the face of it, the collection of all this information and the analysis of relationships between the different elements does not, at first blush, constitute listening. I could try to equate it to a mechanic listening to the sound of a car engine, but that might be stretching the analogy a little, it being more analogous to the battery of diagnostic tests that cars are given to identify any problems.

Listening, as used here, is simply shorthand for all investment made in better understanding customers' needs. In that respect, it is more than simply the time spent listening during conversations with customers, whether as part of everyday activity or research; analysis is an increasingly important part of this process and is critical to improving the service delivered. Defined this way, it is a measure of how genuinely customer-centric the business aspires to be, of how much investment it is making to achieve that.

Ultimately, this is the important point. If marketing is ever to become the eyes and ears of the organization as much as the mouth, it needs to transform its role to become more outside-in in its perspective and rebalance its expenditures towards really understanding customers – retailer and distributor as well as end-user – and away from promotion. Marketers needs to recognize that innate egocentricity has moved them too much to the 'What's in it for me?' end of the spectrum; in so doing they have neglected the customer perspective. If marketing is ever to regain its prominence within the organization, it needs to reclaim its position as the champion of customers' interests and provide their voice in internal conversations.

Calculating a talk–listen ratio will not automatically achieve this. And if the expenditure is not spent on the most valuable form of listening, it could be misleading. However, recognizing the importance of listening, whether by tracking expenditure or by some other method, will force businesses to counterbalance natural inclinations, not unconsciously pander to them. In that respect, it could help marketing take a step towards becoming what it was always supposed to be.

Epilogue

I t's early evening, late summer. As you saunter along the seafront, one by one the stalls and shops start to pack up or close for the night. As if in solidarity, its work for the day done, the breeze dwindles to the lightest zephyr. Seemingly exhausted by their after-noon's exertions, the waves' shoving and dragging of the pebbles subsides to playful teasing. Unable to muster enough incoming force to displace even the tiniest, they shrink rather than rush away, the scrape of stone against stone replaced by gentle lapping.

Despite its descent towards the horizon, the sun still breathes a gentle fire, infusing the sea with its warmth. As if hypnotized by the slow swaying of its rays on the surface, you wade in. With each reaching stride, icy chills surge up your legs until you dive in, cold water enveloping your whole body. Shocked into action, the body responds, stroke after stroke pounding each rolling swell until, acclimatized, you catch your breath, treading water and bouncing gently off the soft seabed. How quickly stone turns to sand.

Lying on your back you paddle in no particular direction, each gentle kick scattering the sun's lazy reflections into fragments that reform with the same ease and zest as they shattered. Turning towards the shore as a respite from the glare, its outline seems unfamiliar, the tide having carried you some way along from where you started. No matter, there is all the time in the world.

A gentle sound pulls you from your reverie. You listen: nothing, then plip... plip... plip. A few seconds later: plip... plip... plip... plip. On tiptoe you peer towards the shingle and see a lanky man in a bright shirt, oblivious to your presence, drawing his arm back and then releasing it, chucking something small into the water. As you take a deep breath to shout out, you hear plip... plip... plip... plip... plip. A grey blur appears, disappears and reappears, your instinctive flinch coming too late to avert your face from the incoming pebble.

Shock then pain then anger; mouthfuls of water rob the expletives you hurl shorewards of their invective; the desire to meet stone with stone rising with each spluttered but unheard insult.

I am probably deluding myself in thinking that anyone thus metaphorically wounded by my verbal skimmings is still reading this book, confirmation bias being what it is. But in case someone is, I'm sorry. Such an apology is unlikely to cut much ice with anyone who feels that their self-concept or economic interests have been attacked and any temptation to return fire is understandable.

Three obvious rocks that could be sent my way are: what evidence do you have to suggest that current practices are as unfit for purpose as you suggest they are? Given your premise that bias permeates our thinking, surely you must accept that your reasoning will be similarly distorted? You challenge the existing paradigm without really outlining any alternative, what value is there in that? I will try to answer all three.

With regard to the first, there is no single compelling piece of evidence proving that a fundamental rethink is necessary, but there are a number that point in that direction. First, we have been through the deepest recession in 60 years. While its cause can be attributed to banking practices, their failure can be traced to how poorly the analytical models relied on for making decisions coped with uncertainty: how easily some of the smartest people on the planet were deceived by wishful thinking into believing that the merry dance would continue; and how personal considerations (in this case the asymmetry of personal returns) created the conditions for organizational irrationality in economic terms.

The recession has already started to reshape attitudes. A new zeitgeist is emerging, particularly a desire to remake capitalism for the better. In business this is manifesting itself in strategy becoming more focused on multiple stakeholders, not only shareholders. In particular, environmental impacts and sustainability are being given additional weight. However, it is also reflected in the adoption of new ways of thinking. Behavioural considerations are also being given more credence.

It is no surprise that the principles of behavioural economics should spread first to the financial sphere, its prodigal son. But what is applicable in finance is also relevant to its stepsibling, strategy. The links between the two are strong, notably in the financial implications of strategic decisions being foremost in the minds of both executives and shareholders. And for asset bubbles and bursts in financial markets, read the cycle of booms and busts that afflicts many sectors in the 'real' economy. The causes are the same: high profitability breeding excessive confidence that induces herd-like investment stampedes, which sow the seeds of inevitable fall-out.

As with financial markets, strategy is full of smart people. Yet as with financial markets, this does not limit overoptimism and over-confidence; if anything, self-admiration may even compound it. How else can the tendency for companies to overpay for acquisitions, a failing that has been recognized since the 1970s, still persist, even when such decisions are supported by the brightest and best analytical talent money can buy?

A failure of strategic thinking is also implied by how poorly stock markets performed in a period of almost unprecedented economic growth between the turn of the millennium and the onset of the financial crisis in late 2007. Over that period, the global economy grew by almost 70 per cent in constant dollar terms, yet only a couple of developed-economy stock markets peaked above their 2000 highs.

In part this stemmed from lower earnings growth than had been enjoyed in the 1980s and 1990s, the low-hanging fruit for productivity-led profit improvements having been picked over those two decades. And despite huge energy directed towards organic growth initiatives, they failed to make up the difference and revenue growth remained stubbornly at the top of CEO priorities until the recession brought other considerations to the fore.

Ultimately, the failure to deliver growth highlights a failure of both strategy and marketing. Marketing in particular has failed to consistently identify and deliver the enhanced value creation for customers that drives organic growth. Instead, it has shrunk to a preoccupation with business-centric rather than customer-centric activities: brand building and lead generation. Despite continuing to pay lip service to how important customers are, actions tell a different tale. In the process of conforming to the internally oriented agenda pushed by other functions, notably finance, marketing has lost the confidence of senior executives across the organization and has seen its role whittled down, with marketers agonizing over their reduced importance in the organizational pecking order.

The credit boom and bust, continued overpayment for acquisitions, an inability to generate organic growth – all of these point the finger towards systematic failings. The reason for such failings becomes clear when the favoured approaches to management research, strategy development and marketing are viewed through a behavioural lens.

Business is hugely complex and, given the many variables involved in strategy and marketing, proving cause and effect with regard to success is almost impossible. In such circumstances, psychological appeal will play a far bigger role than either it should or we recognize. If that demand can be supplied profitably – by business schools, consultants or agencies – the chimera is sustained, with more and more inculcated into the prevailing approach. Results may be randomly distributed, but only the successes are made visible, whether publicized by the companies themselves or codified by researchers. And with that the cycle begins again.

While the flow described above is hugely simplistic, there is validity in each stage – enough to suggest that more than being merely a simple adornment to existing approaches, behavioural science fundamentally challenges popular approaches by highlighting their susceptibility to distortion.

The above argument is all inductive. And as Chapter 4 describes, the inability to prove cause and effect provides fertile ground for bias, which leads to the second charge that I am biased. Well, of course I am. You cannot write about bias without acknowledging its existence in yourself. I have tried to be even-handed, but such a commitment is bound to predispose me to confirmation bias in particular.

Nevertheless, the fact that I am motivated to see behavioural economics as fundamentally challenging existing approaches does not, by definition, mean that I am wrong. Every husband knows that 'No' is the better answer to 'Does my bum look big in this?' But that does not automatically invalidate its truthfulness as an answer. It would be equally valid to argue that those who wish to preserve the current paradigm are biased, either by an economic interest in maintaining it or by straightforward status quo bias.

At an individual level we are all biased. The aspiration of rationalism is that at a societal level we are not; that through debate, discussion and experimentation, reason will prevail. My aim for this book has always been to institute debate by raising awareness of how intellectually precarious some popular presuppositions are, by raising awareness of the idea that we need to reexamine the true value of some of the key building blocks of how businesses are managed today, not simply tinker around with them. I am not trying, certainly not expecting, to convince any reader that my arguments are right, merely that there is a case for a fundamental reappraisal.

That brings me to the final point: it is easier to throw stones, much harder to construct new stuff. While I have tried in each chapter to suggest an alternative approach, it would be hypocritical to argue that these will deliver automatic success. Again, their existence is as much to stimulate the generation of alternative ideas as to provide a recipe for action. However, once more it is my hope that one of the outcomes of widespread discussion will be the generation of alternative ways of expanding knowledge, educating managers and developing business or marketing strategies and implementation approaches to achieve that most elusive of aims, organic growth.

With that, I hand the discussion over to you, for you to do with what you will: tell your friends, agree or disagree on blogs, argue with your professors, challenge your consultants, seek to distract attention from my arguments, hurl rocks in my direction.

In preparation for the last of these, I will get myself a tin hat.

Notes

Chapter 2

1 Irwin Stelzer, Reaganomics, Thatcheromics, and the future, in *Reaganomics and After*, Institute of Economic Affairs, 1989

2 Jack Welch & John Byrne, *Jack: Straight from the Gut*, Warner Books, 2001.

3 The radical fringe: An interview with Gary Hamel, *Business Strategy Review*, Winter 2003.

4 William Niskanen, Reaganomics, *The Concise Encyclopedia of Economics*, http://www.econlib.org/index.html.

5 Alan Beattie, Trading ritual and reality, *Financial Times*, 18 October 2007,

6 IMF World Economic Outlook database, October 2007.

7 Global Capital Flows: Defying Gravity, IMF Finance & Development, March 2007.

8 Erik Brynjolfsson & Lorin Hitt, Beyond computation: Information technology, organizational transformation and business performance, *Journal of Economic Perspectives*, 14(4), 2000.

9 Robert Cringely, *Accidental Empires: How the Boys of Silicon Valley Make Their Millions, Battle Foreign Competition and Still Can't Get a Date*, Addison Wesley, 1992.

10 Nicholas Carr, *Does IT Matter? Information Technology and the Corrosion of Competitive Advantage*, Harvard Business School Press, 2004.

11 *Ibid.*

12 Lorin Hitt & Erik Brynjolfsson, Productivity, business profitability, and consumer surplus: Three different measures of information technology value, *MIS Quarterly*, June 1996.

13 Stephen Oliner & Daniel Sichel, The Resurgence of Growth in the Late 1990s: Is Information Technology the Story?, Federal Reserve Board white paper, February 2000.

14 Carr, *op. cit.*

15 Welch & Byrne, *op. cit.*

16 *Dealogic*, quoted in Martin Wolf, Unfettered finance is fast reshaping the global economy, *Financial Times*, 18 June 2007.

17 Lowell Bryan & Michele Zanini, Strategy in an era of global giants, *McKinsey Quarterly*, 4, 2005.

18 Includes both US companies and foreign companies with ADRs.

19 In 'Creating new growth platforms' (*Harvard Business Review*, May 2006) Donald Laurie, Yves Doz and Claude Sheer state: 'Over time, 65% of acquisi-

tions have destroyed more value than they create.' A more recent article by Clayton Christensen, Richard Alton, Curtis Rising and Andrew Waldeck, 'The new M&A playbook', published in the March 2011 edition of *Harvard Business Review*, points to a higher failure rate, stating 'companies spend more than $2 trillion on acquisitions every year. Yet study after study puts the failure rate of mergers and acquisitions somewhere between 70% and 90%.'

20 Known then as leveraged buy-outs, as debt often constituted 80–90 per cent of financing. According to the CMBOR, the proportion of debt financing peaked in this cycle and currently it is around 50 per cent.

21 Mike Wright *et al.*, Management Buy-outs 1986-2006: Past Achievements, Future Challenges, CMBOR, June 2006. Also Private Equity Smashes all Records in 2006, CMBOR press release. This equates to a compound annual growth rate of 15 per cent.

22 FTSE All-Share: 17.2%, 8.5% and 7.9% per annum for 3-, 5- and 10-year periods to end 2006; Total Private Equity: 31.3%, 20.9% and 19.7% per annum over 3-, 5- and 10-year periods to 2006. Source: BVCA Private Equity and Venture Capital Performance Measurement Survey for 2006.

23 Wright, *op. cit.*

24 Felix Barber & Michael Goold, The strategic secret of private equity, *Harvard Business Review*, September 2007.

25 Wright, *op. cit.*

26 Walter Kiechel, *The Lords of Strategy: The Secret Intellectual History of the New Corporate World*, Harvard Business School Press, 2010.

27 Management Consultancies Association; Number of consultants: 1469 in 1960, 1694 in 1980, 8020 in 1995 and 51,340 in 2005.

28 Cambridge University Press, 2006.

29 Being an academic rather than a consultant, McKenna lacks the CAGR Reflex – the instinctive nominalization of any time series data into a compound annual growth rate. For any consultants reading this, the CAGR for Booz Allen & Hamilton's growth in consultants over the 43-year period from 1960 to 2003 was 7.2% and for McKinsey it was 8.7%.

30 Nicholas Lemann, Kids in the conference room: How McKinsey & Company became the next big step, *New Yorker*, 18 & 25 October 1999.

31 Edward de Bono, *Teach Yourself to Think*, Penguin, 1996.

32 Edward de Bono, *New Thinking for the New Millennium*, Penguin, 2000.

33 When I was looking at business schools for MBA programmes!

34 When my father decided to go to business school in 1950, his only option was to travel to the US.

35 Wafiq Said, who advised Margaret Thatcher's government on the Al-Yamamah arms contract that resulted in British Aerospace (now BAE) winning a multi-billion contract to supply the Saudi Royal Air Force; Sir Paul Judge, who initiated and led the buy-out of Premier Brands from Cadbury Schweppes; Dr Gary Tanaka, co-founder of specialist technology investor Amerindo Investments, who was tried in 2008 and found guilty of conspiracy, securities

fraud and investment adviser fraud and sentenced to five years in prison in early 2010, though the case is still under appeal. In August 2008, the school was renamed Imperial College Business School, with Dr Tanaka's consent, ostensibly to make the link to Imperial College more obvious.

36 John Kay, Research that aids publicists and not the public, *Financial Times*, 30 October 2007.

37 US and World figures from McCann-Erickson's Insider's Report, December 2005, and Bob Coen, *Estimated World Advertising Expenditures*, deflated using US Implicit GNP Price Deflator; reproduced in Vital Signs Online, Worldwatch Institute (www.worldwatch.org). UK figures from *Advertising Statistics Yearbook 2007*.

38 UK GDP Chained Volume Index.

39 John Gapper, Mavericks who made it all up, *Financial Times*, 23 September 2007 – a review of Sam Delaney, *Get Smashed: The Story of the Men Who Made the Adverts that Changed Our Lives*, Sceptre, 2008.

40 Quoted in Mark Tungate, *Adland: A Global History of Advertising*, Kogan Page, 2007.

41 For those who have not heard of him, Taverne was elected as a Labour Member of Parliament in 1962. He became a junior minister in the 1966–70 Harold Wilson government, but resigned the party whip in 1972 following disagreements on party policy. He stood as an independent candidate in the resulting by-election and won. He now sits in the House of Lords as a Liberal Democrat peer.

42 Derren Brown may seem a strange inclusion in this list, given his popularity as an entertainer, but his power as an illusionist relies on his understanding of the tricks our minds play, so he is highly qualified from a practical perspective.

43 John Micklethwait, A special report on religion and public life, *The Economist*, 3 November 2007. A subsequent book on the subject, co-authored with Adrian Wooldridge, *God is Back: How the Global Rise of Faith Is Changing the World*, was published by Allen Lane in 2009.

44 Richard Dawkins, *The God Delusion*, Black Swan, 2007.

45 Dick Taverne, *The March of Unreason: Science, Democracy, and the New Fundamentalism*, Oxford University Press, 2006.

46 Mike Moore, Green zealots need to get out more, *Financial Times*, 3 December 2009.

47 Michael Shermer, Living in denial: When a sceptic isn't a sceptic, *New Scientist*, 18 May 2010.

48 Dan Kahan, Fixing the communications failure, *Nature*, 463, 21 January 2010.

49 www.jonathonporritt.com/pages/2010/03/genetically_modified_fetishism.html

50 Spin, science and climate change, *The Economist*, 18 March 2010.

51 Tim Ball *et al.*, Letter to Royal Society, 26 September 2006.

52 Michael Schrage, Science must be more political, *Financial Times*, 25 September 2007.

53 Gill Ereaut & Nat Segnit, Warm Words: How Are We Telling the Climate Change Story and Can We Tell It Better?, IPPR, August 2006.

54 Erin Biba, Why science needs to step up its PR game, *Wired*, June 2010.

55 HarperCollins, 2008.

56 Kiechel, *op. cit.*

Chapter 3

1   http://stallpoints.executiveboard.com/resources.html#resource2.

2   IMF World Economic Outlook, October 2009. Global GDP based on purchasing-power-parity valuation of component country GDPs, translated at constant currency.

3   See www.inflationdata.com/inflation/Inflation_Rate/Historical_Oil_Prices_Table.asp.

4   Source of all data is Office for National Statistics, www.statistics.gov.uk.

5   Source of all data is Bureau of Economic Statistics, www.bea.gov.

6   Source: Standard & Poor's.

7   Source: Standard & Poor's.

8   Source: Standard & Poor's. Returns are calculated using the S&P500 Total Return index, which includes dividend reinvestment as well as capital appreciation in the return calculation.

9   Source: Datastream. Returns are calculated using the FTA All Share Total Return index, which includes dividend reinvestment as well as capital appreciation in the return calculation.

10 The P/E ratio for a share is the share price divided by the earnings per share. The higher the expected growth in earnings and the higher the quality of that earnings growth (the less risky and inflation-dependent earnings growth is, the higher its quality is deemed to be), the higher the P/E ratio that those shares will command. The P/E for an index is calculated by taking the total value of the constituents divided by the total value of their earnings.

11 Source: Standard & Poor's. Based on trailing earnings for previous 12 months.

12 According to the Bureau of Economic Analysis, inflation was 8.9% in 1981, falling to 5.5% in 1982 and 2.4% in 1986, before rising to 3.5% in 1987 and 4% in 1988.

13 A rule of thumb used by some investment managers for deciding whether a stock market is over or undervalued is comparing the prospective (i.e. based on forecast earnings over the next twelve months) P/E ratio for the market as whole to a benchmark of 20 minus the forecast rate of inflation.

14 The radical fringe: An interview with Gary Hamel, *Business Strategy Review*, Winter 2003.

15 The growth boosters, *Harvard Business Review*, July–August 2004.

16 Andrew Campbell & Robert Park, Stop kissing frogs, *Harvard Business Review*, July–August 2004.

17 David Garvin, What every CEO should know about creating new businesses, *Harvard Business Review*, July–August 2004.

18 Michael Treacy, Innovation as a last resort, *Harvard Business Review*, July–August 2004.

19 The CEO Challenge: Top Marketplace and Management Challenges 2001, A CEO Survey by Accenture and The Conference Board; CEO Challenge 2004 and 2007, Top 10 Challenges, The Conference Board (www.conference-board-org).

20 Bull session, *The Economist*, 6 January 2007.

21 Growth as a process, interview with Thomas A Stewart, *Harvard Business Review*, June 2006.

Chapter 4

1 Tversky died in 1996. It is generally believed that had he been alive in 2002, he would have shared the award with Kahneman.

2 Amos Tversky & Daniel Kahneman, Judgment under uncertainty: Heuristics and biases, *Science*, 27 September 1974.

3 The full title of the book is *Inevitable Illusions: How Mistakes of Reason Rule Our Minds* (John Wiley) and it is an excellent primer on cognitive bias.

4 Amos Tversky & Daniel Kahneman, The framing of decisions and the psychology of choice, *Science*, January 1981.

5 B McNeil, S Pauker, H Sox & A Tversky, On the elicitation of preferences for alternative therapies, *New England Journal of Medicine*, May 1982.

6 Dan Ariely, *Predictably Irrational*, HarperCollins, 2008.

7 Humphrey Neill, *The Art of Contrary Thinking*, Caxton Press, 2003.

8 Ariely, *op. cit.*

9 For more see Maurice Schweitzer, Lisa Ordonez, Adam Galinsky & Max Bazerman, Goals gone wild: The systematic side-effects of over-prescribing goal-setting, Knowledge@Wharton, 18 February 2009.

10 Amos Tversky & Daniel Kahneman, Extensional versus intuitive reasoning: The conjunction fallacy in probability reasoning, *Psychological Review*, October 1983.

11 Tversky & Kahneman, *op. cit.*

12 Amos Tversky & Eldar Shafir, Thinking through uncertainty: Non-consequential reasoning and choice, *Cognitive Psychology*, 24(4), 1992.

13 Ariely, *op. cit.*

14 *Ibid.*

15 Jamil Zeki, Jason Mitchell & Jessica Schirmer, Social influence modulates the neural computation of value, *Psychological Science*, 2011.

16 Sara Solnick & David Hemenway, Is more always better? A survey on positional concerns, *Journal of Economic Behavior & Organization*, 37(3), 1998.

17 My wife is an honourable exception in this regard, but given that she is a care-oriented speech and language therapist this is not a huge surprise. As a money-centric management consultant, I just wished she earned twice as much.

18 Do economists need brains? *The Economist*, 26 July 2008.

19 James Surowiecki, *The Wisdom of Crowds: Why the Many Are Smarter than the Few*, Abacus, 2005.

20 Terence Burnham High testosterone men reject low ultimatum game offers, *Proceedings of the Royal Society*, published online 5 July 2007.

21 When we become parents, the 'me' bit expands to include our offspring, evidenced by our desire to share pictures of our children exceeding our desire to look at those of others.

22 One recent example is Andrew Campbell, Jo Whitehead & Sydney Finkelstein, Why good leaders make bad decisions, *Harvard Business Review*, February 2009.

23 Dan Ariely, Count on irrational decision making, *Harvard Business Review*, July–August 2009.

Chapter 5

1 *Financial Times*, 6 September 2010.

2 Jeffrey Pfeffer & Christina Fong, The end of business schools? Less success than meets the eye, *Academy of Management Learning & Education*, September 2002.

3 Warren Bennis & James O'Toole, How business schools lost their way, *Harvard Business Review*, May 2005.

4 Henry Mintzberg, Managers not MBAs, Berret Koehler, 2004.

5 Marcus Alexander & Harry Korine, When you shouldn't go global, *Harvard Business Review*, December 2008.

6 I first heard research described as codification by David Pettifer, a former PwC partner, around 2002. However, I also recall that David knew Marcus Alexander, so which of the two (if either) deserves the credit for the originality of this particular insight, I do not know.

7 *Fawlty Towers* was a brilliant 1970s British sitcom that epitomized the expression of leaving the audience wanting more, as only two series of six episodes were ever made; over 20 years after the second was filmed, it was ranked first by industry professionals in a 2000 BFI poll of the best British television programme ever made. Equally popular at the time was the quiz show *Mastermind*, in which contestants faced two rounds of questions, one on general knowledge having been preceded by one on a specialist subject of their choosing – though usually something more specific and learned, such as the works of Jane Austen or the life of Martin Luther King, rather than the 'bleeding obvious'.

8 Michael Hammer, Deep change: How operational innovation can transform your company; George Stalk & Rob Lachenauer, Hardball: Five killer strategies for trouncing the opposition, both in the *Harvard Business Review* of April2004. Hammer's article is excellent, Stalk and Lachenauer's is a classic example of macho, testosterone-fuelled competitive strategy to which we will return later.

9 Dana Carney, Andy Yap, Brian Lucas & Pranjal Mehta, People with power are better liars, Columbia University working paper, 2009.

10 Joris Lammers, Diederik Stapel & Adam Galinsky, Power increases hypocrisy: Moralizing in reasoning, immorality in behavior, *Psychological Science*, May 2010.

11 Quoted from The Science of Thinking Smarter, Harvard Business Review, May 2008

12 Jereker Denrell, Selection bias and the perils of benchmarking, *Harvard Business Review*, April 2005.

13 Adrian Wooldridge, The world turned upside down, A special report on innovation in emerging markets, *The Economist*, 17 April 2010.

14 Henry Petroski, Look first to failure, *Harvard Business Review*, October 2004.

15 Or if they are a consultant, 'in my twelve cumulative years of experience', consultants' perception being that the longer hours worked justifies a factor of at least 1.2 to be applied to actual years to calculate the more relevant cumulative years figure.

16 Mark Gottfredson, Steve Schaubert & Hernan Saenz, New leader's guide to diagnosing the business, *Harvard Business Review*, February 2008.

17 Jeffrey Pfeffer & Robert Sutton, Evidence-based management, *Harvard Business Review*, January 2006.

18 Eric Bonabeau, The perils of the imitation age, *Harvard Business Review*, June 2004.

19 Warren Buffett, Berkshire Hathaway Annual Report, 1989. The full list he cites is: (1) as if governed by Newton's First Law of Motion, an institution will resist any change in its current direction; (2) just as work expands to fill available time, corporate projects or acquisitions will materialize to soak up available funds; (3) any business craving of the leader, however foolish, will quickly be supported by detailed rate-of-return and strategic studies prepared by his troops; and (4) the behaviour of peer companies, whether they are expanding, acquiring, setting executive compensation or whatever, will be mindlessly imitated.

Chapter 6

1 As an example, my father crossed the Atlantic to attend The Wharton School of the University of Pennsylvania in 1950. There were about 30 in his class, with the foreign contingent being him, an Irishman and a Frenchman.

2 Joel Podolny, The buck stops (and starts) at business school, *Harvard Business Review*, June 2009.

3 Henry Mintzberg, *Managers not MBAs*, Berret Koehler, 2004.

4 National Center for Education Statistics.

5 London Business School, Manchester Business School, Cranfield School of Management.

6 *Academy of Management Learning & Education*, September 2002.

7 Anthony Mayo, Nitin Nohria & Laura Singleton, *Paths to Power*, Harvard Business School Press, 2006.

8 *Time*, 4 May 1981.

9 Source: www.businessschooladmission.com.

10 Rakesh Khurana & Nitin Nohria, It's time to make management a true profession, *Harvard Business Review*, October 2008.

11 Lyman Porter & Lawrence McKibbin, *Management Education and Development:*

Drift or Thrust into the 21st Century?, McGraw Hill, 1988.

12 Warren Bennis & James O'Toole, How business schools lost their way, *Harvard Business Review*, May 2005.

13 When I started doing research for this book I asked a friend still working at Fidelity whether copies of these pieces still existed, but unfortunately no record could be found.

14 *Harvard Business Review*, October 2008.

15 This was brilliantly parodied in a *SatireWire* piece on Larry Ellison fictionally giving a speech to the graduating class at Yale, calling them losers who would never reach the ranks of the super-rich because they were the preserve of the diploma-less. www.satirewire.com/news/0006/satire-ellison.shtml.

16 Richard Barker, No, management is not a profession, *Harvard Business Review*, July–August 2010.

17 Though such an idea could appeal to the European Commission.

18 Jamie Whyte, *Bad Thoughts*, Corvo, 2003.

Chapter 7

1 *Harvard Business Review*, January 2008.

2 *Harvard Business Review*, September 2009.

3 Edward de Bono, *Teach Yourself to Think*, Penguin, 1996.

4 Special report on design thinking, *BusinessWeek*, 30 September 2009.

5 Something I quite clearly wasn't. During a performance review in the early 1990s, Iain chastised me with: 'We don't do 80:20 at LEK, we take analysis to the 99th percentile', an attitude that probably explains his somewhat fractious relationship with another of the firm's founders, Richard Koch, author of *The 80:20 Principle*; *The 80:20 Revolution*; *The 80:20 Individual*; and *Living the 80:20 Way* (all from Nicholas Brealey Publishing).

6 www.lek.com/services/strategy.cfm, 11 January 2011.

7 www.bcg.com/about_bcg/vision/mission.aspx, 11 January 2011.

8 www.bcg.com/about_bcg/vision/values.aspx, 11 January 2011.

9 www.marakon.com/firm_difference.asp, 11 January 2011.

10 http://origin.mckinsey.com/aboutus/whatwebelieve/, 11 January 2011.

11 http://origin.mckinsey.com/aboutus/whatwedo/, 11 January 2011.

12 In *Hard Times*, Charles Dickens caricatured the utilitarians of his day in the character of Thomas Gradgrind, a retired merchant who becomes a Member of Parliament and runs a school. The book opens with the following exhortation to a new school teacher: 'Now, what I want is, Facts. Teach these boys and girls nothing but Facts. Facts alone are wanted in life. Plant nothing else, and root out everything else. You can only form the minds of reasoning animals upon Facts: nothing else will ever be of any service to them. This is the principle on which I bring up my own children, and this is the principle on which I bring up these children. Stick to Facts, sir!'

13 Michael Porter's big ideas, *Fast Company*, February 2001.

14 This represents the distinction of risk from uncertainty first defined by Frank Knight in *Risk, Uncertainty and Profit* (Houghton Mifflin, 1921). A more recent definition by Douglas Hubbard in his book *How to Measure Anything* (John Wiley & Sons, 2007) equates the two, with risk differing only in terms of 'some of the possibilities involve a loss'. While any future event is, by definition, uncertain, so that any evaluation of risk based on huge tracts of historical data will always contain an intractable element of uncertainty and an implicit assumption that the future will be similar to the past, I still believe that there is a difference between a distribution of possible outcomes that can be predicted with a reasonable degree of confidence versus those where the limits have been developed as best guesses. Fundamentally, the distinction is in the knowledge-to-assumption ratio: how much is known and how much has had to be assumed, which is why I prefer the Knightian definition.

15 Quoted from the 1985 annual report of Berkshire Hathaway, repeated in Lawrence Cunningham, *The Essays of Warren Buffett, Lessons for Investors and Managers*, John Wiley & Sons (Asia).

16 Sven Smit, Caroline Thompson & Patrick Viguerie, Do or die battle for growth, *McKinsey Quarterly*, 3, 2005.

17 Tesco and Harrah's spring immediately to mind, but see Thomas Davenport, Competing on analytics, *Harvard Business Review*, January 2006 for more examples.

18 Dan Goldstein, Gain an instant insight, *Strategy Magazine*, December 2009.

19 Joseph Bower & Clayton Christensen, Disruptive technologies: Catching the wave, *Harvard Business Review*, January 1995.

20 David Garvin, What every CEO should know about creating new business, *Harvard Business Review*, July–August 2004.

21 Rand, 2003.

22 C West Churchman, Wicked problems, *Management Science*, December 1967.

23 Horst Rittel & Melvin Webber, Dilemmas in a general theory of planning; *Policy Sciences*, 4, 1973; available at www.uctc.net/mwebber/Rittel+Webber+Dilemmas+General_Theory_of_Planning.pdf.

24 Roger Martin, *The Design of Business: Why Design Thinking Is the Next Competitive Advantage*, Harvard Business School Press, 2009.

25 Customers to replace Marketing Departments, *MarketingWeek*, 22 July 2004.

26 W Edwards Deming, *Out of the Crisis*, MIT Press, 1982.

27 www.kaushik.net/avinash/2006/05/overview-importance-of-qualitative-metrics.html.

28 Henry Mintzberg, *Managers not MBAs*, Berret Koehler, 2004.

29 If presented with such an analysis, try asking 'Do we get free prawn crackers with that?'

30 Edward de Bono, *Teach Yourself to Think*, Penguin Psychology, 1996.

31 Penguin Psychology, 2000.

32 This should obviously include some right-brained hypothesis generation, but it will be analysis that confirms that such an opportunity exists.

33 Magnus Lindkvist, Trendspotting in an age of uncertainty, *Strategy Magazine*, December 2009.
34 Anthony Mayo, Nitin Nohria & Laura Singleton, *Paths to Power*, Harvard Business School Press, 2006.

Chapter 8

1 Those of you of a thoughtful bent might argue that ironic usage should score 2 points, as it highlights what common currency such an expression has become. But I only award half a point because the speaker obviously finds the expression useful, if a little crass. Sarcastic usage obviously merits zero points.
2 Cynthia Montgomery, Putting leadership back into strategy, *Harvard Business Review*, January 2008.
3 Michael Porter, *Competitive Advantage*, Free Press, 1985.
4 One example being Michael Porter's big ideas, *Fast Company*, February 2001.
5 Robert Buzzell, Bradley Gale & Ralph Sultan, Market share – A key to profitability, *Harvard Business Review*, January–February 1975.
6 Crown Books, New York, 2002.
7 George Stalk Jr & Rob Lachenauer, Hardball: Five killer strategies for trouncing the competition, *Harvard Business Review*, April 2004.
8 *The Economist*, 28 August 2004.
9 The best global brands/Online extra, *Business Week*, 2 August 2004,
10 What's a Business For?, *Harvard Business Review*, December 2002. Speaking on Packard's death, his co-founder Bill Hewlett commented: 'As far as the company is concerned, the greatest thing he [Packard] left behind him was a code of ethics known as the HP Way.'

Chapter 9

1 *Harvard Business Review*, September 2005.
2 Michael Hammer, Deep change: How operational innovation can transform your company, *Harvard Business Review*, April 2004.
3 www.bain.com/bainweb/home.asp.
4 Rita Gunther McGrath & Ian MacMillan, Discovery-driven planning, *Harvard Business Review*, January 1995.
5 Kathleen Eisenhardt & Donald Sull, Strategy as simple rules, *Harvard Business Review*, January 2001.
6 The thinking behind the stakeholder scorecard was developed in conjunction with Richard Sanders and was first published in the December 2010 edition of *Strategy*, the journal of the Strategic Planning Society.
7 For two examples: Jeffrey Pfeffer, Shareholders first? Not so fast, *Harvard Business Review*, July 2009; and Nathan Washburn, Why profit shouldn't be your top goal, *Harvard Business Review*, December 2009.
8 HarperCollins, 2010.

Chapter 10

1 *Harvard Business Review*, July–August 1960.
2 http://hbr.org/2004/07/marketing-myopia/ar/1.
3 Al Ries and Laura Ries, *The 22 Immutable Laws of Branding*, HarperCollins, 2002.
4 Roland Rust, Valarie Zeithami & Katherine Lemon, Customer-centred brand management, *Harvard Business Review*, September 2004. See also Roland Rust, Christine Moorman & Gaurav Bella, Rethinking marketing, *Harvard Business Review*, January 2010.
5 Harvard Business School Press, 2010.
6 The Outside-In Approach to Customer Service, Harvard Business School Working Knowledge, 16 February 2010.
7 Naomi Klein, *No Logo: Taking Aim at the Brand Bullies*, Knopf Canada, 2000.
8 Not bitter.
9 Jacqui Hill, Opinion: Marketing Society – Rebuilding FMCG brand value, *Marketing*, 6 April 2005.
10 Special report: The future of advertising, *The Economist*, 26 June 2004.
11 In part this was due to my experience of nearly five years in a marketing role in an investment management company, working for a managing director who 'reinvested' a significant proportion of the company's profits in brand building to create an impression that the company was larger than it was. The cynical among us thought that the fact that his name was that of the company also had something to do with it.
12 George Miller, The magical number seven, plus or minus 2: Some limits on our capacity for processing information, *Psychological Review*, 63, 1956.
13 www.lippincott.com/services/brand_strategy.shtml, 11 January 2011.
14 www.futurebrand.com/about/what-we-do/brand-strategy/, 11 January 2011.
15 www.landor.com/index.cfm?do=brandexpertise.experience, 11 January 2011.
16 Marc Andreessen, Act II, *Fast Company*, January 2001.
17 The best global brands/Online extra, *BusinessWeek*, 2 August 2004.
18 *Ibid.*
19 Simultaneous Media Usage Survey (SIMM 14), BIG Research, June 2009.
20 Jeff Bezos on word-of-mouth power, *BusinessWeek*, 2 August 2004.
21 Howard Schulz & Dori Jones Yang, *Pour Your Heart into It: How Starbucks Built a Company One Cup at a Time*, Hyperion, 1999.
22 http://starbucksgossip.typepad.com/_/2007/02/starbucks_chair_2.html.
23 Roland Rust, Christine Moorman & Gaurav Bella, Rethinking marketing, *Harvard Business Review*, January 2010.
24 A Lafley, What I learned from Peter Drucker: The purpose of a company is to create a customer, *Harvard Business Review*, November 2009.
25 *Ibid.*
26 Peter Kim, Reinventing the marketing organization, *Forrester Big Idea*, 13 July 2006.

27 This law was inspired by my former colleague who informed me that brand strategy conversations at P&G typically included a range of functions. Despite this I will grudgingly grant a semi-exemption to CPG companies given the importance of perception to their value propositions.

28 Rust, Moorman & Bella, *op. cit.*

Chapter 11

1 Peter Kim, Reinventing the marketing organization, *Forrester Big Idea*, 13 July 2006.

2 www.marketingweek.co.uk/home/philip-kotler-causes-uproar-at-marketing-forum-with-tv-ads-a-waste-of-money-claim/2046903.article.

3 *Ibid.*

4 www.prophet.com/downloads/whitepapers/shift-survey-2009.pdf Survey of 150 marketers, from Director level to Chief Marketing Officer, at group and business unit level in large and small businesses.

5 www.mrs.org.uk/media/2009/11une09.htm.

6 www.adassoc.org.uk/aa/index.cfm/adstats/.

7 The MRS changed the way market research spend is calculated, resulting in an increase of 33% between 2006 and 2007, compared to the more usual 5-6% per annum growth that had been shown before. For the period 1997-2006, the multiple was around 13.

8 The Future of Advertising: the Harder Hard Sell, The Economist, 26 June 2004.

9 Robert McChesney, *The Political Economy of Media: Enduring Issues, Emerging Dilemmas*, Monthly Review Press, 2008.

10 Shaun Smith, Customer Experience Management: The Next Frontier for Support Centres, www.shaunsmithco.com.

11 http://customer-engagement.ning.com/.

12 Nick Evans, Moving from monologue to dialogue, www.jaywingdmg.com, 31 March 2008.

13 Gene Alvarez, Kimberly Collins & Adam Sarner, Predicts 2010: CRM Marketing Is Building Demand on a Limited Budget, Gartner Inc, 23 November 2009.

14 www.beingpeterkim.com/2010/01/the-marketers-new-clothes.html.

15 Philip Kotler, Neil Rackham & Suj Krishnaswamy, Ending the War between Sales and Marketing, *Harvard Business Review*, July–August 2006.

Index